Myla Kabat-Zinn, B.S.N., R.N., has worked a⸳⸳⸳⸳⸳⸳⸳⸳⸳⸳ educator, birthing assistant and environmental advocat⸳⸳⸳⸳⸳⸳⸳⸳ mindful parenting workshops in the U.S. and in ⸳⸳⸳

Jon Kabat-Zinn, Ph.D., is the founder of ⸳⸳⸳⸳⸳⸳⸳⸳ Reduction (MBSR), which is used in hospitals and clinics wo⸳⸳⸳⸳⸳⸳ professor of medicine emeritus at the University of Massachusetts Medical School, he founded its Center for Mindfulness in Medicine, Health Care, and Society. A scientist and meditation teacher, he is the author of numerous books and leads workshops throughout the world on mindfulness and its applications. The Kabat-Zinns are parents of three, and grandparents.

Praise for *Everyday Blessings*:

'Myla and Jon Kabat-Zinn's personal and professional insights in this accessible, story-filled classic volume enable us to become the kind of parent we want to be – open, attuned, flexible and compassionate to our children and to ourselves. This revised and updated edition of the original source for "mindful parenting" gives us new guidance to create the life of love our children deserve'
Daniel J. Siegel, M.D., author of *Brainstorm: The Power and Purpose of the Teenage Brain*

'Reading this book could be a life-changing event'
Marian Wright Edelman, president, The Children's Defense Fund

'I urge parents to take refuge in this beautiful book, and to be inspired to embrace each day as an opportunity for learning, growing, and loving more deeply'
Susan Stiffelman, author of *Parenting without Power Struggles*

'This book is a treasure, especially for these fast-paced, accelerating times when many of us seek more balance and wholeness in our lives and relationships'
Nancy Carlsson-Paige, author of *Taking Back Childhood: A Proven Roadmap for Raising Confident, Creative, Compassionate Kids*

Mindfulness for Beginners:
Reclaiming the Present Moment—and Your Life

Mindfulness:
Diverse Perspectives on Its Meaning, Origins, and Applications
(co-editor with Mark Williams)

The Mind's Own Physician:
A Scientific Dialogue with the Dalai Lama on the Healing Power of Meditation
(co-editor with Richard Davidson)

Letting Everything Become Your Teacher:
100 Lessons in Mindfulness

Arriving at Your Own Door:
108 Lessons in Mindfulness

The Mindful Way Through Depression:
Freeing Yourself from Chronic Unhappiness
(with Mark Williams, John Teasdale, and Zindel Segal)

Coming to Our Senses:
Healing Ourselves and the World Through Mindfulness

Wherever You Go, There You Are:
Mindfulness Meditation for Everyday Life

Full Catastrophe Living:
How to Cope with Stress, Pain and Illness Using Mindfulness Meditation

everyday
blessings
mindfulness for parents

Myla & Jon Kabat-Zinn

piatkus

PIATKUS

First published in the US in 1997 by Hyperion
This revised edition published in 2014 by Hachette Books, a division of
Hachette Book Group, Inc.
First published in Great Britain in 2014 by Piatkus

A CIP catalogue record for this book
is available from the British Library.

ISBN 978-0-349-40479-0

Printed and bound by CPI Group (UK) Ltd, Croydon, CR0 4YY

Papers used by Piatkus are from well-managed forests
and other responsible sources.

MIX
Paper from
responsible sources
FSC® C104740

Piatkus
An imprint of
Little, Brown Book Group
100 Victoria Embankment
London EC4Y 0DY

An Hachette UK Company
www.hachette.co.uk

www.piatkus.co.uk

for our children and grandchildren
and
for parents and children everywhere

Acknowledgments

In writing this book together, we wrote chapters by ourselves initially, then gave each other feedback on them through many iterations and changes. For this revised and updated edition, we followed the same approach. We each went over our individual chapters first, making whatever changes we felt necessary, and then, side by side, we went over it all, revising drafts and writing new material. Every chapter became the product of our dual scrutiny in both the thinking and the writing. The final product is truly a collaborative effort of our hearts and our minds, and, of course, of our lives together.

We want first and foremost to thank our children—for their honesty and insight, and their forbearance with our sharing something of their lives with the world beyond our family. Ultimately the stories from their childhoods reflect precious moments that are truly theirs alone. We are blessed by their being and their love.

We also want to acknowledge our parents, Sally and Elvin Kabat and Roslyn and Howard Zinn, for their love, for everything we learned from them, and for the remarkable ways they manifested their love in the world.

At various stages of the writing of the first edition, we asked for feedback from our friends. We wish to express our thanks and gratitude to them. Larry Rosenberg, Sarah Doering, Robbie Pfeufer Kahn, Becky Sarah, Norman Fisher, Jack Kornfield, and Trudy Goodman read the manuscript and gave us invaluable perspectives and suggestions. We also thank Hale Baycu-Schatz, Kathryn Robb, Jenny Fleming-Ives, Mary Crowe, Nancy Wainer Cohen, Sala Steinbach, Sally Brucker, Barbara Trafton Beall, and Nancy Bardacke for their suggestions.

A number of people contributed their own writing and, in that way, a part of their own hearts and souls to our effort. We are deeply indebted to them for their generosity and their eloquence: Caitlin Miller for her poems in "Letters to a Young Girl Interested in Zen"; Lani Donlon for the story in "Family Values"; Cherry Hamrick for her letter in "Mindfulness in the Classroom"; and Rebecca Clement, her student, for hers; Ralph and Kathy Robinson for the poem written by their son Ryan Jon Robinson, and for Ralph's account of Ryan's life and untimely death in "Impermanence"; and Susan Block for the material in "It's Never Too Late."

Rose Thorne, Becky Sarah, Hale Baycu-Schatz, Kathryn Robb, Robbie Pfeufer Kahn, and Levin Pfeufer also contributed material to the book, for which we are grateful.

I (mkz) would like to thank Robbie Pfeufer Kahn for our many conversations over the years regarding the needs of children. Gayle Peterson's seminal work on the mind/body connection in birthing, and her book *Birthing Normally: A Personal Growth Approach to Childbirth*, published in 1984, informed my view of labor and birth and some of the content of the childbirth education classes I taught in the 1980s.

We also want to express our appreciation to all of the people who shared stories about their parenting experiences with us. Many of those stories are included anonymously at their request. Some, for reasons of space and content, we were unable to include in the book.

Nonetheless, we are grateful to those people who reached out to us with their poignant stories.

It was from Robert Bly that I (mkz) first heard the story of "Sir Gawain and the Loathely Lady," told in his wonderfully soulful, heart-stirring way. Robert in turn credits Gioia Timpanelli. She in turn credits the medieval oral tradition, Chaucer's "The Wife of Bath's Tale," and the Goddess Mysteries of Great Britain. We have based our version primarily on Rosemary Sutcliff's in *The Sword and the Circle*, and have made ample use of her beautiful prose in our retelling.

Our publisher at Hyperion/Hachette, Martha Levin, gracefully midwived this second edition in a time of transition at Hyperion. We deeply appreciate the care, attention, and thoughtfulness she brought to the process. We also thank our editor Lauren Shute for all her help and skillful shepherding of the book to completion, and Bob Miller for bringing this book to Hyperion in the first place. We wish to acknowledge the British Museum, London, for allowing us to photograph one of its statues, from which the lotus flower graphic was designed.

Contents

Once the realization is accepted that even between the closest human beings infinite distances continue to exist, a wonderful living side by side can grow up, if they succeed in loving the distance between them which makes it possible for each to see the other whole against the sky.

RAINER MARIA RILKE, *Letters*

Introduction to the Revised Edition

Have you ever weeded a garden? The more you weed, the more weeds you see. One minute, you think you have gotten them all. The next minute there are more. So you have to be very patient and appreciate the process itself, and not just the desired end point. Revising a book on parenting eighteen-plus years after writing it the first time is not dissimilar, and a bit humbling. It was inevitable that our views would change some with the additional years of experience as parents and, now, as grandparents. No matter how clearly we felt we saw things in the past, with the perspective of more time and the continued cultivation of mindfulness, our capacity for seeing and understanding evolved, deepened, and what we were so certain of became more nuanced. This is a never-ending process, which hopefully allows us to continue learning across the life span. Through this lens, we revisited the entire book, preserving the essence of the original edition. We fine-tuned the writing and clarified what we were saying wherever we felt something was unclear, or where we felt a need to illuminate a point or perspective that we hadn't seen before. We reworked the text in both tone and content to reflect the ways in which our views have changed since we first wrote it, and in part, of course, because the world has changed so much as well, for both parents and children.

Indeed, the world children are being born into now is in many ways enormously different from the era in which we were raising our children. For one, our children were born into a solely analog, and therefore slower, world. Now, with the advent of the Internet and wireless connectivity, there is also the digital world and its ever-increasing speed to contend with, an alternate reality that, for all its wonders and uses, easily entrains us into self-distraction and disembodied experience just when we most need to be more present and embodied to face the emotional challenges of parenting and of life and to fully experience the joys as well. Mindfulness is more necessary than ever to navigate this new territory in raising our children and in continuing to grow and lead satisfying lives ourselves. These two life trajectories, nurturing our children and growing ourselves, are intimately intertwined.

Mindfulness as a way of being and as both an informal and a formal meditation practice has moved into the mainstream of society to a degree unimaginable in 1997. There is now a rapidly growing and increasingly robust science of the practice of mindfulness and its effects on our biology, our psychology, and our social interactions. The practice of mindfulness affects our brains and our genes, our capacity for attention, emotion regulation, impulse control, perspective taking, executive functioning in general, and many other important traits that make us who we are, such as our ability to realize our deep connectedness with each other through our innate capacity for attunement, empathy, compassion, and kindness.

Never has the scientific evidence been more compelling that cultivating greater mindfulness can have significant benefits for oneself and for those with whom we share our lives. And never has it been more important for parents to cultivate this capacity we all have for openhearted present-moment awareness, and ultimately for greater wisdom to lead lives of purpose and meaning in ways that are emotionally and socially intelligent.

We hope that this revised edition of *Everyday Blessings* speaks to you and inspires you to actively cultivate greater mindfulness and heartfulness in your parenting and in your life.

Myla and Jon Kabat-Zinn

February 22, 2014

Prologue—jkz

First child off at college freshman year, arrives home 1:30 a.m. for Thanksgiving, driven by a friend. When he had called earlier to say he would not make it home for dinner as we had hoped, we were all disappointed, and for a few moments there had been more than a slight current of annoyance in me. We leave the door unlocked, as arranged, having told him to wake us when he arrives. No need. We hear him come in. The energy is young, vital, spilling over even in his attempts to be quiet. He comes upstairs. We call to him, whispering, so as not to wake his sisters. He comes into our darkened room. We hug. My side of the bed is closer to him than Myla's. He lies down across my chest, backward kind of, extends himself, and embraces us both with his arms, but even more with his being. He is happy to be home. He lies here, draped over my body sideways, as if it were the most natural thing in the world. Any trace of annoyance at the lateness of the hour and disappointment about him not making it by dinnertime evaporate instantly.

I feel happiness radiating from him. There is nothing over-exuberant or manic here. His energy is joyful, content, calm, playful. It feels like old friends reunited and, beyond that, familial celebration. He is at home now, here in our darkened room. He belongs. The bond is palpable among the three of us. A feeling of joy fills my chest and is joined by a series of images of my life with him, captured in the fullness of this moment. This huge nineteen-year-old, lying across me, who I held in my arms as much as possible until he could and would wriggle out and run in the world, now with his scruffy beard and powerful muscles, is my son. I am his father. Myla is his mother. We know this wordlessly. What a blessing, bathing in our different happinesses that unite as we lie here.

After a while he leaves us to watch a movie. He has too much energy to sleep. We try to go back to sleep, but we can't. We toss for hours in a daze of sleepless exhaustion. It crosses my mind to go into his room to spend more time with him, but I don't. There is nothing to chase after here, not him, not even needed sleep. The depths of our contentedness finally hold sway, and we sleep some. I am gone to work in the morning long before he wakes up. My whole day is suffused with knowing that I will see him when I get home.

✳

Such moments, when they are not subverted by us, as I could easily have done in my initial annoyance, and when they are not passed over entirely unnoticed, as we do with so many of our moments, are part of the blessing and the bliss of parenting. Are they special? Is it just at the moment of arrival, the first time home from college, or at the birth of a child, or the first word or the first step, that we taste such deep connection and its blessing, or do such moments occur more frequently than we suspect? Might they not be abundant rather than rare, available to us virtually in any moment, even the more difficult ones, if we stay attuned to both our children and to *this* moment?

In my experience, such moments are abundant. But I find that they too easily go by unnoticed and unappreciated unless I make an effort to see them and capture them in awareness. I find I have to continually work at it, because my mind is so easily veiled from the fullness of any moment by so many other things.

As I see it, all parents, regardless of the ages of our children at any point in time, are on an arduous journey, an odyssey of sorts, whether we know it or not, and whether we like it or not. The journey, of course, is nothing other than life itself, with all its twists and turns, its ups and its downs. How we see and hold the full range of our experiences in our minds and in our hearts makes an enormous difference in the quality of this journey we are on, and what it means to us. It can influence where we go, what happens, what we learn, and how we feel along the way.

A fully lived adventure requires a particular kind of commitment and presence, an attention that to me feels exquisitely tenacious, yet also gentle, receptive. Often the journey itself teaches us to pay attention, wakes us up. Sometimes those teachings emerge in painful or terrifying ways that we would never have chosen. As I see it, the challenge of being a parent is to live our moments as fully as possible, charting our own course as best we can, and above all, nourishing our children and, in the process, growing ourselves. Our children, and the journey itself, provide us with endless opportunities in this regard.

This is clearly a life's work, and it is for life that we undertake it. As we all know down to our very bones, there is no question about doing a perfect job, or always "getting it right." It seems more a quest than a question of anything. "Perfect" is simply not relevant, whatever that would mean in regard to parenting. What is important is that we be authentic, and that we honor our children and ourselves as best we can, and that our intention be to, at the very least, do no harm.

To me, it feels like the work is all in the attending, in the quality of the attention I bring to each moment, and in my commitment to live and to parent as consciously as possible. We know that unconsciousness in one or both parents, especially when it manifests in rigid and unwavering opinions, self-centeredness, and lack of openhearted presence and attention, invariably leads to sorrow in the children. These unfortunate habits of being and relating are often symptoms of underlying sorrow in the parents as well, although they may never be seen as such without an experience of awakening to something larger and more spacious in our lives and relationships.

Maybe each one of us, in our own unique ways, might honor Rilke's insight that there are always infinite distances between even the closest human beings, including with our own children. If we truly understand and accept that perspective, terrifying as it sometimes feels, perhaps we can choose to live in such a way that we can indeed experience the "wonderful living side by side" that can grow up when we embrace and love the distance that lets us see the other whole against the sky.

I see this as our work as parents. To take it on, we need to continue to nurture, protect, and guide our children and bring them along until they are ready to walk their own paths. In parallel, we also need to continue growing and developing ourselves—each of us in our own way, as our own unique person, with a life of our own—so that when they look at us, they will be able to see our wholeness against the sky.

This is not always so easy. Mindful parenting is hard work. It means getting to know ourselves inwardly, and working at the interface where our lives meet the lives of our children. It is particularly hard work in this era, when the culture is intruding more and more into our homes and into our children's lives in so many new ways, and our attention spans are becoming shorter and shorter and our minds more and more distracted.

One reason I practice meditation is to maintain my own balance and clarity of mind in the face of such huge challenges, and to be able to stay more or less on course through all the weather changes that, as a parent, I encounter day in and day out on this journey. Making time each day, usually early in the morning, for a period of quiet stillness, even for a few minutes, helps me to be calmer and more balanced, to see more clearly and more broadly, to be more consistently aware of what is really important and to over and over again make the choice to live by that awareness.

For me, mindfulness, cultivated in periods of stillness and during the day in the various things I find myself doing, hones a greater sensitivity to the present moment that helps me keep my heart at least a tiny bit more open and my mind at least a tiny bit clear, so that I have a chance to see my children for who they are, recognize what they might need from me, and be more present for the moments we share.

But the fact that I practice meditation doesn't mean that I am always calm or kind or gentle, or always present, for that matter. There are many times when I am not. It doesn't mean that I always know how to be or what to do, or that I never feel confused or at a loss. But being even a little more mindful helps me to see things I might not have seen and take small but important, sometimes critical, steps I might not otherwise have taken.

Following a workshop in which I read the above story of our son coming home for Thanksgiving, I received a letter from a man in his sixties who wrote:

I want to thank you for a special gift you gave me on that day. It was when you read us the account of your son's homecoming for Thanksgiving. It touched me very deeply, particularly when you described how he enveloped you with his being, or words to that effect, when he lay down across your chest on the bed. Since then, I have experienced the first genuinely loving feelings towards my own son that I have felt for a long, long time. I don't know what has happened exactly, but it is as if up to now I needed another kind of son to love, and now I don't anymore.

It may be that the feeling of needing another kind of child to love visits all of us as parents from time to time when things feel particularly bad or hopeless. Sometimes, that feeling can, if unexamined, turn from a short-lived impulse into a steady current of disappointment and a yearning for something we think we don't have. But if we look again, as this father did, we may find that after all, we can know and love well the children who are ours to love.

Prologue—mkz

The fiercely protective love I feel for my children has propelled me to do the inner work we call mindful parenting. This inner work has yielded unexpected gifts and pleasures. It has helped me to be more present for the day-to-day richness of being a parent. It has also given me a way to see my children more clearly, to see through the veils of my own fears, expectations, and needs, and to see what might be called for in each moment. Bringing mindfulness to my parenting helps me to see myself as well, and gives me a way to work with the difficult moments and the automatic reactions that can arise so easily in me at such times, reactions that can be limiting, harsh, or hurtful to my children's well-being.

Although I have never had a formal meditation practice, I have always needed some time and space for nondoing, for being still, in silence. This was especially hard to find when my children were little. Moments of solitude and inner reflection would come as I lay in bed in the morning, awake but unwilling to move, aware of the images from my dreams, sometimes clear, sometimes elusive, receptive to whatever thoughts visited me in that place somewhere between wakefulness and sleep.

This was my inner, self-nourishing meditation. It brought some balance to my outer meditations—the ongoing, moment-to-moment awareness, the tuning, responding, holding, and letting go that my children needed from me.

Meditative moments have come in many forms—sitting up in the middle of the night nursing my newborn, soaking in the peace and quiet, feeding her as I am being fed by the sweetness of her being; or walking with a crying baby, finding ways to soothe and comfort, chanting, singing, rocking, as I work with my own tiredness; or looking into the face of an unhappy, angry teenager, trying to discern the cause and intuit what might be needed.

Mindfulness is about paying attention, and paying attention takes energy and concentration. Every moment brings something different and may require something different from me. Sometimes I am blessed with understanding. Other times I am at a loss, confused, off balance, not really knowing, but trying to respond instinctively, creatively, to whatever is presented to me. There are deeply satisfying moments of pure bliss, when a child is thriving and glowing with a sense of well-being. There are plenty of difficult, frustrating, painful moments, when nothing I do is right, and I feel completely at a loss. I've found it especially hard to see clearly with older children. The issues are much more complex and the answers rarely simple.

But what I have come to see is that each time I feel I have lost my way as a parent, when I find myself in a dark wood, the ground rough and uneven, the terrain unfamiliar, the air chilled, there is often something to be found in my pocket when I finally find my way back. I have to remember to stop, to breathe, to reach in, and look closely at what it is.

Each difficult moment has the potential to open my eyes and open my heart. Each time I come to understand something about one of my children, I also learn something about myself and the child

I once was, and that knowledge can act as a guide for me. When I am able to empathize and feel compassion for a child's pain, when I am more accepting of the contrary, irritating, exasperating behaviors that my children can manifest, try on, experiment with—the healing power of unconditional love heals me as it nourishes them. As they grow, I also grow.

Rather than being a disadvantage, my sensitivity has become an ally. Over the years, I have learned to use my intuition, my senses, my emotional antennae to try to see into the heart of whatever I am faced with. An essential part of this is attempting to see things from my child's point of view. I have found this inner work to be very powerful. When I can choose to be kind instead of cruel, to understand rather than judge, to accept rather than reject, my children, no matter what their ages, are nourished and strengthened.

This kind of parenting is trust building. I work hard to maintain that trust and the underlying feelings of connectedness that have been built over many years of hard emotional and physical work. Moments of carelessness or the unconscious surfacing of old destructive patterns are betrayals of my children's trust, and I have had to consciously work to rebuild and strengthen our relationship after such moments.

Over the years I have tried to bring some awareness to my moment-to-moment experiences as a parent: observing, questioning, looking at what I most value and what I think is most important for my children. Although there are myriad aspects of parenting that are not touched on in this book, it is my hope that in describing this inner process to you, we can evoke the richness of experience and potential for growth and change that reside in mindful parenting.

PART ONE

The Danger

and the Promise

The Challenge of Parenting

Parenting is one of the most challenging, demanding, and stressful undertakings on the planet. It is also one of the most important, for how it is approached influences in great measure the heart and soul and consciousness of the next generation, their experience of meaning and connection, their repertoire of life skills, and their deepest feelings about themselves and their possible place in a rapidly changing world. Yet those of us who become parents do so virtually without preparation or training, with little or no guidance or support, and in a world that values producing far more than nurturing, doing far more than being.

When we first wrote this book, in the mid-1990s, there were few if any books addressing the inner experience of parenting. In fact, this book launched the term *mindful parenting* and even a field of research on that subject. The best parenting manuals of that era served as helpful and authoritative references, giving parents new ways of seeing situations and reassuring us, especially in the early years of child rearing or when facing particular challenges, that there were various ways to handle things and that we were not alone. They also offered an understanding of age-appropriate landmarks of child development and thus helped parents to have more realistic expectations of their children.

But for the most part, they did not address the inner experience of parenting. What are we to do, for instance, with our own mind? How do we avoid getting swallowed up and overwhelmed by our doubts, our insecurities and fears? What about the times when we feel carried away and lose touch with our children and ourselves? Nor did they address the critical importance of being present with and for our children, and how we as parents might develop greater understanding and appreciation for the inner experiences of our children.

To parent consciously requires that we engage in an inner work on ourselves as well as in the outer work of nurturing and caring for our children. The how-to advice that we can draw upon from books to help us with the outer work has to be complemented by an inner authority that we can only cultivate within ourselves through our own experience. Such inner authority only develops when we realize that, in spite of all of the things that happen to us that are outside of our control, through our choices in response to such events and through what we initiate ourselves, we are still, in large measure, "authoring" our own lives. In the process, we find our own ways to be in this world, drawing on what is deepest and best and most creative in us. Realizing this, we may come to see the importance for our children and for ourselves of taking responsibility for the ways in which we live our lives and for the consequences of the choices we make.

Inner authority and authenticity are developed through that inner work. Our authenticity and our wisdom grow when we purposely bring awareness to our own experience as it unfolds. Over time, we can learn to see more deeply into who our children are and what they might need, and take the initiative in finding appropriate ways to nourish them and support their growth and development. We can also learn to interpret their many different, sometimes puzzling signals and to trust our ability to find a way to respond appropriately. Attention, inquiry, and thoughtfulness are essential to this process.

Parenting is above all uniquely personal. Ultimately, it has to come from deep inside ourselves. Someone else's way of doing things may not be appropriate or useful. We each need to find a way that is our own, certainly consulting other perspectives as we go along, but above all, learning to trust our own instincts while continuing to examine and question them.

Still, in parenting, what we thought and did yesterday that "worked out well" is not necessarily going to help today. We have to stay very much in the present moment to sense what might be required. And when our inner resources are depleted, it is helpful to have healthy ways to replenish them and restore ourselves.

Becoming a parent may happen on purpose or by accident, but however it comes about, parenting itself is a calling. It calls us to re-create our world every day, to meet it freshly in every moment. Such a calling is in actuality nothing less than a rigorous spiritual discipline, a quest to realize our truest, deepest nature as human beings. The very fact that we are parents impels us to continually seek and express what is most nurturing, wise, and caring within ourselves, to be, as much as we can be, our best selves.

As with any spiritual discipline, the call to parent mindfully is filled with enormous promise and potential. At the same time, it also challenges us to approach our parenting with consistent intentionality, so that we can be fully engaged in this fundamentally human enterprise, this remarkable and decades-long unfolding passage of life and learning from one generation to the next.

People who choose to become parents take on this hardest of jobs for no salary, often unexpectedly, at a relatively young and inexperienced age, or under conditions of economic strain and insecurity.

Typically, the journey of parenting is embarked upon without a clear strategy or overarching view of the terrain, in much the same intuitive and optimistic way we approach many other aspects of life. We learn on the job, as we go. There is, in fact, no other way.

But to begin with, we may have no sense of how much parenting augurs a totally new set of demands and changes in our lives, requiring us to give up so much that is familiar and to take on so much that is unfamiliar. Perhaps this is just as well. Each child is unique and each situation different. We have to rely on our hearts, our deepest human instincts, and our memories of our own childhoods, both positive and negative, to encounter the unknown territory of having and raising children.

And just as in life itself—faced with a range of familial, social, and cultural pressures to conform to frequently unstated and unconscious norms, and with all the inherent stresses of caring for children—as parents we often find ourselves, in spite of all our best intentions and our deep love for our children, running more or less on automatic pilot and plagued by the vagaries of our minds, which are ordinarily exceedingly reactive and usually caught up in unnoticed but incessant thinking.

To the extent that we are chronically preoccupied and invariably pressed for time, we may be significantly out of touch with the richness of what Thoreau called the "bloom" of the present moment. This moment—any moment, actually—may seem far too ordinary, routine, and fleeting to single out for attention. If we are in fact caught up in such habits of mind, the unexamined automaticity of it all can easily spill over into a similar automaticity as far as our parenting is concerned. We might be assuming that whatever we do will be okay as long as the basic love for our children and desire for their well-being is there. We can rationalize such a view by telling ourselves that children are resilient creatures and that the little things that happen to them may be just that, little things that may have no effect on them at all. Children can take a lot, we tell ourselves. And there is some truth in that.

But, as I (jkz) am reminded time and again as people recount their stories in the Stress Reduction Clinic and in mindfulness workshops and retreats around the country, for many people, childhood was a time of either frank or subtle betrayals, of one or both parents out of control to one degree or another, often raining down various combinations of unpredictable terror, violence, scorn, and meanness on their children, much of it coming out of their own experiences of trauma and neglect and the addictions and deep unhappiness that often follow. Sometimes, in the deepest of ironies, accompanying such terrible betrayals, come protestations of parental love, making the situation even crazier and harder for the children to fathom. For others, there is the pain of having been invisible, unknown, neglected, and unappreciated as children. And there is also the sense that what with the rising stress on virtually all fronts in society and an accelerating sense of time urgency and insufficiency, things are strained to, and often beyond, the breaking point in families and getting worse, not better, generation by generation.

A woman who attended a five-day mindfulness retreat said:

I noticed this week as I was doing the meditation that I feel like I have pieces missing, that there are parts of me that I just can't find when I become still and look underneath the surface of my mind. I'm not sure what it means but it's kind of made me a little bit anxious. Maybe when I start to practice the meditation a little more regularly, maybe I'll find out what is stopping me from being whole. But I really feel holes in my body or in my soul that keep me pushing mountains in front of myself everywhere I go. My husband says: "But why did you do that? There was a big opening here." And I just say: "I don't know, but if there is a way to block it up, I will." I feel a little like a Swiss cheese. I have felt this from when I was small. I had some losses when I was small. I think parts of me were removed and taken from [me by] deaths and [by] other people; my sister died when I was young, and my parents went into a sort of depression, I think until they died. I think parts of me just got taken to feed them. I feel that. I was a very lively, young go-getter when I was young, and I felt parts of me just being taken, and I can't seem to be able to regain those parts now. Why can't I be that way? What happened to me? Parts of me have gotten lost, and when I'm sitting here today, meditating, I realized that I'm looking for those parts and I don't know where they are. I don't know how to become whole until I find those parts that are gone. Now my whole family has died. They've taken all the parts and left, and I'm still here with the Swiss cheese.

A chilling image, that parts of this woman were taken to feed her parents. But this happens, and the consequences to the children reverberate throughout their lives.

What is more, some parents cause deep hurt and harm to their children, as when they beat them to teach them lessons, saying things like "This is for your own good," "This hurts me more than it hurts you," or "I'm only doing this because I love you," often the very words that were said to them as children when they were beaten by their parents, as was shown by the Swiss psychiatrist Alice Miller in her seminal work. In the name of "love," frequently unbridled rage, contempt, hatred, intolerance, neglect, and abuse are inflicted on children from parents who are unaware of or have ceased to care about the full import of their actions. This happens across all social classes in our society.

In our view, an automatic, unexamined, lowest-common-denominator approach to parenting, whether it manifests in overt violence or not, can cause deep and frequently long-lasting harm to children and their developmental trajectories. Unconscious parenting can arrest our own potential to grow as well. From such unconsciousness can come, all too commonly, sadness, missed opportunities, hurt, resentment, blame, restricted and diminished views of self and the world, and ultimately isolation and alienation on all sides.

If we can remain awake to the challenges and the calling of parenthood, this does not have to happen. On the contrary, we can use all the occasions that arise with our children to break down the barriers in our own minds and hearts, to see more clearly into ourselves, and to be more effectively present for them. These opportunities lie at the heart of cultivating greater mindfulness in our parenting.

*

We live in a culture that does not uniformly value parenting as valid and important work. It is considered perfectly acceptable for people to give one hundred percent to their careers, or to their "relationships," or to their passions, but not to their children.

Society at large and its institutions and values, which both create and reflect the microcosms of our individual minds and values, contribute in major ways to the undermining of parenting. Who are the highest-paid workers in our country? Certainly not day-care workers, or teachers, whose work so much supports the work of parents. Where are the role models, the support networks, the paid parental leave for young parents, the job sharing and part-time jobs for mothers and fathers who want to stay home with their children for more than a few weeks after they are born? Where is the support for parenting classes? By their prevalence, such programs would tell us that healthy parenting is of utmost importance and is valued highly in our society. But their prevalence is depressingly low.

Certainly there are bright spots and reasons for hope. Countless parents across the country see parenting as a sacred trust, and manage to find heartful and creative ways to guide and nurture their children, often in the face of great obstacles and odds. There are imaginative efforts by people all across the country involved in programs that teach parenting skills, communication skills, violence prevention, and stress reduction, and that offer counseling services to parents and families. There are also many groups engaged in community building and political lobbying on behalf of children, such as the Children's Defense Fund. For many years La Leche League International and Attachment Parenting International have given invaluable support to parents for meeting the needs of their children through breast-feeding and other practices that promote secure parent-child attachment. The Searses' *The Baby Book* has for decades provided practical information and a framework for honoring the needs of infants and babies. A number of books connect mindful awareness and attunement with parenting (see the Suggested Reading at the end of this book). Laura Kastner's *Wise-Minded Parenting* and Susan Stiffelman's *Parenting Without Power Struggles* are valuable resources for parents. Dan Hughes's book *Attachment-Focused Parenting: Effective Strategies to Care for Children* and Dan Siegel and Mary Hartzell's book *Parenting from the Inside Out* connect interpersonal neuroscience, attachment research, and awareness. Nancy Bardacke's book *Mindful Birthing: Training the Mind, Body, and Heart for Childbirth and Beyond* is a ground-breaking work on mindfulness-based childbirth and parenting. New research and new books are coming out on these subjects all the time.

Whatever the era in which we are raising our children, we are always subject to large social, cultural, and economic forces that shape our lives and the lives of our children. Nevertheless, we always have at least some latitude as individuals to make conscious and intentional choices about how we are going to relate to the circumstances and the era in which we find ourselves. To one degree or another, usually far more than we think, we have the potential to inquire deeply about the path we are on and how it reflects what we most care about and long for. We always have the option of bringing greater attention and intentionality to our lives, especially where it concerns our children. Charting such a path for ourselves can be made significantly easier and more robust if we have a larger framework within which we can examine what we are doing and develop insight into what else may be needed—a framework that can help keep us on course, even though things may be constantly changing and our next steps unclear. Mindfulness can provide such a framework.

New and important doors in our own minds can open just by entertaining the possibility that there are alternative ways of perceiving situations and that we may have more options open to us in any moment than we may realize.

Bringing mindfulness to the various aspects of our day as it unfolds may be a practical as well as a profoundly positive alternative to the driven, automatic-pilot mode in which we can function much of the time without even knowing it. This is particularly important for us as parents, as we try to juggle all the competing responsibilities and demands that we carry from day to day while at the same time providing for our children and meeting their unique inner and outer needs in an increasingly stressful and complex world.

What Is Mindful Parenting?

Mindful parenting calls us to wake up to the possibilities, the benefits, and the challenges of parenting with a new awareness and intentionality, not only as if what we did mattered, but also as if our conscious engagement in parenting were virtually the most important thing we could be doing, both for our children and for ourselves.

This book is a series of meditations on various aspects of parenting. It is about recognizing and meeting our children's needs as wisely as possible by cultivating greater familiarity and intimacy with a capacity we already have and therefore don't have to acquire, namely awareness itself. All that is required is to bring this capacity to our moment-to-moment lives. *Mindfulness* is a synonym for *awareness*. It also includes different ways to systematically cultivate greater access to our own awareness. When we bring awareness to our parenting through the cultivation of mindfulness as a practice, it can lead to deeper insight into and understanding of our children and ourselves. Mindfulness has the potential to penetrate past surface appearances and behaviors and allow us to see our children more clearly, to look both inwardly and outwardly and act with some degree of wisdom and compassion on the basis of what we see.

As we shall see in Part 4, from the perspective of mindfulness, parenting can be viewed as a kind of extended and, at times, arduous meditation retreat spanning a large part of our lives. And our children, from infancy to adulthood and beyond, can be seen as perpetually challenging live-in teachers who provide us with ceaseless opportunities to do the interior work of understanding who we are and who they are so that we can best stay in touch with what is important and give them what they most need in order to grow and flourish. In the process, we may find that this ongoing moment-to-moment awareness can liberate us from some of our most confining habits of perception and relating, the straitjackets and prisons of the mind that have been passed down to us or that we have somehow constructed for ourselves. Through their very being, often without any words or discussion, our children can inspire us to do this inner work. The more we are able to keep in mind the intrinsic wholeness and beauty of our children, especially in those moments when those qualities are particularly difficult for us to see, the more our ability to be fully present and compassionate deepens. In seeing more clearly, we can respond to them more effectively with greater generosity of heart and a degree of wisdom.

As we devote ourselves to caring for our children, nurturing them, and trying to understand who they are, these live-in teachers of ours, especially in the first ten to twenty years of our "training," will provide endless moments of wonder and bliss and opportunities for the deepest feelings of connectedness and love. They will also, in all likelihood, push all our buttons, evoke all our insecurities, teach us things we never could have imagined, test all our limits and boundaries, and touch all the places in us where we fear to tread and feel inadequate or worse. In the process, if we are willing to attend carefully to the full spectrum of what we are experiencing, they will remind us over and over again what is most important in life, including its mystery, as we share in their lives and shelter and nourish and love them and give them what guidance we can.

Being a parent is particularly intense and demanding, in part because our children can ask things of us no one else could or would, in ways that no one else could or would. They see us up close as no one else does, and constantly hold mirrors up for us to look into. In doing so, they give us over and over again the chance to see ourselves in new ways, and to work at consciously asking what we can learn from any and every situation that comes up with them. We can then make choices out of this awareness that will nurture both our children's inner growth and our own. Our interconnectedness and our interdependence enable us to learn and grow together.

*

To bring mindfulness into our parenting, it is helpful to know something about what mindfulness is. Mindfulness is the awareness that arises from paying attention on purpose, in the present moment, nonjudgmentally. It is cultivated by gently reminding ourselves over and over again to pay attention in that way. As best we can, we then intentionally sustain that attention over time. When our attention gets carried away, as it invariably will, we bring it back to the present moment over and over again. In the process, we become much more in touch with our lives as they are unfolding. You might say that we learn to "inhabit" our own awareness.

Ordinarily, we live much of our lives on automatic pilot, paying attention only selectively and haphazardly, taking many important things completely for granted or not noticing them at all, and judging everything we do experience by forming rapid and often unexamined opinions based on what we like or dislike, what we want or don't want. Mindfulness brings to parenting a powerful method and framework for paying attention to whatever we are experiencing in each moment, and seeing past the veil of our automatic thoughts and feelings to a deeper actuality. By the way, cultivating mindfulness doesn't mean that we won't have plenty of judgments. It does mean that we will work at recognizing them as such, be willing to suspend them as best we can, at least momentarily, and not judge our judging. As you will see, we also differentiate between judging, which tends to be reactive and very black or white, and *discerning*, which is much more nuanced, seeing many gradations between any two extremes.

Mindfulness lies at the heart of Buddhist meditation, which itself is all about cultivating attention, openhearted presence or "wakefulness," and compassion. The practice of mindfulness has been kept alive and developed within various meditative traditions across Asia for over twenty-six hundred years. In the past thirty-five years, it has found its way into mainstream society in many different contexts, including medicine, neuroscience, psychology, health care, education, the law, sports, social programs, and even government. In the past fifteen years, scientific research on mindfulness has grown exponentially. As a consequence, there is now widespread interest in cultivating mindfulness in many different domains of our lives.

Mindfulness is a meditative discipline. There are many different meditative disciplines. We might think of them all as various doors into the same room. Each doorway gives a unique and different view into the room. Once inside, however, it is the same room, whichever door we come through. Meditation, whatever the method or tradition, is tapping into the order and stillness embedded in and behind all activity, however chaotic it may appear, using our faculty of attention and our ability to comprehend what we are perceiving, or to know it when we don't. And what could be more chaotic at times than parenting?

While it received its most elaborate articulation in the Buddhist tradition, mindfulness is an important part of all cultures and is truly universal, since it is simply about cultivating the capacity we all have as human beings for awareness, clarity, and compassion. There are many different ways to engage in this work of cultivation. There is no one right way, just as there is no one right way to parent.

Mindful parenting involves keeping in mind what is truly important as we go about the activities of daily living with our children. Much of the time, we may find we need to remind ourselves of what that is, or even admit that we may have no idea at the moment, for the thread of meaning and direction in our lives is easily lost. But even in our most trying, sometimes horrible moments as parents, we can deliberately step back and begin afresh, asking ourselves as if for the first time, and with fresh eyes, "What is truly important here?"

In fact, mindful parenting means seeing if we can *remember* to bring this kind of attention and openness and wisdom to our moments with our children. It is a true *practice*, its own inner discipline, its own form of meditation. And it carries with it profound benefits for both children and parents, to be discovered in the practice itself.

For us to learn from our children requires that we pay attention and learn to be still within ourselves. In stillness, we are better able to see past the endemic turmoil and cloudiness and reactivity of our own minds, in which we are so frequently caught up, and in this way, cultivate greater clarity, calmness, and insight, which we can bring directly to our parenting.

Like everybody else, parents have their own needs and desires and lives, just as children do. Our needs as parents in any given moment may be very different from those of our child. Rather than pitting our needs against our children's, parenting mindfully involves cultivating an awareness, right in such moments, of how our needs are *interdependent*. Our lives are undeniably deeply connected. Our children's well-being affects ours, and ours affects theirs. If they are not doing well, we suffer, and if we are not doing well, they suffer.

This means that everyone benefits when we are aware of our children's needs as well as our own, emotional as well as physical, and, depending on their ages, work at finding ways for everybody to get some of what they most need. Just bringing this kind of sensitivity to our parenting will enhance our sense of connectedness with our children. Through the quality of our presence, our commitment to them is felt, even in difficult times. We may find that our choices in moments of conflicting and competing needs will come more out of this heartfelt connection, and as a result, will have greater kindness and wisdom in them.

✻

We see parenting as a sacred responsibility. Parents are nothing less than protectors, nurturers, comforters, teachers, guides, companions, models, and sources of unconditional love and acceptance. If we are able to keep this sense of parenting as a sacred responsibility in mind, and we bring a degree of mindfulness to the process as it unfolds moment by moment, our choices as parents are much more likely to come out of an awareness of what this moment, this child—at this stage of his or her life—is asking from us right now, through his or her very being and behavior. In rising to this challenge, we may not only come to do what is best for our children, but we may also uncover and come to know, perhaps for the first time, what is deepest and best in ourselves.

Mindful parenting calls us to acknowledge and name the challenges we face daily in trying to parent with awareness. For awareness has to be inclusive. It has to include recognizing our own frustrations, insecurities, and shortcomings, our limits and limitations, even our darkest and most destructive feelings, and the ways we may feel overwhelmed or pulled apart. It challenges us to "work with" these very energies consciously and systematically.

Taking on such a task is asking a great deal of ourselves. For in many ways, we ourselves are products, and sometimes, to one degree or another, prisoners of the events and circumstances of our own childhoods. Since childhood significantly shapes how we see ourselves and the world, our histories will inevitably shape our views of who our children are and "what they deserve," and of how they should be cared for, taught, and "socialized." As parents, we all tend to hold our views, whatever they are, very strongly and often unconsciously, as if in the grip of powerful spells. It is only when we become aware of this shaping that we can draw on what was helpful and positive and nurturing from the way we were parented, and grow beyond those aspects that may have been destructive and limiting.

For those of us who had to shut down, to "not see," to suppress our feelings in order to survive our own childhoods, becoming more mindful can be especially painful and difficult. In those moments when we are ruled by old demons, when old beliefs, destructive patterns, and nightmares visit us and we are plagued by dark feelings and black-or-white thinking, it is particularly difficult to stop and see freshly.

By no means are we suggesting that to parent mindfully, there is some ideal standard we have to measure ourselves against or strive to achieve. Mindful parenting is a continual process of deepening and refining our awareness and our ability to be present and act wisely. It is not an attempt to attain a fixed goal or outcome, however worthy. An important part of the process is seeing ourselves with some degree of kindness and compassion. This includes seeing and accepting our limitations, our blindnesses, our attachments, our humanness, our fallibility, and working with them mindfully as best we can. The one thing we know we can always do, even in moments of darkness and despair that show us we don't know anything, is to begin again, fresh, right in that moment. Every moment is a new beginning, another opportunity for tuning in, for opening, and perhaps in that very moment, seeing, feeling, and knowing ourselves and our children in a new and deeper way.

For our love for our children is expressed and experienced in the quality of the moment-to-moment relationships we have with them. It deepens in everyday moments when we hold those moments in awareness and dwell within them. Love is expressed in how we pass the bread, or how we say good morning, and not just in the big trip to Disney World. It is in the everyday kindnesses we show, in the understanding we bring, and in our openness. Our love is also in the boundaries, limits, and frameworks we establish and then stand by with clarity, firmness, and kindness. Love is expressed by embodying love in our actions. So whether we are facing good times or hard times on any given day or in any moment, the quality of our presence is a deep measure of our caring and of our love for our children.

*

This book is for people who care about the quality of family life and the well-being of their children, born and unborn, young or grown. We hope it will support parents in their efforts to show their love through their being and their actions in their everyday lives. It is not likely that we can do this unless we can be authentic in our own lives and in touch with the full range of feelings we experience—in a word, awake.

Parenting is a mirror in which we get to see the best of ourselves and the worst, the richest moments of living and the most frightening. The challenge to write about it sensibly is daunting. During the years when our children were growing up, there were plenty of times when we felt that things were basically sound in our family. The children seemed happy, strong, and balanced. However, the very next day, or moment, all hell could break loose. Our world filled with confusion, despair, anger, frustration. What we thought we understood was of no use. All the rules seemed to have changed overnight, or in an instant. We had no idea what was going on or why. We felt like the biggest of failures. We felt as if we didn't know or understand anything.

In such moments, we tried to remind ourselves as best we could to hold on to the thread of some kind of awareness of what was happening, no matter how unpleasant or painful things were. Hard as it was, we tried to acknowledge what was actually taking place and what might have been needed from us. The alternative was to get caught up in our own reactivity and automatic behaviors, and surrender whatever compassion and clarity we had to our fear or fury or denial. And even when this happened, as it inevitably does at times, we tried to reexamine it later, with greater calmness, in the hope of learning something from it.

This book comes out of our own experience as parents. It was originally written when our children were in middle school, high school, and college. Now, at the time of this revised edition, our children are grown and we are grandparents. Our experience will undoubtedly differ in many ways from your experience as a person and as a parent. You may find some of the specific ways we chose to parent to be very different from how you were parented or how you have parented your children. You may find yourself reacting with strong feelings to some of the things we say or to some of the choices we have made. The whole topic of parenting can arouse deep emotions in all of us, because it is so intimately connected with how we think of ourselves and with how we have chosen to live our lives.

We are not suggesting that you should do everything as we have done it, or if you didn't, that you were lacking in any way. As we all know, there are few easy answers and consistently simple solutions in parenting. Nor are we saying that mindfulness is the answer to all life's problems, or to all questions regarding parenting. We are simply trying to point to a way of seeing and a way of being that can be integrated in many different fashions into your way of parenting and into your life. Ultimately, we all have to make our own individual decisions about what is best for our children and for ourselves, drawing most of all on our creativity and our capacity to be awake and aware in our lives.

We share with you our experiences and this orientation we call mindful parenting in the hope that some of its transformative potential will resonate with your values and your intentions, and be of some use as you chart your own path in your parenting.

Ultimately, mindful parenting is about the possibility of seeing our children with greater clarity and of listening to and trusting our own hearts. It gives form and support to the daily challenges of parenting. It can also help us find ways to act with greater wisdom and be sources of unconditional love for our children, moment by moment, and day by day.

How Can I Do This?

No two families ever have exactly the same situations to deal with or resources to call upon. But no matter what the circumstances of people's lives, we believe that all families and individuals, by virtue of being human, have deep inner resources that can be called upon and cultivated, resources that can help enormously in making important choices as we struggle to bring balance into our lives and into our families.

At every level of economic and social well-being or lack of it, and no matter what enormous difficulties they are faced with, there are people who find ways to put their children first. But what does it mean to put our children first? This is worth thinking about. Of course, whatever it means to you, it will change with the ages of your children, and it may be different for each child. It certainly does not mean being obsessed with your children and hovering over them incessantly (which is what the term *helicopter parenting* refers to). Nor does it mean to sacrifice your own needs in ways that are essentially unwise and potentially unhealthy all around. Mindfulness is not about being so focused on a child that you lose yourself. It helps us develop and nurture embodied self-awareness, the lived experience of being grounded in our bodies and in our own lives.

Like a relay race with a long overlap in which the baton is passed—lasting at least eighteen years and often longer—our job as parents is to position our children to run their solo laps effectively. To do that optimally, we need to give our all during our run alongside them. There are many ways to do this. There is no one right way, and there is no formula. It is not just about doing, either. In fact, in the long run, it may be more about "how we *be*" in our own lives than it is about "what we *do*." But no matter what our circumstances, if the will and the motivation and caring are present, we can learn to draw on the interior resources of strength and wisdom, creativity and caring, that reside within us all. Moreover, each moment provides us with new occasions to do this, so it is important to learn to pace ourselves and understand that we need to be gentle with ourselves, as we are in it for the long haul. This is what the practice of mindful parenting offers us.

Mindful parenting takes energy and commitment, as does any deep spiritual practice or consciousness discipline. We may find ourselves wondering from time to time whether we are capable of taking on such a task that is really the work of a lifetime, asking ourselves, "How can I do this on top of everything else I am already doing?" We may find it reassuring and inspiring to discover that to a large degree, important elements of both the systematic discipline and the methods of mindful parenting are already familiar to all of us as parents. Mindful parenting as a practice and as an inner discipline is possible and practical, because it arises naturally out of the experiences and challenges we already face every day as parents.

For instance, as parents, we are already constantly called upon to pay attention and we are already highly disciplined. We have to pay attention and be disciplined in waking up on time every morning; in getting the children up, fed, and ready for school; in getting ourselves ready for work and getting to it if we work outside the home. We are disciplined and attentive in arranging our children's complex schedules and our own, and in planning and then doing everything that needs to be done: all the shopping, cooking, cleaning, the countless repetitive tasks of daily life in a family.

We are also already highly accomplished. We deal every day with constant crises, juggle competing demands on our time and energy, and utilize the incredible sixth sense that parents develop early on, which allows us to be continually aware of where our little ones are in each moment and of potential danger. We are also skilled at having conversations while doing other things, and dealing with constant interruptions while trying to keep a train of thought. People may sometimes feel hurt or put off when it seems as if we are not giving them our full attention, but as parents, we develop an ability to give our attention to many things at once; we can speak to them at the same time that we are watching our child, or buttoning a jacket, or grabbing her before she gets into something harmful. Such skills and such disciplines go with the territory of parenting. The more we use and develop them, as we have to as parents, the better we get at them. They become a way of being.

We can make exceedingly good use of these skills and the discipline that is natural to us as parents in our efforts to parent more mindfully. The one is a natural extension of the other. Mindful parenting asks us to direct some of that energy and discipline and caring inwardly, toward our own minds and bodies and experiences, and toward attending more consistently to the inner as well as the outer lives of our children, to their emotional and soul needs as well as to their needs for clothing, food, and shelter.

We can bring mindfulness to any moment, no matter how brief or how stressed, no matter how off we may be feeling. But to do so requires a strong commitment to cultivate mindfulness through some kind of regular daily practice. This can be done in a variety of ways, but the overall approaches, which are highly complementary and mutually supporting, are *formal meditation practice* and *informal meditation practice*. The latter, also known as mindfulness in everyday life, is the primary practice we are recommending for parents. If you can also make formal meditation practice a part of your everyday life, even for relatively brief periods of time, say five or ten minutes a day, or longer, that of course can be extremely helpful in strengthening the muscle of mindfulness. But ultimately, mindful parenting involves dropping into the present moment over and over again, and learning from this intentional opening into awareness, which is its own remarkably powerful practice (see "Four Mindfulness Practices for Everyday Life" in the Epilogue).

Most of the tens of thousands of people who have completed the Mindfulness-Based Stress Reduction (MBSR) Program at the Center for Mindfulness at the University of Massachusetts Medical Center and other MBSR programs around the country and throughout the world are parents. All have significant stress in their lives. Many come with serious, sometimes life-threatening medical problems, many with difficult social, economic, and personal problems as well. Some have horrifying family histories. Many already do remarkable things, day in and day out, to cope with extremely difficult situations in the present and from the past. In the eight-week MBSR program, they work at cultivating mindfulness in their lives through both formal and informal mindfulness practices on a daily basis, building on the foundation of what they are already doing to maintain their well-being and that of their families. In the process, their lives and their attitudes and the ways in which they see and relate to others, including their children, often change profoundly and enduringly. In spite of the inherent challenges in cultivating and sustaining the discipline of mindfulness in day-to-day situations, many people report that in paying attention in new ways, they feel more relaxed, more hopeful, cope better with stress both at home and at work, and have greater peace of mind and self-confidence. They are able to see new openings in their lives through which to navigate, using the practice of mindfulness itself. Some report feeling a greater sense of freedom, a greater sense of inner control and security, than they had thought possible before.

In MBSR, the instructors introduce people to the various aspects of the meditation practice and make general suggestions for how it might be applied to daily life and to challenging and stressful situations. But for the most part, it is the participants themselves, while they are going through the program, who discover how to apply mindfulness in meaningful ways to the unique circumstances of their everyday lives. This is a creative and intuitive process that emerges naturally out of the practice itself.

It is the same with mindful parenting. We are not telling you what you should do, or what choices you need to make. Only you can determine that, because only you are living your life and could possibly know what your specific situation calls for in any moment. We are not even directing you in applying the practice, except in the most general terms. The detailed applications of mindfulness, and the specific choices you will be drawn to make, can only come out of your own motivation to practice, from your own commitment to honor each present moment by bringing your full awareness to it, and from the yearnings of your own heart. Mindful choices will then come out of the very situations you find yourself in with your children. They will come out of your own creativity, imagination, love, and genius, which, being human, are profound and virtually limitless.

Besides, what with so many people now carrying all the parenting responsibilities alone as single parents; with the sharing of the parenting in divorced families; with people having children later in life; gay and lesbian parents; grandparents sometimes parenting their children's children; couples who get along together and see more or less eye to eye about parenting; couples who don't get along a good deal of the time or who see parenting very differently; couples where the division of labor and parenting responsibilities are highly skewed; families where both parents work full-time and more; families with children with life-threatening diseases, physical challenges, or developmental differences; families with closely spaced children, with children widely separated in age, or with twins or triplets; or families with vastly different numbers of children, with all boys or all girls, or different combinations, there is no single way of parenting or body of knowledge that could be relevant and useful in all circumstances.

But mindfulness, precisely because it not formulaic, and because it has to do with the quality of our experience as human beings and the degree to which we can pay attention in our lives, is truly universal in scope and therefore relevant in virtually all circumstances. Everybody has a mind, everybody has a body, everybody can pay attention intentionally, and everybody's life unfolds only in moments. Mindfulness doesn't tell us what to do, but it does give us a way to listen, a way to pay close attention to what we believe is important, and to expand our vision of what that might be in any situation, under any circumstances.

As parents and as people, no matter what we are facing in our lives, we are all capable of remarkable growth and transformation if we can learn to recognize and tap our deep inner resources and chart a path that is true to our values and to our own hearts. It does take work, but not much more than we are already doing. What it really involves is a rotation in consciousness, a new way of seeing that comes out of present-moment awareness, and that both invites and allows what is best in us and in our children to emerge.

*

To enter now the world of mindful parenting and what it asks of us as well as what it has to offer, we begin by telling a story. For a time, we will be stepping outside of time, into the domain of the mythological, of the psyche, to return with perhaps a better sense of what it might mean to see in a deeper way, and to trust the mystery of our own hearts. It may be helpful to keep in mind that in this realm, all the characters in the story can be seen as different aspects of our own being, and that male and female, beauty and ugliness, kindness and hard-heartedness reside to varying degrees within each of us.

PART TWO

Sir Gawain and the

Loathely Lady:

The Story Holds the Key

Sir Gawain and the Loathely Lady

Long ago, in the days of King Arthur, for reasons we don't have to go into here, Arthur found himself on Christmas Day taking up a just cause that brought him face to face with his own impotence even though he was the King of the Land. His nemesis took the form of the Knight of Tarn Wathelan, "huge beyond the size of mortal man and armed from crest to toe in black armor, mounted on a giant red-eyed warhorse the color of midnight." As Arthur charged toward him to do battle on the plain before the knight's dark castle, the knight cast a spell upon Arthur which drained him and his horse of all power. "Like an icy shadow, a great fear fell upon him, the more terrible because it was not of the knight or of anything in this world; a black terror of the soul that came between him and the sky, and sucked the strength from him so that sword arm and shield arm sank to his sides and he was powerless to move."

"What—would you—of me?" gasped Arthur.

Rather than killing him or flinging him into his dungeons "to rot among other valiant knights who lie there, and take your realm for my own by means of the magic that is mine to wield," the Knight of Tarn Wathelan offers Arthur his life and freedom if he returns in seven day's time, on New Year's Day, with the answer to the question: "What is it that all women most desire?"

Filled with shame and rage, but helpless to do anything other than agree, Arthur made the bargain and rode off.

That entire week he wandered the land, posing the question to every woman he met, whether she was a girl herding geese, an alewife, or a great lady, dutifully writing down their answers, knowing all the while that none rang true. And so, on the morning of New Year's Day, with a heavy heart, he turned his horse in the direction of the knight's castle, his one chance for life having eluded him, knowing now that he must submit and die at the knight's hand.

"The hills looked darker than they had done when last he rode that way, and the wind had a keener edge. And the way seemed much longer and rougher than it had done before, and yet it was all too quickly passed."

Not far from the knight's castle, as he rode chin on breast through a dark thicket, Arthur heard a woman's voice, sweet and soft, calling out to him, "Now God's greeting to you, my Lord King Arthur. God save and keep you."

He turned and saw a woman in a vivid scarlet gown the color of holly berries, sitting on a mound of earth beside the road between an oak tree and a holly tree. Expecting her face to be as sweet as her voice, he is shocked to see "the most hideous creature he has ever seen, with a piteous nightmare face that he can scarcely bear to look upon, sprouting a long wart-covered nose bent to one side and a long hairy chin bent to the other. She had only one eye, and that set deep under her jutting brow. Her mouth was no more than a shapeless gash. Her hair hung in gray twisted locks and her hands were like brown claws, though the jewels that sparkled on her fingers were fine enough for the Queen herself."

Arthur is struck dumb by the sight of her, and has to be reminded by her of his code of chivalry and how a knight is to comport himself in the presence of a lady. She, mysteriously, knows on what errand he rides. She knows that he has asked many women what it is that all women most desire, and that all have given him answers, and that not one is the right answer. She then informs the astonished king that she and she alone knows the answer he is seeking, and that for her to tell him, he will have to swear a solemn oath that he will grant her whatever she asks of him in exchange. To this, he readily agrees. She beckons him to bend his ear to her lips, and whispers into it the answer he is looking for, so that "not even the trees may hear."

The moment he heard it, Arthur knew in his very soul that it was the true answer. He caught his breath in laughter, for it was such a simple answer, after all.

The answer that he was given to the question, "What is it that all women most desire?" was *"Sovereignty."*

Arthur asked what she would have in return, but the lady refused to say until he had tested the answer on the Knight of Tarn Wathelan. So Arthur went off, and after some good sport at the expense of the huge knight, finally gave the true answer and with it, won his freedom. He then made his way back to the spot where the loathely lady was waiting for him.

Upon his return, the reward that Dame Ragnell, for that was the lady's name, asked of the King was that he bring to her from his court one of his own knights of the Round Table, brave and courteous, and good to look upon, to take her as his loving wife. Arthur, staggered and repulsed by this inconceivable request, has to be reminded that he owes his life to her and had made a knightly and kingly promise in exchange for her help.

Of course, for Arthur to assign the task to someone would be to disrespect the sovereignty of one of his own knights. The choice must be made freely. When Arthur returned to court and told the full story of his week's adventure to an astonished gathering of knights, his nephew Sir Gawain, out of loyalty to his uncle, the King, and out of his own goodness, offered to marry the lady himself. Arthur, ashamed and heavy hearted, would not let Gawain make the vow without seeing her first.

So the knights rode out in company the next morning to the woods, and after some time, they caught a glimpse of scarlet through the trees. Sir Kay and the other knights were sickened by the sight of Lady Ragnell, and some were even insulting to her face. Others turned away in pity or busied themselves with their horses.

But Sir Gawain looked steadily at the Lady, and something in her pathetic pride and the way she lifted her hideous head caused him to think of a deer with the hounds about it, and something in the depth of her bleared gaze reached him like a cry for help.

He glared about him at his fellow knights. "Nay now, why these sideways looks and troubled faces and ill manners. The matter was never in doubt. Did I not last night tell the King that I would marry this lady? And marry her I will, if she will have me!" And so saying, he jumped down from his horse and knelt before her, saying, "My Lady Ragnell, will you take me for your husband?"

The Lady looked at him for a moment out of her one eye, and then she said in that voice, so surprisingly sweet, "Not you, too, Sir Gawain. Surely you jest, like the others." "I was never further from jesting in my life," he protested.

She tried then to dissuade him. "Think you before it is too late. Will you indeed wed one as misshapen and old as I? What sort of wife should I be for the King's own nephew? What will Queen Guinevere and her ladies say when you bring such a bride to court? And what will you secretly feel? You will be shamed, and all through me," said the Lady, and she wept bitterly, and her face was wet and blubbered and even more hideous.

"Lady, if I can guard you, be very sure that I can also guard myself," Gawain said, glowering around at the other knights with his fighting face on him. "Now Lady, come with me back to the castle, for this very evening is our wedding to be celebrated."

To which Dame Ragnell replied, with tears falling from her one eye, "Truly, Sir Gawain, though it is a thing hard to believe, you shall not regret this wedding."

As she rose to move toward the horse they had brought for her, they saw that, beside all else, there was a hump between her shoulders and that she was lame in one leg.

Gawain then helped her into the saddle, mounted his own horse beside hers, and the whole group wended their way back to the King's castle.

Word ran ahead of them from the city gates and the people came flocking out to see Sir Gawain and his bride go by. All were horrified beyond even their expectations.

That evening, the wedding took place in the chapel, with the Queen herself standing beside the bride, and the King serving as groomsman. Sir Lancelot was the first to come forward and kiss the bride on her withered cheek, followed by the other knights, but the words strangled in their throats when they would have wished her and Sir Gawain joy in their marriage, so that they could scarcely speak. "And the poor Lady Ragnell looked down upon bent head after bent head of the ladies who came forward to touch her fingertips as briefly as might be, but could not bear to look at her or kiss her cheek. Only Cabal, the dog, came and licked her hand with a warm wet tongue and looked up into her face with amber eyes that took no account of her hideous aspect, for the eyes of a hound see differently from the eyes of men."

Dinner conversation was feverish and forced, a hollow pretense of gladness, through which Sir Gawain and his bride sat rigidly beside the King and Queen at the High Table. And when the tables were cleared away and it was time for dancing, many thought that now Sir Gawain might be free to leave her side and mingle with his friends. "But," he said, "Bride and groom must lead the first dance together," and offered his hand to the Lady Ragnell. She took it with a hideous grimace that was the nearest she could come to a smile, and limped forward to open the dance with him. And throughout the festivities, with the King's eye upon the company and Sir Gawain's as well, no one in the hall dared look as though anything was amiss.

At last, the forced festivities came to a close and it was time for the newlyweds to go to the wedding chamber in the castle. There, "Gawain flung himself into a deeply cushioned chair beside the fire and sat, gazing into the flames, not looking to see where his bride might be. A sudden draught drove the candle flames sideways and the embroidered creatures on the walls stirred as though on the edge of life. And somewhere very far off, as though from the heart of the enchanted forest, he fancied he heard the faintest echo of a horn.

"There was a faint movement at the foot of the bed, and the silken rustle of a woman's skirt; and a low sweet voice said, "Gawain, my lord and love, have you no word for me? Can you not even bear to look my way?"

"Gawain forced himself to turn his head and look and then sprang up in amazement, for there between the candle sconces stood the most beautiful woman he had ever seen."

"Lady," he said at half-breath, not sure whether he was awake or dreaming. "Who are you? Where is my wife, the Lady Ragnell?'"

"I am your wife, the Lady Ragnell," said she, "whom you found between the oak and the holly tree, and wedded this night in settlement of your King's debt—and maybe a little, in kindness."

"But—but I do not understand," stammered Gawain, "you are so changed."

"Yes," said the maiden. "I am changed, am I not? I was under an enchantment, and as yet I am only partly freed from it. But now for a little while I may be with you in my true seeming. Is my lord content with his bride?"

She came a little towards him, and he reached out and caught her into his arms. "Content? Oh, my most dear love, I am the happiest man in all the world; for I thought to save the honor of the King my uncle, and I have gained my heart's desire. And yet from the first moment I felt something of you reach out to me, and something of me reach back in answer…"

In a little, the lady brought her hands down and set them against his breast and gently held him off. "Listen," she said, "for now a hard choice lies before you. I told you that as yet I am only partly free from the enchantment that binds me. Because you have taken me for your wife, it is half broken; but no more than half broken."

Dame Ragnell explained that she was now able to appear in her natural form for but half of each day, and Gawain must choose whether he wanted her to be fair by day and foul by night, or fair by night and foul by day.

"That is a hard choice indeed," said Gawain.

"Think," said the Lady Ragnell.

And Sir Gawain said in a rush, "Oh my dear love, be hideous by day, and fair for me alone!"

"Alas!" said the Lady Ragnell. "And that is your choice? Must I be hideous and misshapen among all the Queen's fair ladies, and abide their scorn and pity, when in truth I am as fair as any of them? Oh, Sir Gawain, is this your love?"

Then Sir Gawain bowed his head. "Nay, I was thinking only of myself. If it will make you happier, be fair by day and take your rightful place at court. And at night I shall hear your soft voice in the darkness, and that shall be my content."

"That was indeed a lover's answer," said the Lady Ragnell. "But I would be fair for you, not only for the court and the daytime world that means less to me than you do."

And Gawain said, "Whichever way it is, it is you who must endure the most suffering; and being a woman, I am thinking that you have more wisdom in such things than I. Make the choice yourself, dear love, and whichever way you choose, I shall be content."

Then the Lady Ragnell bent her head into the hollow of his neck and wept and laughed together. "Oh, Gawain, my dearest lord, now, by seeing that it is for me to decide, by giving me *my own way*, by according me the very sovereignty that was the answer to the original riddle, you have broken the spell completely, and I am free of it, to be my true self by night and day."

For seven years Gawain and Ragnell knew great happiness together, and during all that time Gawain was a gentler and a kinder and more steadfast man than ever he had been before. But, after seven years she left. No one knew where she went. And something of Gawain went with her.

PART THREE

The Foundations

of Mindful Parenting

Sovereignty

Let's look at the mysterious jewel lying at the heart of the Gawain story. It is the concept of *sovereignty*, offered up as the answer to the riddle "What is it that all women most desire?"

As the answer to the riddle, the *knowledge* of sovereignty saved Arthur from certain death. But a deeper *feeling* for sovereignty that came out of Gawain's empathy and compassion for Ragnell solved (actually dissolved) a dilemma that no amount of thinking could have ever dispelled. By giving the choice back to her, he accorded (literally, opened his heart to) her sovereignty, and out of that came transformation.

This is the key to mindful parenting. In honoring our children's sovereignty, we make it possible for them to show themselves in their "true seeming" and find their own way. Both are necessary to come to full adulthood.

How many times do our children seem to be caught up in spells of their own, captivated by energies that carry them away, turned suddenly into demons, witches, trolls, ogres, and imps? Can we as parents in those moments, as Gawain did, see past the surface appearance, at which a part of us may recoil, to the true being behind the spell? Can we make room in ourselves to love them as they are without having them have to change to please us? And how many times do we as parents get caught up in spells of our own, show our children our ferocious side, the ogre within, or the witch? How much do we secretly yearn to be accepted as we are by others, and to find our own way in our lives?

In *Reviving Ophelia*, Mary Pipher points out that the answer to Sigmund Freud's patronizing question, "What does a woman want?" is revealed over and over in her therapy sessions with women, and that although they all want "something different and particular...each woman wants the same thing—to be who she truly is, to become who she can become," to be "the subject of her life, not the object of others' lives."

If sovereignty means being who one truly is and becoming who one can become, then could it not also be the answer to the larger question, "What does everyone at heart most desire?" And even, "What does everyone most deserve?"

In our view, sovereignty, understood in this way, is not an external seeking of power, although to be in touch with it is supremely powerful. It can be thought of as deeply connected to the Buddhist concept of *Buddha Nature*, which is another way of saying *our true self*. The figure of the Buddha represents the embodiment of a state of mind and heart, best described as in touch with itself, conscious, knowing, awake. The Buddhist view is that our individual mind and Buddha mind are fundamentally the same, and that our deepest work as human beings is to realize that essential unity. Buddha Nature underlies everything. Everything is perfectly and uniquely what it is, and yet nothing is separate and isolated from the whole. So everybody's true nature is Buddha Nature, and in that we are all the same. Everybody's true nature is sovereign. We have only to recognize it and honor it in other people, in all beings, in our children, and in ourselves.

Of course, having "only to recognize it" isn't so easy. It is the work of a lifetime. We may not know or may have lost touch with what is most fundamental in ourselves, with our own nature, with what calls to us most deeply. When we don't recognize our true nature, and live far from it, we can create a lot of suffering for ourselves and for others.

The Buddha is sometimes called, "One who has Sovereignty over Himself or Herself." Events carry us away, and we lose ourselves. Walking meditation helps us regain our sovereignty, our liberty as a human being. We walk with grace and dignity, like an emperor, like a lion. Each step is life.

THICH NHAT HANH
The Long Road Turns to Joy

Honoring what is deepest in people is symbolically reflected in the custom of greeting others by bowing to them. In many countries, instead of shaking hands in greeting, people put their palms together over their hearts and bend slightly toward each other. This means "I bow to the divinity within you." It signifies a shared recognition of each other's intrinsic wholeness, of what is deepest and most fundamental, already and always present. You are bowing from your true nature to theirs, recalling that at the deepest level, they are one and the same, even as we recognize that on other levels, we are all different, unique expressions of this oneness. Sometimes, people bow to cats and dogs, sometimes to trees and flowers, sometimes to the wind and the rain. And sometimes the cats and dogs, the trees and the flowers, even the wind and the rain, bow back. For everything has its intrinsic nature that makes it what it is and helps it take its place within the whole, and the relationship between them is always reciprocal. As parents, we sometimes find ourselves bowing inwardly to our babies and our children.

*

At different ages, with different children, and in different circumstances, our choices as parents about how to go about according our child or children sovereignty will be very different. But what will not change, hopefully, is a deep commitment to recognize it and honor it as a fundamental attribute and birthright of each child. This calls for us as parents to remember and, ultimately, to trust the sovereignty, the intrinsic goodness, and the beauty in our children, even when we are least in touch with it or it is least in evidence.

As every parent knows or soon finds out, each child comes into this world with his or her own attributes, temperament, and genius. As parents, we are called to recognize who each of them uniquely is, and to honor them by making room for them as they are, not by trying to change them, hard as that sometimes is for us. Since they are already always changing as part of their own nature, it may be that this kind of awareness on our part is precisely what is called for to make room for them to grow and change in those very ways that are best for them and that we cannot impose through our will.

Children are born with sovereignty, in that they are born perfectly who and what they are. While sovereignty is fundamental to our very nature as human beings, our ability to feel it and draw upon it deepens through our life experience, beginning with how we are treated when we are young. As adults, our intrinsic sovereignty can be damaged by traumatic life experiences and by our own neglecting of this essential domain of being.

Even so, what we are calling sovereignty is so deep, so tenacious, so vital, so integral to our nature because it *is* our true nature, that many people manage to draw sustenance and strength from it even through extremely difficult childhood circumstances. At times, someone other than a parent may assume a key role in a child's life by seeing who he really is and offering kindness and encouragement, appreciation and acceptance. Many people credit one special person who gave them recognition and encouragement to be who they already were and to become what they longed to become as the source of their success in life.

The mentoring of children and adolescents by people who themselves know in some way their own wholeness, and can thus recognize the beauty and wholeness in others, is the sacred responsibility of the adults in any healthy society.

*

The experience of sovereignty deepens as a child learns to encounter the world and overcome obstacles, developing inward strength and confidence, secure in herself, knowing that she is loved and accepted *as she is*.

At first blush, the very notion of the intrinsic sovereignty of children might easily be misconstrued to suggest that we are advocating our children should be treated as kings and queens and therefore waited on hand and foot. We are not. In fact, nothing could be further from an understanding of sovereignty as we are using the term. According sovereignty to our children does not mean letting them run rampant over everyone, or promoting a sense of false "self-esteem" disconnected from their behavior and life experiences. It does not mean that they have license to do whatever they like, that whatever they do is fine, or that they should always get whatever they want because they have to have their own way and they have to always be happy.

Sovereignty, in the sense of one's true nature, is a universal quality of being, and life, above all, an occasion to understand what that true nature is and how it expresses itself for each of us. Children are sovereign within themselves, and so is everyone else, including their parents. We might reflect on how we can honor sovereignty in them while also respecting our own. How do we help them to grow into all aspects of their being? How can we encourage them to see and respect the sovereignty of others?

Sovereignty is very different from unbridled entitlement. It does not mean that children should be given everything they want, or that others should do their work for them. It is our job to protect and nurture sovereignty in our children without fostering an attitude that whatever they do is fine regardless of its effects, because only they are important, only their views or their desires count. Each person's sovereignty is interdependent and interconnected with everybody else's. We are all part of a larger whole, and everything we do affects each other.

Another way of putting this is that actually our children *are* entitled. They are entitled to a great deal. Adults are entitled as well, but there are important asymmetries in the relationship. The adults are responsible for the children. Children are *entitled* to be loved, cared for, and protected by their parents and by other adults. As adults and as parents, we cannot look to children to meet our emotional needs. We have to look to ourselves and to other adults for that. But we do get to bask in the endless blessings that our children bestow on us unbidden, just by their being.

Indeed, as adults and as parents, we may very well need to explore, nourish, and deepen a more abiding connection to our own underlying sovereignty, since it is so fundamental and, at the same time, so elusive. This is the great work of awareness, of mindfulness, the opportunity to awaken to and embody our own true nature as human beings. Of course, most of the time, if we think about it at all, we might say that we are too busy to pay attention to such notions, for all the injunctions such as Socrates', to "know thyself." But it may be that we can't afford *not* to pay attention to our own true nature and learn to live in accordance with it. For if we don't, in a very real way, we may sleepwalk through large parts of our lives and at the end not know who we are or were, and not know who our children are, either, for all our thinking we did.

As we have seen, one vehicle for that inward journey of growth and discovery is mindfulness, cultivated in two complementary ways: as attentiveness brought to all aspects of daily life, and in the daily practice of a more formal meditative discipline in which we stop for a period of time and observe in stillness and quiet the moment-to-moment activity of our own minds and bodies. Bringing mindfulness to our lives in one or both of these ways and to the whole question of who we really are can help us perceive our own sovereign nature as we accord sovereignty to our children.

＊

What might a fundamental honoring of a child's own way look like, practically speaking, for us as parents? After all, what does it really mean to *have one's way*? What is one's true Way, with a capital *W*? How is sovereignty experienced as an adult or as a child? How is it experienced at different ages and stages of life, and for children with vastly different temperaments?

For one, the honoring of a child's sovereignty means acknowledging to ourselves the reality of those very stages and temperaments. It might mean that the messages an infant gives us are responded to because we are the baby's major interface with the world. If the baby cries, we pick her up, we hold her, we move in with our presence, our listening. We attempt to provide comfort and a sense of well-being. By doing so, we honor her power to have the world respond to her; we accord her that respect and teach her that the world does respond, and that there is a place for her, that she belongs. And we do this as an intentional practice, whether we feel like it at any given moment or not.

According sovereignty might mean child-proofing our house so that our toddler is free to explore her environment safely. Yet, even in a relatively safe environment, toddlers need to be attended to. Just keeping an eye out accords a toddler sovereignty. It is a form of honoring, a statement that the child deserves that attention at arm's length that becomes, in parents of children that age, a sixth sense, like knowing when the glass is too close to the edge of the table and moving it just before the child grabs for it, even as we may be in midconversation with another person.

On the other hand, a steady diet of fearful warnings, such as "Don't do that, you'll hurt yourself" whenever the child is exploring something can undermine a child's confidence and instill our fears in her. An alternative might be to give her the chance to find her own way out of a difficulty, quietly positioning ourselves to assist her if it becomes necessary. In this way, we allow her to adventure and problem-solve without injecting our own fears into her bold explorations.

With adolescents, according sovereignty might mean being willing to see past the ways they choose to appear or assert themselves, which, as expressions of their inner power, often shock or repulse their elders, relating instead to their underlying goodness. We accord them sovereignty by listening to them and trying to understand and appreciate their views, insights, skills, and strengths. We can also do so by staying abreast of the various forces that may exert themselves on adolescents in these times. It might mean knowing when to be silent and leave them alone, and when to reach out, verbally and nonverbally, in ways that respect their growing autonomy. And sometimes it means setting definite and clear limits and sticking to them with kindness and firmness.

These are just a few passing examples of how we might accord sovereignty to children at different ages. As with Dame Ragnell, our true nature is not always so apparent. The clarity that enables us to see past the veil of appearances and act in the best interest of our children comes out of our moment-to-moment awareness. Sovereignty can neither be fully tapped in oneself nor fully accorded to another by one hopeful act, however important that act or moment may be. It emerges out of the practice of embracing the present moment with an open, discerning heart.

✳

Not a day will go by when we do not feel challenged in one way or another, when we might question our own sovereignty or feel it is in conflict with our child's. This is another way of saying that parenting is exhausting at times, and involves hard work in the same way that being mindful is hard work. As we have seen, it is a discipline, a calling upon ourselves to remember to be present, to see and accept our children for who they are, and in doing so, to be and share with them our best self.

Part of this work is keeping in mind that we cannot solve all our problems or our children's problems through thinking alone. For there are other, equally important intelligences at work in our lives, and as parents, we need to develop fluency in them ourselves in order to help them emerge in our children. One is the intelligence of *empathy*. Gawain *felt* something for Lady Ragnell. In trusting his feelings, what we could call his intuition, his heart, he penetrated past appearances, and past the either-or veil of his own thinking. It was only when he let go of his attachment to a particular outcome and accepted both the dilemma *and* Ragnell's sovereignty that—in that very moment—an opening occurred, and with it, a seemingly impossible liberation.

If each moment is truly an opportunity for growth, an occasion to be true to oneself, a potential branch point leading to one of an infinite number of possible next moments depending on how this one is seen and held, according sovereignty to a child in one moment makes room right then and there for his or her true nature to emerge, to be seen and silently celebrated. In this way, self-acceptance, self-confidence, and trust in one's own true nature and path take root, develop, and mature in the growing child.

The power of empathy and acceptance is immense, and deeply transformative of both the person receiving them and the person according them. More than anything else, a careful nurturing of a child's sovereignty, and an honoring of it through empathy and acceptance, lie at the heart of mindful parenting.

✻

Here is a striking example of a gift of sovereignty from a father to his son:

> "Daddy's going to be very angry about this," my mother said. It was August 1938, at a Catskill Mountains boarding house. One hot Friday afternoon three of us—9-year-old city boys—got to feeling listless. We'd done all the summer-country stuff, caught all the frogs, picked the blueberries and

shivered in enough icy river water. What we needed, on this unbearably boring afternoon, was some action.

To consider the options, Artie, Eli and I holed up in the cool of the "casino," the little building in which the guests enjoyed their nightly bingo games and the occasional traveling magic act.

Gradually, inspiration came: the casino was too new, the wood frame and white sheetrock walls too perfect. We would do it some quiet damage. Leave our anonymous mark on the place, for all time. With, of course, no thought as to consequences.

We began by picking up a long, wooden bench, running with it like a battering ram, and bashing it into a wall. It left a wonderful hole. But small. So we did it again. And again...

Afterward the three of us, breathing hard, sweating the sweat of heroes, surveyed our first really big-time damage. The process had been so satisfying we'd gotten carried away. There was hardly a good square of sheetrock left.

Suddenly before even a tweak of remorse set in, the owner, Mr. Biolos, appeared in the doorway of the building. Furious. And craving justice: When they arrived from the city that night, he-would-tell-our-fathers!

Meantime, he told our mothers. My mother felt that what I had done was so monstrous she would leave my punishment to my father. "And," she said, "Daddy's going to be very angry about this."

By six o'clock Mr. Biolos was stationed out at the driveway, grimly waiting for the fathers to start showing up. Behind him, the front porch was jammed, like a sold-out bleacher section, with indignant guests. They'd seen the damage to their bingo palace, knew they'd have to endure it in that condition for the rest of the summer. They too craved justice.

As to Artie, Eli and me, we each found an inconspicuous spot on the porch, a careful distance from the other two but not too far from our respective mothers. And we waited.

Artie's father arrived first. When Mr. Biolos told him the news and showed him the blighted casino, he carefully took off his belt and—with practiced style—viciously whipped his screaming son. With the approbation, by the way, of an ugly crowd of once-gentle people.

Eli's father showed up next. He was told and shown and went raving mad, knocking his son off his feet with a slam to the head. As Eli lay crying on the grass, he kicked him on the legs, buttocks and back. When Eli tried to get up he kicked him again.

The crowd muttered: Listen, they should have thought of this before they did the damage. They'll live, don't worry, and I bet they never do that again.

I wondered: What will my father do? He'd never laid a hand on me in my life. I knew about other kids, had seen bruises on certain schoolmates and even heard screams in the evenings from certain houses on my street, but they were those kids, their families, and the why and how of their bruises were, to me, dark abstractions. Until now.

I looked over at my mother. She was upset. Earlier she'd made it clear to me that I had done some special kind of crime. Did it mean that beatings were now, suddenly, the new order of the day?

My own father suddenly pulled up in our Chevy, just in time to see Eli's father dragging Eli up the porch steps and into the building. He got out of the car believing, I was sure, that whatever it was all about, Eli must have deserved it. I went dizzy with fear. Mr. Biolos, on a roll, started talking. My father listened, his shirt soaked with perspiration, a damp handkerchief draped around his neck; he never did well in humid weather. I watched him follow Mr. Biolos into the casino. My dad—strong and principled, hot and bothered—what was he thinking about all this?

When they emerged, my father looked over at my mother. He mouthed a small "Hello." Then his eyes found me and stared for a long moment, without expression. I tried to read his eyes, but they left me and went to the crowd, from face to expectant face.

Then, amazingly, he got into his car and drove away! Nobody, not even my mother, could imagine where he was going.

An hour later he came back. Tied onto the top of his car was a stack of huge sheetrock boards. He got out holding a paper sack with a hammer sticking out of it. Without a word he untied the sheetrock and one by one carried the boards into the casino.

And didn't come out again that night.

All through my mother's and my silent dinner and for the rest of that Friday evening and long after we had gone to bed, I could hear—everyone could hear—the steady bang bang bang bang of my dad's hammer. I pictured him sweating, missing his dinner, missing my mother, getting madder and madder at me. Would tomorrow be the last day of my life? It was 3 A.M. before I finally fell asleep.

The next morning, my father didn't say a single word about the night before. Nor did he show any trace of anger or reproach of any kind. We had a regular day, he, my mother, and I, and, in fact, our usual sweet family weekend.

Was he mad at me? You bet he was. But in a time when many of his generation saw corporal punishment of their children as a God-given right, he knew "spanking" as beating, and beating as criminal. And that when kids were beaten, they always remembered the pain but often forgot the reason.

I also realized years later that, to him, humiliating me was just as unthinkable. Unlike the fathers of my buddies, he couldn't play into a conspiracy of revenge and spectacle.

But my father had made his point. I never forgot that my vandalism on that August afternoon was outrageous.

And I'll never forget that it was also the day I first understood how deeply I could trust him.

MELL LAZARUS,

CREATOR OF THE COMIC STRIPS

MOMMA AND *MISS PEACH*,

AND A NOVELIST

(from: "Angry Fathers," About Men, *New York Times,* May 28, 1995)

Empathy

Empathy played a key role in Sir Gawain's ability to free Dame Ragnell from the spell she was under. He sensed her pain and he glimpsed, through her eyes, a beauty and soulfulness beyond appearance, hidden, but there nonetheless: "Something in her pathetic pride and the way she lifted her hideous head caused him to think of a deer with the hounds about it. Something in the depth of her bleared gaze reached him like a cry for help."

The dog of the castle shows an empathy that puts the humans to shame. "Only Cabal, the dog, came and licked her hand with a warm wet tongue and looked up into her face with amber eyes that took no account of her hideous aspect." Often, if we are paying attention, dogs and cats can teach us about sovereignty, empathy, and acceptance. Perhaps that is why we live with them and they with us. They provide the basic course. Raising children is advanced training. We enroll whether we are ready for it or not. And who is ever ready?

✦

Reflecting on empathy in our own lives, perhaps it is useful to ask ourselves, "What did I most want from my parents when I was a child?" We might take a minute or two to reflect, and see what words or images come to mind....

For many people, what is most deeply desired is to have been seen and accepted in the family for who they were, a desire to have been treated with kindness, compassion, understanding, and respect; to have been accorded freedom, safety, and privacy, and a sense of belonging. All of these depend on a parent's ability to empathize. It is easy to empathize with a child when he is hurting. It is much harder to do when he is kicking and throwing things and screaming. It is also hard to do when his interests or views conflict with ours. Our ability to empathize in a broader range of situations takes intentional cultivation.

When we cultivate empathy, we try to see things from our child's point of view. We try to understand what he or she may be feeling or experiencing. We attempt to bring a sympathetic awareness to what is happening in each moment. This includes an awareness of our own feelings, as well.

What might it be like to empathize with a newborn baby, to imagine how she might feel arriving in this world after nine months of being in a very different one? We could start by imagining what it was like in the uterus, in a place that is warm, wet, and protected, with constant, rhythmic sounds, a feeling of being contained, held, rocked...an experience of undifferentiated wholeness, where there is nothing wanting, nothing missing.

In a letter written by a young man of nineteen to his mother on Mother's Day, we are given a heartfelt glimpse into this world:

Much peace and strength from my heart to you. For the nine months of sweetest meditation. In which, water I could breathe like fish. When food was so pure not the mouth nor throat were used...Blessings.

When we are born, we leave this harmonious world and emerge into a new and totally different one. There may be harsh light and cold air. We may hear loud, unpredictable noises and feel roughness or hardness against our skin. We feel hunger for the first time. All of this is occurring as raw, pure sensory experience, with no filters of knowing anything. Imagine being thrust into this foreign environment, where you depend entirely on the inhabitants' ability to understand your language and to be sensitive and responsive to your whole being, and to what you may need in any given moment.

Why is it so hard sometimes for us to see our infants as fully feeling, fully experiencing beings? Why is it okay to let them "cry it out" when we would never ignore the cries of a friend or a lover or even a stranger? What might we be resisting, or protecting ourselves from, when we distance ourselves from a baby's distress?

One thing we may be protecting ourselves from, of course, is more work. It's much more labor-intensive in the short run to parent moment by moment in responsive ways. Tuning in to a child's body language, trying different things, being sensitive not to underrespond or overrespond, holding, comforting, crooning, all take time and energy. More often than not, they can also interrupt our sleep, literally and metaphorically. It is certainly easier to empathize with our children when it also meets our own needs. The real test for us comes when it feels as if their needs are in conflict with ours.

A lack of empathy in such situations may also be a way of protecting ourselves from the pain we may have experienced when our own physical or emotional needs were not responded to when we were little. Empathizing with a child's vulnerability can be a painful reminder of our own.

One way to avoid having to acknowledge, as adults, our suffering as children is to revert to a coping mechanism we may have relied on when we were babies ourselves. In the face of an unresponsive environment, many babies close off emotionally, withdraw, and tune out. If that is the way we learned to deal with pain and frustration when we were children, we may continue to do this as adults, in ways that may be entirely automatic and below our level of awareness. Rather than tuning in to our baby's feelings and our own feelings in response, we might instead ignore them or minimize them with rationalizations such as "Kids are tough, she'll adjust," "Crying won't hurt her," and "We don't want to spoil her." Then, we may try to ease our own distress by reaching for food, alcohol, TV, our electronic devices, or the newspaper to calm ourselves and tune out the pain.

We may not realize that we have powerful inner resources that extend far beyond such vehicles of escape. Tuning in and connecting empathically in such moments is a healthier alternative, and far more satisfying for both parent and child. Even if we did not learn this in childhood, our babies and children can call up this primordial capacity from the depths of our being, if we are prepared to give ourselves over to such deep callings.

In studies where researchers asked mothers to deliberately over- or underrespond to their infants, rather than matching their feelings in an attuned, empathic way, the infants responded with immediate dismay and distress. Reporting on these studies, Daniel Goleman, in his seminal book *Emotional Intelligence*, writes:

> Prolonged absence of attunement between parent and child takes a tremendous toll on the child. When a parent consistently fails to show any empathy with a particular range of emotion in the child—joys, tears, needing to cuddle—the child begins to avoid expressing, and perhaps even feeling, those same emotions. In this way, presumably,

entire ranges of emotion can begin to be obliterated from the [child's] repertoire for intimate relations, especially if through childhood those feelings continue to be covertly or overtly discouraged.

The implications of such studies are profound. According to researcher and psychiatrist Daniel Stern, as cited by Goleman, the small, repeated exchanges that take place between parent and child form the basis for the most fundamental lessons of emotional life. If this is so, the importance of parents engaging wholeheartedly in this dance of interconnectedness with their children is vital to their children's ongoing development as whole, emotionally competent, sovereign beings.

From this point of view, the "good" baby who stops crying after ten minutes and goes to sleep may be a baby who has learned to give up. But is giving up what we want to teach them? Is adapting to not getting their needs met the way we want our children to develop "independence"? Is shutting down emotionally and losing some of their aliveness and openness what we want for our children? Or do we want to teach them that their feelings count, that we will respond to them, that there are people who they can trust and rely on to be sensitive to them, and that it is safe to be open, expressive, to ask for what they need, to be *interdependent*?

*

As babies become toddlers and start to explore the world, they have a natural curiosity and pleasure in everything around them. At the same time, the world offers many experiences of frustration as they try to do things they cannot yet do, limited by motor skills and strength they have yet to develop. While they are continually venturing out, they still need a loving, emotionally available person to come back to. Toddlers depend on their parents' sensitivity and understanding to create an environment (or in the case of child care, to choose an environment) that feeds their curiosity, gives them the freedom to safely explore and discover, and at the same time gives them appropriate limits and boundaries, as well as the warmth and security they need, in the form of a welcoming lap or being held or carried.

As our children get older, empathy takes a less physical form, although there are times when what a child needs is a silent hug, or for us to hold his hand. The cues we get from older children can be confusing and at times difficult to understand. One day (or one minute) they may be friendly and communicative, and the next they can be angry and rejecting. Our ability to communicate with them, or even its possibility, will depend a great deal on the sense of an enduring and strong commitment to them on our part, even when they may be questioning their relationship with us, or rejecting our overtures or inquiries.

Being empathic in the face of rejection requires us to not let our own hurt feelings get in the way of seeing what our child may be struggling with or what stresses he or she may be experiencing. In some sense, our children have to feel us staying connected with them, no matter what repugnant (to our mind) spells come over them, no matter what dark disguises they try on. We can reject their behavior without rejecting them. This mindful persistence on our part comes not out of a desire to control them, or to hold them back, or to cling to them out of our own neediness, but out of a commitment to be appropriately present for them, to let them know that they are not alone, that we have not lost sight of who they are and what they mean to us.

And isn't it true for all of us that when we are feeling lost, sad, and often quite toadlike, it helps enormously to feel that the people closest to us are still our allies, are still able to see and love our essential self? So, as parents, it is our job to continually rebuild and restore our relationships with our children. This takes time, attention, and commitment. If we are perpetually absent, or present in our bodies and absent in our attention and in our hearts, it is less likely that our child will feel the trust and sense of safety needed to let us know what problems she or he is facing.

Children have a wonderful ability to cut to the heart of an issue. A friend told us the following story: One night when her daughter was eight years old, she sat with her as she tried to go to sleep. Her daughter was overwhelmed by an acute fear of robbers and kidnappers, something that had surfaced at nighttime for a number of years. The mother sat on the bed, listening, struggling inwardly with her desire to reassure her child, to convince her that there was nothing to fear, and knowing the futility of trying to use reason in the face of her daughter's deep and persistent dread.

Taking a different tack, she told her that when she was her age, she also was very fearful at night. The young girl looked at her mother solemnly and said, "You were?" She responded with a nod. The daughter was thoughtful for a moment and then asked with great seriousness, "Could you tell your mommy?" Her mother paused, thinking back to when she was a child, and said, "No, I couldn't."

At eight years old, her daughter knew from her own direct experience how important it is to be able to tell someone close to you how you feel. She knew what it was like to feel an openness and acceptance, an empathic presence from a parent. Her fears weren't dismissed, joked about, or belittled. In the grip of this very real terror, she unquestioningly felt safe enough to tell her mother. She didn't have to feel alone in her fear.

As parents, we can learn a great deal about ourselves by bringing mindfulness to the thoughts and feelings that come up when a child is sharing something difficult with us. If we can observe our own discomfort—brought on by certain feelings—and any impulse that might arise in us to smooth over, dismiss, or belittle particular concerns or fears, the possibility exists of changing our own automatic behavior and becoming a more empathic and supportive parent.

Sometimes, in moments when we are called upon to listen, to empathize, to respond in a caring manner, we may instead find ourselves overwhelming a child with our own strong feelings and reactions. She may end up feeling that she has to take care of us, rather than the other way around.

If we can bring mindfulness to those moments in which we find ourselves moving down a tributary we didn't mean to take, carried away by our own emotions, we may be able to sense what is happening within us at that particular moment, stop, and perhaps change course, choosing a more relational and empathic alternative. This kind of moment-to-moment awareness reminds us that we can decide in a more conscious way when it is helpful to share our own feelings and when it is unnecessary or even destructive. We can learn through an inner listening when to reach out and when to let things be, when to speak and when to keep silent, and how to be present in silence so that it is felt by another as empathic presence rather than as rejection and withdrawal. No one can teach us these things. We have to learn from our own experience, from attending to the clues and cues we are given, and to our own mind states as they come and go.

Of course this isn't easy, and in particularly fraught moments of upset and conflict, we may find ourselves becoming emotionally reactive and saying things or acting in ways we will later regret. These "ruptures," moments of alienation and disconnection, are an inevitable part of any relationship. Children need to experience this, too, namely that their parents are human, that at times we can be insensitive, misattuned, even unempathic—that we can get upset and angry. Much can be learned from such moments of stress and disconnection, and from the important process of repair and recovery. As family therapist Daniel Hughes points out in his book *Attachment-Focused Family Therapy*, the strength of the parent-child relationship, which is sometimes referred to as *secure attachment*, is based as much on this tumultuous process of rupture followed by repair as it is in feelings of closeness and safety. Out of such moments can come a felt experience that parents and children can see and experience things very differently and still be safe within a loving and trustworthy relationship. Not only is the relationship strengthened by going through this process, but so, too, is the child's sense of autonomy and connection, both of which are essential for healthy development.

The continual weaving and restoring of empathic connections with our children is a foundation of mindful parenting. Trying to see things from our child's point of view can guide us in the choices we make and help us to navigate these complex and always-changing currents of connectedness.

Acceptance

Sovereignty and empathy are augmented by acceptance, a third fundamental element of mindful parenting. The three complement each other and are intimately interconnected. You can think of them as together forming the sides of an equilateral triangle. Acceptance is an interior orientation that recognizes and acknowledges that things are as they are, independent of whether they are the way we want them to be or not, no matter how terrible they may be or seem to be at certain moments. This is not easy to actualize in everyday life, even if you feel that it makes sense. The practice of mindfulness is about developing awareness of our relationship to the present moment, and noticing when we are struggling against the way things are. The stories we just visited illustrate the openings that can happen when we manage to not be caught by our strongly aversive thoughts and emotions.

Gawain accepted Ragnell as she was. Mell Lazarus's father accepted that what the boys had done was already done. In doing so, he saw that the next moment called for something new, something to further healing, completion, and respect. Acceptance of what is underlies our ability to choose *how* to be in relationship to whatever is actually happening. Acceptance is not passive resignation or defeat.

Just as sovereignty does not mean unbridled entitlement, so acceptance does not mean that everything our children do is okay with us. Even as we are clear with our children that certain behaviors are not acceptable, they can still feel that we accept them completely, including their strong emotions. Acceptance is a door that, if we choose to open it, leads to seeing in new ways and finding new possibilities to navigate in difficult moments, as well as being more in touch with the harmonious and joyful ones.

The process of attempting to see things as they actually are is key to cultivating even a modicum of acceptance. Thus, working with acceptance itself becomes a form of mindfulness practice. Part of the practice involves bringing awareness to how much resistance we sometimes feel when things are not going "our way." All sorts of emotions arise under such circumstances, including frustration and anger. There is a paradoxical opening and a loosening that may come about when we hold these afflictive emotions with kindness and clarity. A large part of this is not taking personally things that are not fundamentally personal. Not so easy to do when it comes to our children's behavior, or anything else that we may find upsetting or threatening.

＊

I (mkz) am in a shoe store with my daughters. One is four and the other is an infant. The four-year-old needs new shoes, and there are none that are quite right. As we are leaving, she starts to yell and scream and grabs a shoe on display, refusing to let go. Holding her baby sister in one arm, I grab her hand and get to the door of the store, where I ask an employee to take the shoe from her. A tugging match ensues. I'm feeling angry and helpless and out of control. I finally manage to get us outside. She is still screaming and crying, her face bright red. She is wild, furious that she cannot have new shoes. It is a struggle to get her into her car seat. In the process, her foot kicks the half-open car door and breaks the plastic side panel.

How I respond to this whole episode is determined by how I see or don't see my child in that moment. At the time, feeling completely overwhelmed by the intensity of her reaction, I felt angry and not very sympathic. I wasn't feeling particularly empathic, but I didn't lash out at her, either. It took all my attention and effort just to get us home and keep her from hurting anyone. It was only later that I was able to look at what had gone on and feel some sympathy for her as I started putting together clues in an attempt to understand what had happened.

The possible causes were as disparate as her being overtired, hungry, perhaps reacting to the fumes from the leather products in the store, coupled with her frustration over not getting what she wanted, made worse by the larger picture of having to share me with her baby sister. In all likelihood, it was a combination of these factors.

In looking back on what happened, I could see that she wasn't kicking and crying and destroying the car out of maliciousness or to drive me crazy or to control me. Her anger over not getting shoes set off a huge reaction that she couldn't control. She was in the grip of something, as if under a spell.

*

There are so many different ways to view what we often call "difficult" or "negative" behaviors in our children. What might be unacceptable to someone else might be normal behavior to me, and vice versa. Very often we're locked into seeing things in only one way, conditioned by views and emotions that are frequently unexamined, and that may put social decorum—what other people might be thinking, or how embarrassed we are feeling—above the emotional well-being of our children. In such moments, it is easy to feel controlled and manipulated by our children, to feel completely helpless, and then of course to feel tremendously angry. We might find ourselves lashing out at them in an attempt to assert our authority and regain control of the situation.

Since such occasions abound in parenting, we are given plenty of opportunities to work with these reactive patterns and develop, out of our awareness and discernment, a more appropriate and nurturing repertoire of emotional responses. This is where mindfulness of our emotional reactions can combine with even a modest engagement in formal meditation practice to help us deepen our natural capacity to be more aware and to see more clearly, as we describe in Part 4. Formal meditation can function as a kind of laboratory, in which we can develop a high degree of familiarity with our mind states and feeling states and how they affect us. We get to watch our thoughts and feelings arise from moment to moment and to see them as impersonal events in the mind, much like weather patterns, to which we do not have to react in a particular way, or in any way at all. Awareness of our emotions simply means consciously acknowledging that they are there. We simply or not so simply accept that they are our feelings in the moment, whether we like them or not, without judging them (which usually means without judging how much we in fact *are* judging them).

As we learn to observe and accept our own wide range of feelings, including very turbulent ones, as part of our effort to be more mindful, we naturally become more aware of other people's feelings, especially our children's. We come to know something of the landscape of feelings and their changing nature and are more likely to be sympathetic and less likely, at the same time, to take them personally. We are better able to accept our children's experience and their feelings, even if we may not like how they are behaving. In doing so, we are able to step out of the limited realm in which we as parents can often find ourselves, where we are so carried away by our own feelings and our attachment to our view of things that we cut ourselves off from our children and in some deep way, from ourselves, and thus, from our ability to work creatively with what is in front of us in such moments.

How we view what is happening, whether it is with judgment and disapproval or with an openness to trying to see beneath the surface, strongly affects our relationships with our children. Viewing our children's problematic behaviors (for example, hurting others, being rude or disrespectful) in a less harsh and judgmental manner allows us to remain their ally and keep a heartfelt connection with them even though their behavior is not okay, and we need to let them know that clearly and firmly, and establish some kind of boundary or limit.

Our children will give us countless opportunities to practice seeing and accepting things as they are through the veils of our own emotional reactivity, and then acting as best we can based on our understanding of the larger picture.

*

How we see things always colors what we choose to do. When a baby is crying, do we see it as a willful attempt to control us or as an expression of discomfort and her needing something from us? When children begin crawling and exploring the world around them, do we view their unstoppable curiosity as a sign of intelligence, strength, and spirit, or as a threat to our control, or—when they get a bit older—as an act of disobedience? How do we view it when a son is wildly teasing his sisters, or when a teenage daughter is moody and distant, critical and demanding, or when a child is so angry that he threatens to run away from home?

Accepting our children as they are. It sounds so simple. But how often do we find ourselves wanting our children to act, look, or be different from the way they actually are in *that* moment? How often do we want them to be, or look, or relate the way they were in a different moment, at a different time, and not accepting—despite all the evidence—that right here, right now, things are not the way we want them to be but are undeniably the way they are?

When things feel out of control, the impulse may be to reach for whatever methods we have at our disposal to "discipline" the offender and restore order. This cycle of "bad behavior" followed by some kind of discipline imposed by us often does not include any attempt to empathize with what the child is experiencing. Rather than a difficult moment leading to a greater sense of understanding and trust between parent and child, distance and alienation can be created instead.

The alternative to this is a process that is much less clear-cut. There is no set formula for it. But we can say that it begins with an attempt to be open, to see our child freshly in that very moment. When we try to do this, we often find that our view is colored by our own needs, fears, and expectations, and by the extent of our resources in that moment. These can combine either to filter our vision so that everything is colored in one particular way or to cloud our vision completely. In either case, we are no longer seeing the whole picture. Only certain colors and certain details come through. Our own partial seeing can lead to habitual negative labeling and judging of our child's behavior and to sustained anger and emotional distancing.

If we bring mindfulness into those very moments when we sense ourselves losing perspective or clarity, perhaps using our breath to ground us in the body, and if we try looking carefully at what is really happening with our child, we often find that there is much more going on than what we are reacting to on the surface. If we assume that there is some underlying reason for a child's "difficult" behavior, even if we don't see it immediately or understand what is going on, we may be able to be a little more sympathetic and accepting. When we are able to put aside our habitual, often critical ways of seeing disruptive or difficult behavior, we may begin to see that wild, loud, or even angry behavior is not necessarily "negative." Sometimes children are acting out as a way of regaining their equilibrium. They may have felt constrained by school or by the demands of homework and need outlets for their energy, their vitality, their agency.

Over the years, in moments when our children have been particularly wild, silly, goofy, or generally provoking, it has helped me (mkz) to view such behaviors as a form of discharging or releasing, an important way for them to let things out rather than hold them in. Sometimes young children are bursting with uncontrolled energy. At other times, they may be expressing deep, subterranean emotion. Even when they are falling apart, yelling, screaming, kicking and banging, seeing such behavior as a passing expression of their inner state makes me more tolerant. Resisting simply isn't helpful in such situations. As much as I want to control and change things in moments like this, I usually can't. Viewing such behavior as a normal release helps me to get some perspective on it and not take it so personally. I can choose to be more sanguine. It also gives them the freedom to express their feelings and try out different behaviors that often arise spontaneously, instead of being locked by a rigid parental authority into a narrowly defined framework of what is acceptable in the domain of being.

There are times when we might find it helpful to view an emotional outburst the way we view suddenly inclement weather. Sometimes we just have to sit out such an eruption the way we might sit out a thunderstorm. Do we think of thunderstorms as manipulative—a word that often comes up when children are not acting the way we want them to? Sometimes the only way our children have to start fresh is to erupt. When disequilibrium builds up for whatever reason, discharging it may be the only way to achieve the peace that follows in its wake, the sigh, the letting go. Children sometimes have to push us away and find a new space within themselves before there can be the possibility of a reconciliation, a reconnecting, and a new beginning.

Every time that we resisted, fought with, attempted to control, or commented negatively about this energy, we only made it worse. In such moments, it helps to find ways to move *with* our children rather than only to offer resistance, to work with them, rather than against them.

Sometimes this calls for engaging their energy directly. If a toddler or even a school-age child is getting wild and a bit out of control, he might like to wrestle with you, or play some other very physical game that allows him to let out his energy but in a more focused, grounded way. Once you have connected with him, you can more easily help him to make the transition to whatever it is he needs in that moment.

If we are observant, over time we can begin to identify the early warning signs that a storm is brewing. We can then work with our children in peaceful moments, when they are more receptive, and encourage them to pay attention to how they feel in those prestorm moments. They can begin to ask themselves: "Am I tired?" "Am I hungry?" "Am I mad, or sad?" Slowly, over time, as they get older, our children can learn to ask for what they need, whether it's a quiet time in their room alone, or a hug, or a warm bath, or a snack, or a rough-and-tumble game. We can also look back at what happened and talk about it together. Depending on their age, we can share what we sensed and saw in terms of what they might have been feeling ("You sounded really frustrated." "You seemed really upset with me." "You wanted this very badly, and I said no.") and listen to what they say in response. Going through this kind of process can strengthen our relationships in the aftermath of these inevitable emotional storms.

We can also let them know how their behavior affects us and others around them (for example, making it difficult to listen to them, pushing us away, etc.). With school-age children, we can ask them if they have any ideas about how they might express their feelings and needs so that they can be better heard. In this way they learn that they can reflect on their experience and perhaps see that they have some choices in regard to expressing their strong feelings. They can also begin to recognize and become more familiar with strong emotions in general: "Anger feels like this," "Sadness feels like this," "Fear feels like this."

*

Being accepting doesn't mean that we have to be naïve or passive in regard to our children. There will inevitably be many times when we need to step in and act decisively and wisely. Of course, what we do will depend very much on a child's age and the particular circumstances. At times, our children may be simply doing too much, moving too fast, flying too high. Learning to self-regulate happens slowly over time throughout childhood and adolescence. Our children may need us to rein them in, give them more structure and boundaries, provide something to come up against to slow them down, to bring them down to earth.

There are also times when our child may be waving a red flag at us, sending a serious distress signal, saying, "Pay attention! Something is not right!" These red flags can take many different forms, such as a pattern of angry outbursts, fearfulness, being withdrawn, physical symptoms, or not wanting to go to school. At such times, if we automatically attribute the worst motives to their behavior and react with punitive harshness, or we ignore them, we diminish our children as well as ourselves. We cannot be sure what our children's motivations are, any more than we can with anyone else. When we label their behavior as "manipulative" and react with disapproval and discipline, we essentially cut ourselves off from our children in those moments, just when they may need us the most. Our judging throws up a barrier. It becomes a dead end. We miss an opportunity to build trust and a sense of connectedness. We also miss an opportunity to deal with what may be very real problems and empathize with the underlying pain that accompanies them.

At such times we have to look beneath the surface and see what is going on. It can be hard to track down the source of these red flags. But rather than a negative, fearful, judging perspective, we might try cultivating a more open, curious, and caring perspective: "What do these signs mean?" "What can we work with here?" If we are more sensitive and attentive to the cues and clues our children give us, and combine them with what we know about them, we can usually begin to see what the underlying issues are and what may be needed.

Of course, when a toddler is kicking and screaming, or a school-age child is yelling and slamming doors, these are not the best times to wonder what is really going on. First, we need to get through the immediate crisis. Whatever the cause, when children are upset, they are not in a thinking mode. They are immersed in strong feelings, and they don't want us to try to reason with them. In such moments, they are unable to hear us, never mind understand us. They need us to stay with them through the storm and to not lose our own center just because they have lost theirs. We might imagine that we are a large sheltering oak tree in this storm, a solid, overarching friend, not necessarily understanding or having answers, but offering a sympathetic presence.

Once the storm has passed, that is the time to ask ourselves what may be going on here. We can become detectives and consider the possible source of his or her unhappiness or disequilibrium. Is it something at school or something at home? Is it physical, emotional, or both? Is it something relatively simple, like needing more structure, or less, being overtired, hungry, or overstimulated? Is there a pattern of behaviors that we need to pay attention to? Has something troubling happened that our child can't share with us? What are the possible stressors in our child's life? What inner and outer resources does he or she have to draw upon or need to develop?

Being accepting of who our children are and what they are going through means asking these kinds of questions and, to whatever degree possible, looking deeply into what we may find.

*

My ten-year-old daughter, in bed, lights out, says to me:

> "Mommy, I feel so confused."
> I reply: "What are you confused about?"
> She says: "I don't know, I just feel confused."
> I struggle with my urge to make it better…"It's okay to feel confused."
> She says: "It is?"
> I say: "Yes, it is."
> She is silent and drifts off to sleep.

She didn't need a discussion or a solution in that moment. Feeling held by me, she was able to accept uncertainty, confusion. My acceptance led her to an acceptance in herself.

*

It can be much harder for us to show teenagers the warmth and affection that may have come from us so easily when they were little.

We need to find ways to remind them that we are on their side, that they are as precious to us as they were when they were adorable, red-cheeked cherubs. But this is not so easy, especially on those occasions when everything they say seems to be a direct criticism of us. This usually happens at the end of a long day when everybody is feeling tired and depleted. Along with what sometimes feels like a steady stream of negative comments often come requests for us to do things for them and complaints about how tired they are and how much they have to do. The more alienated we feel from them, the angrier and more critical and demanding they become. In turn, we might feel angry and even more unaccepting and rejecting of them.

My teenage daughter comes into the kitchen, shivering, dressed in a T-shirt, and we have the following exchange:

Her: "It's cold in here."

Me: "Put something else on."

Her: (annoyed) "I don't need to put something more on—it's cold in here."

Me: "It's not very cold in here. Why don't you go and put something warmer on?"

Her: (getting angry) "I shouldn't have to put something on. It's cold in here."

It seems so inconsequential, yet each interaction pushes us farther apart. I am annoyed by her behavior and not feeling sympathetic because of all the times recently when I have felt relentlessly picked on by her. Later, things dissolve into a hugely upsetting scene in which she is in her room and refusing to talk to me. This has the effect of throwing cold water on me and waking me up, and I am finally able to see past my own anger and glimpse the difficult time she is going through. I see that the more distant we have grown in the past few weeks, the angrier she has become, and the more she has snapped at me, the angrier and more alienated from her I have become. A horribly vicious cycle, culminating in this present impasse. How does it end?

Clearly, I have to end it. I see that she can't get what she needs from me. She wants something, but she doesn't want it from me...she does and she doesn't. In that lies a conundrum.

When she complained of being cold and refused to put something on, I could have been sympathetic and just turned up the heat, which would have given her warmth in a way she might have accepted. Sometimes teenagers are asking for our attention and love and yet at the same time, they need more distance from us and are pushing us away. I could have responded in any number of ways, but instead I let my anger from the previous days make me intolerant. I closed myself off from her and made her the problem.

During this time, she needed me to not take her criticisms of the past few weeks so personally but to see them as a sign of her own internal struggles and the pressures she was under. I couldn't change things in the rest of her life, but I could have been more empathic and made an effort to hear the feelings behind her words and actions. At the same time, it would have been helpful if I had addressed her hostile behavior when it occurred in all those earlier moments, letting her know how it felt to me, so that my own resentment hadn't built up and she had more awareness of the effect of her behavior on others.

Our children's feelings are their own, but how they express them affects us and others. When their behavior is off-putting, hurtful, alienating, rude, or disrespectful, it does not serve them or us to ignore our own feelings and the effect their behavior is having on us and on the relationship. Figuring out when and what to say—or whether to say anything at all—is a creative process and requires us to be in touch with the present moment. There is no formula, no one right answer. The creativity arises in response to the particulars of each situation, with each child, and with ourselves. For this reason, a mindful response can only come from our willingness to stay in the situation with openness and not jump to finding "solutions" out of our own discomfort and our desire to fix or correct or teach in such moments.

*

Some of the ways in which our children behave may on occasion trigger volcanic feelings and destructive behaviors in us. These reactive patterns might have been part of the landscape of our own childhood, and we may have absorbed them without even knowing it. They tend to surface in particular situations when similar conditions arise. Our reactions can take the form of unconscious posturing, tension, self-righteousness, contempt, intolerance, cruelty, and catastrophic thinking.

Any behavior can be seen in its worst light, but most behaviors can be seen in a more understanding and accepting way. When we have been raised in an environment of mistrust, when we have been hurt by suspicion and judgment, when we have been belittled or ridiculed, we are primed to fall into these familiar patterns and repeat them with our children. To break out of them takes ongoing moment-to-moment awareness. It helps to be aware of *what* we are saying, *how* we are saying it, and *the effect* we are having on our children. Every time we are able to see a little more clearly our own reactive patterns and where they come from, we have the possibility of embodying new and healthier responses.

Too many children and adults live with the feeling that they are not accepted for who they are, that somehow they are "disappointing" their parents or not meeting their expectations—that somehow they don't "measure up." How many parents spend their time focusing on the ways in which their child is "too this" or "too that," or "not enough of this or that"? A great deal of unnecessary pain and grief is caused by this withholding, judging behavior. When has parental disapproval in the form of shaming or humiliating or withholding ever been a positive influence on a child's behavior? It might result in obedience, but at what cost to the child, and the adult the child becomes?

Parents don't have to like or agree with everything their children do, or the ways in which they choose to live when they are older. There are always going to be differences. But when a child, no matter how old, feels our acceptance, when he feels our love, not just for his easy-to-live-with, lovable, attractive, and agreeable self, but also for his difficult, repulsive, exasperating self, it can free him to become more balanced and whole. Children can face all sorts of difficulties and challenges if they can come back to the well of our unconditional love. For it is in our recognizing and accepting them as they are that inner growth and healing take place.

PART FOUR

Mindfulness:

A Way of Seeing

Parenting Is the Full Catastrophe

When we become parents, whether intentionally or by happenstance, our whole life is immediately different, although it may take some time to realize just how much. Being a parent compounds stress by orders of magnitude. It makes us vulnerable in ways we weren't before. It calls us to be responsible in ways we weren't before. It challenges us as never before and takes our time and attention away from other things, including ourselves, as never before. It creates chaos and disorder, feelings of inadequacy, occasions for arguments, struggles, irritation, noise, seemingly never-ending obligations and errands, and plenty of opportunities for getting stuck, angry, resentful, hurt, and for feeling overwhelmed, old, and unimportant. And this can go on not only when the children are little, but also even when they are full grown and on their own. Having children is asking for trouble.

So why do it? Maybe the folksinger Pete Seeger said it best: "We do it for the high wages...kisses." Children give us the opportunity to share in the vibrancy of life itself in ways we might not touch were they not part of our lives. Especially when children are young, our job as a parent is to be there for them and, as best we can, nurture them and protect them so that they are free to experience the innocence and genius of childhood, gently providing what guidance we can out of our own hearts and our own wisdom as they learn to find and define their own paths.

Children embody what is best in life. They live in the present moment. They are part of its exquisite bloom. They are pure potentiality, embodying vitality, emergence, renewal, and hope. They are purely what they are. And they share that vital nature with us and call it out of us as well, if we can listen carefully to the calling.

Once we have children, we are in touch with the rest of the universe in an entirely different way. Our consciousness changes, rotates from one way of seeing to another. We may find ourselves feeling connected to the hopefulness and the pain in others in ways that we might not have felt before. Our sphere of compassion tends to broaden. Concern for our children and their well-being may give us a different perspective on poverty, the environment, war, and the future.

As for trouble, Zorba, the crusty old character played by Anthony Quinn in the classic movie version of Nikos Kazantzakis's novel *Zorba the Greek*, who, when asked whether he had ever been married, replied, "Am I not a man? Of course I've been married. Wife, house, kids, the full catastrophe," also said, "Trouble? Life is trouble. Only death is no trouble."

Ultimately, we make our own choices, mindfully or not, and we live with their consequences. Even so, we never know what is coming next. Immanent uncertainty is a big part of the full catastrophe. The question is, can we learn to use all of life's circumstances, even the most trying and stressful ones, to grow in strength and wisdom and openheartedness, much as a sailor makes skillful use of all kinds of wind conditions to propel a sailboat toward a particular destination? For our own ongoing growth is an absolute necessity if we are to serve as effective parents of our children over the long haul, so that they may be sheltered and grow well in their own ways and in their own time.

Live-in Zen Masters

Although we are not Buddhists, we were married in a Zen ceremony in which our wedding vows were to help each other "attain 'big mind' for the sake of all beings." The Zen tradition has had a deep appeal to me (jkz) from my first contacts with it many years ago. Zen training is arduous and demanding, intense and unpredictable, wild and crazy, and very loving and funny. It's also very simple and at the same time not so simple. It's all about mindfulness and nonattachment, knowing who we are at the deepest of levels, and knowing what we are doing, which paradoxically includes both not knowing and nondoing.

For me, the wild ride of Zen training in the years that I was immersed in it seemed like it had a lot in common with parenting. They both appeared to be about waking up to life itself, with no holds barred. So it was not such a big jump to think that I could see our babies—who, like all babies, really do look like little Buddhas, with their round bellies, big heads, and mysterious smiles—as live-in Zen Masters. Zen Masters don't explain themselves. They just embody presence. They don't get hung up in thinking or get lost in theoretical musings about this or that. They are not attached to things being a certain way. They are not always consistent. One day does not necessarily have to be like the next. Their presence and their teachings can help us break through to a direct experiencing of our own true nature and encourage us to find our own way, now, in this moment. They do this not by telling us how, but by giving us endless challenges that cannot be resolved through thinking, by mirroring life back to us in its fullness, by pointing to wholeness. More than anything, Zen Masters embody wakefulness and call it out of us.

Children are similar in many ways, especially when they are babies. The older they get, the harder it is for us to see it. But a child's true nature is always present, and always mirroring our own, if we are willing to look, and to see.

Children have what might be called "original mind," open, pure, unencumbered. They are undeniably and totally present. They are constantly learning, developing, changing, and requiring new responses from us. As they grow, they seem to challenge every place that we might be holding an expectation, a fixed opinion, a cherished belief, a desire for things to be a certain way. As babies, they so fill our lives and require so much attention to their physical and emotional needs that they continually challenge us to be present, to be sensitive, to be patient with our sometimes impatience, to inquire into what is actually happening, to be willing to try different things, and to learn from their responses to our attempts. They teach us how to be attuned to them and to find joy and harmony in our connectedness with them. There is little time for theory, and it doesn't seem to help much anyway unless it is connected to practice.

Of course, children are not really Zen Masters. Children are children and Zen Masters are Zen Masters. No point in idealizing the one or the other. But if we are able to look at our children with openness and receptivity, and see the purity of life expressing itself through them, at any age, it can wake us up at any moment to their true nature and to our own.

Nothing anyone ever tells us prepares us for what it is actually like to be a parent. We learn on the job, in the doing, charting our own paths, relying on our inner resources, including the ones we never knew we had, taking our cues from our children and from every new situation that presents itself. We have to live inside of parenthood to know what it is. It is a deep and abiding inner work, a spiritual training all its own, if we choose to let it speak to us in that way, literally moment to moment.

We can ignore entirely, or resist as inconvenient or unimportant, or too messy or difficult, the continual stream of teachings from our children and from the circumstances we find ourselves in, or we can look deeply into them, letting them serve as indicators of where we need to pay attention and discern what is happening and what needs doing in any moment. It is entirely our choice. If we resist, we may occasion a great deal of unnecessary struggle and pain, for to ignore or struggle against the life force of children exploring and learning and growing, to not recognize and honor their sovereignty, denies a reality that is fundamental and will make itself known and felt one way or another.

For example, to forget momentarily that a two-year-old is a child and to rigidly and unfeelingly impose our own expectations about how she should be behaving is to forget that what she is doing is what two-year-olds do. If we want it to be different from what is happening in that moment, and we resist or contract in our mind and try to force what we want on the situation, we will be creating a lot of trouble all around. We have all undoubtedly experienced the consequences of such a situation at one point or another as parents.

On the other hand, if we can let go of our idea in such a moment of how things "should be" and embrace how they actually are with this child—in other words, if we can remember that we are the adult and that we can look inside ourselves at that very moment and find a way to act with some degree of understanding and kindness—then our emotional state and our choices of what to do will be very different, as will be the unfolding and resolution of that moment into the next. If we choose this path, she will have taught us something very important. She will have shown us how attached we can be to having things happen a certain way, that our mind wavers when we are challenged, and that we have various choices available to us. One of those choices would be to allow ourselves to be carried away by our own reactivity and ignorance, forgetting that two-year-olds do two-year-old kinds of things; another might be to affirm that we are capable of seeing our own reactivity and choose to go a different route, one in which we work both with our reaction and with what is actually happening with our child. We may have "known" all this, theoretically speaking, the moment before, or in another circumstance, but perhaps not in a way that prevented us from reacting automatically. So our two-year-old showed us, through her being, that we can easily lose ourselves in emotional reacting and that we don't have to. An important lesson, applicable in many different areas of our life. After all, our mind goes everywhere we do, and it usually reacts in a similar way whenever it doesn't feel in control or like what is happening.

If we can bring attention and intentionality to our own growing edges, in parenting and elsewhere in our lives, painful and frightening as that can be, that very orientation, that tenacious willingness to be present and to look at *anything* can bring us into greater harmony with the way things actually are. But for that to happen, we need to learn to listen carefully to what the world offers us, and look with a greater openness into our experience as it is unfolding.

The funny thing is that if we bring awareness to what is in front of us in every moment, without insisting on it being a certain way, then the discipline of doing just that gives rise to a stability of mind and an openness and clarity of heart that are unattainable by struggling to achieve them through forcing a particular resolution or outcome. For such harmony underlies everything. It is here now, in us, and in our children, if we can but make room, over and over again, for it to emerge.

*

First we braid grasses and play tug of war,
then we take turns singing and keeping a kick-ball in the air.
I kick the ball and they sing, they kick and I sing.
Time is forgotten, the hours fly.
People passing by point at me and laugh:
"Why are you acting like such a fool?"
I nod my head and don't answer.
I could say something, but why?
Do you want to know what's in my heart?
From the beginning of time: just this! just this!

RYOKAN

EIGHTEENTH-CENTURY

JAPANESE ZEN MASTER, HERMIT,

CALLIGRAPHER, POET

An Eighteen-Year Retreat

Just as it might be useful to look at our children as little Buddhas or Zen Masters in order to help us to parent them better and to continue to grow ourselves, I (jkz) have often felt that parenting could be looked at as an extended meditation retreat, an opportunity to do a certain kind of deep and concentrated inner work of potentially profound and continuing benefit to children and parents alike within a family.

Usually meditation retreats last for days, weeks, or months, but in this case, the "parenting retreat" would last on the order of at least eighteen years per child. Of course, the demands of parenting from day to day are very different from those of a secluded and intensive meditation retreat, but seeing them as related ways of engaging in sustained inner work has energized and buoyed me at times in bringing a tenacious and overarching perspective to the calling of parenting and to the years of attention, caring, and wisdom that it asks of us.

What then is a meditation retreat? What is its purpose? And how might seeing parenting as a kind of retreat help us understand and deepen what is being asked of us when we engage in mindful parenting, even for those of us who don't meditate regularly or who have no personal experience of such retreats? And how might looking at parenting in this way contribute to our own growth and development?

A meditation retreat is an opportunity to do a certain kind of inner work on ourselves that is extremely difficult to do outside of the retreat setting because of all the competing obligations, distractions, and enticements of everyday life. On retreat, because we are off in a special place for an extended period of time, away from the demands of family and work, we have a rare and precious chance to simplify our lives and give great care and attention to the domain of being.

Meditation retreats are often guided by one or more skilled teachers who serve to encourage, inspire, guide, instruct, and listen to the experiences of the retreatants. The basic practice consists mostly of periods of sitting and walking, all in silence, typically from early morning to late at night. Just sitting. Just walking. Usually there is a period of work as well, also silent, so that the same mind that we cultivate in sitting and walking can be brought to cleaning the bathroom, or washing pots, or weeding the garden. What the task is is not so important...the mind that we bring to it is exquisitely important.

Attention is directed primarily inwardly, toward a few basic aspects of life experience that are ordinarily taken completely for granted, such as the breath flowing in and out, and what there is to be perceived moment by moment in your own body and in your own mind. Other than that, you eat, also in silence, and you sleep. Usually there is no reading, no writing, no computers, no Internet, no devices of any kind, and either very limited or no phone calls, so you are really on your own, except for occasional interviews with the teacher. Such retreats can be extremely arduous and challenging, and deeply healing.

Initially the mind can be very active or agitated, but over time it can gradually settle and become deeply concentrated and one-pointed. Sometimes it can remain focused and relatively balanced and still over extended periods of time. Through the disciplined cultivation of attention, coupled with recognition and acceptance of what you are observing, you can come to know the landscape of your own mind and your own heart in radically new ways. A highly penetrative awareness can develop, providing a deep look into the very nature of your own being, underneath surface appearances, attachments, and personal history. Intensive and sustained attention of this kind can sometimes catalyze profound insights—awakenings that are truly enlightening—and can reveal you to yourself and illuminate life in ways you may never have known or thought possible.

Intensive meditation practice is both a mirror and also a profound purification process. We may come to a larger and more accurate way of seeing, which can give rise to deep learning about ourselves and an equally deep letting go, perhaps most importantly, a letting go of whatever we find we identify with in absolute and rigid ways...our attachments to things, our ways of seeing, our fixed ideas.

In paying sustained attention to your own mind, you can discover that the mind actually behaves in fairly structured ways, in patterns that are recognizable, if sometimes excruciatingly repetitive and unrelenting. You might come to see, just by sitting and walking in silence, how ceaselessly the stream of thinking flows, how chaotic the thought process is (the order within it is sometimes difficult to discern), and how unreliable and inaccurate most of our thoughts are. You might come to see how reactive the mind is and how powerful its emotional storms are.

You might see that the mind spends enormous amounts of time in the past (reminiscing, resenting, or blaming) and in the future (worrying, planning, hoping, and dreaming). You might see that the mind tends constantly to judge itself and everything else depending on whether an experience is felt to be pleasant, unpleasant, or neutral at any particular moment. You might see how strong the mind's attachments are, its incessant identification with things and opinions, and how so much of the time it is driven by wishful thinking and the desire to be somewhere else, to have things and relationships be different from how they actually are.

You might see how hard it is for the mind to settle into the present moment as it is, but also that over time, the mind can actually calm down enough to see much of this ceaseless activity that it is engaged in and come to an inner stillness and calmness and balance that is less easily disturbed by its own activity.

If you are motivated enough to stick with the practice through the hard times, if you can stay with the pain in your body that may come from long periods of sitting still, if you can stay with the yearning in the mind for talk, or for entertainment and distraction and novelty, if you can stay with the boredom, the resistance, the grief, the terror, and the confusion that can and do arise on occasion, and if, all the while, you ruthlessly and with utter kindness and gentleness, without expectations, persist in simply observing whatever comes up in the field of your awareness, moment by moment, you may come to encounter, at certain points in your practice, great oceanlike depths of silence, well-being, and wisdom within your own mind.

For in many ways, the mind does resemble a body of water, a veritable ocean. Depending on the season, the weather, and the winds, the surface can be anything from completely calm and flat to hugely tumultuous and turbulent, with forty-foot waves or higher. But even at its most stormy, if one goes down deep enough, the water is still.

Persisting in the practice, we might come to see on such a retreat that our own mind is much the same, that calmness and deep stillness are intrinsic to its nature, that they are always present, and that even when we are caught up in huge storms of emotional turmoil, for whatever reasons, the calmness and the stillness and the capacity to be aware are still here, underneath, embedded in and an integral part of our being. They can be called upon and used, not to extinguish the surface turbulence of the mind (just as we don't try to flatten the waves on the ocean), but to understand it and to provide a larger container for it, a context in which the very turbulence itself can be held, seen, and even used to deepen our understanding.

We may come to see that our thoughts and emotions do not have to carry us away or blind us in one way or another, as so frequently happens in life. Nor do we have to make any effort to suppress them to be free from much of the suffering they contain or engender.

Working in this way with the activity of our own mind, we might also come to see that it is a fiction that we are isolated, separate, and alone. We might see that "I," "me," and "mine" are themselves thoughts—powerful, deeply rooted, and tenacious habits of mind, but thoughts all the same. Beneath the sense of ourselves as being separate and preoccupied so much of the time with concerns about our individual self and our own personal gains and losses, we might see that we are part of a flowing movement of wholeness that is larger than we are and to which we belong.

We might see that there is a deep mystery in our individual life emerging from the union of our parents and, before them, of their parents, and so on back into time; that we are an intermediary between our parents and our children, between all those who have come before, who we will never know, and all those who will come after our children's children's children, who we will also never know.

We may come to see that the deepest nature of the universe is that it is one seamless whole, and that everything that is is an aspect of everything else. We may come to see that everything is embedded in and reflected in everything else, part of a larger wholeness, and that interconnectedness and interdependence are the root relationships out of which meaning and the particulars of our fleeting and constantly changing individual lives arise.

And you may come to see with fresh eyes and a new understanding and appreciation that, together with the ways in which the unfolding of life is impersonal, it is all the same, very personal. You may realize directly, as the veils of thinking and strong attachment thin, that right now and right here, you are who you are, that the being that is you is unique, with your own face and character and desires, with a particular history that is the legacy of having the parents that you had and growing up the way you did, and with your own unique and mysterious path or calling that can infuse your life with vision and passion. You work where you work, you live where you live, your responsibilities are your responsibilities, your children are your children, your hopes are your hopes, your fears your fears.

We might come to see that "separate" and "not separate" are just thoughts attempting to describe a deeper reality that is us. We might see the possibility of living more gracefully, knowing that the things that happen to us are happening to us, yet also knowing that it is not entirely wise to take them personally, because everything is also impersonal, and it is problematic—Buddhists would say impossible— to point to a solid, permanent "you" who is there to take them personally. You are certainly who you are, and you are responsible for many things, but you are certainly not who you think you are, because thinking itself is limited, and your true nature is limitless.

On retreat, we might also come to know that we are not our body, not our thoughts, not our emotions, not our ideas and opinions, not our fears and our insecurities and our woundedness, even though they are an intimate part of our experience and can influence our lives enormously, much like the weather can influence the surface of the ocean. Their influence is particularly strong if we form strong and unconscious attachments to them, to which we cling for dear life, and through which we see everything as through dark, or light, or colored, or kaleidoscopic glasses.

We are not our ideas and opinions. If we could live our lives knowing this, and take off the glasses through which we filter our experience, what a difference it might make in the way we see, in our choices, and the way we conduct our lives from day to day. This insight alone might cause us to see ourselves very differently, to see our parenting very differently, and indeed, to live differently.

We may also see that like everybody else, we are only here very briefly, but that brief moment we call a lifetime is also infinitely long if we can bring awareness to our moments, since there are, to a first approximation, infinite moments in any lifetime. In living in the present, we step out of clock time into a timeless present. Such experiences may show us that we are not entirely bound by time.

We might, thus, also begin to know something about impermanence, since nothing we focus our attention on endures for long. Each breath comes and goes, sensations in the body come and go, thoughts come and go, emotions come and go, ideas and opinions and desires come and go, moments come and go, days and nights come and go. We may see that, similarly, seasons and years come and go, youth comes and goes, jobs and people come and go. Even mountains and rivers and species come and go. Nothing is fixed. Nothing is permanent, although things may appear that way to us. Everything is always moving, changing, becoming, dissolving, emerging, evolving, in a complex dance, the outer dance of the world not so different from the inner dance of our own mind. We might see that our children are also part of this dance... that, like us, they, too, are only brief visitors to this beautiful and strange world, and our time with them even briefer, its duration unknown.

Might not this realization strike us deeply and teach us something of great value? Might it not suggest how precious the time we do share together with our children is, and how to hold our essentially fleeting moments with them in awareness? Might it not influence how we hug and kiss our children, and say good night to them, and watch them sleep, and wake them in the morning? Might such understanding not influence how we respond to them when, in seeking to find their own ways, they scrape up against our ideas and opinions, the limits of our patience, and our ego investments in being right and all-knowing, forgetting in those moments what we actually know that is far larger and more life-affirming?

Perhaps taking on parenting as a kind of meditation retreat, and doing the inner work of mindful parenting day by day and moment by moment in the same spirit of concentrated and sustained effort of attention and presence as on a retreat would help us to realize the enormous power in seeing and remembering the larger context of wholeness so that we are not lost in the surface waves of our own minds and our sometimes narrowly conceived and clung-to lives. Perhaps we would hold our moments differently. Perhaps they would not slip by so unnoticed.

Perhaps we would care more, and care differently, and attend more, and attend differently, if we held in our own minds and hearts what we already deeply know but usually forget. Perhaps we would know how to stand in our own life, on our own feet, and feel the earth beneath us and the wind in our face and around our body, and know the place as here, and the time as now, and honor the mysterious wisdom that resides within all beings and within our children.

These glimpses are some of what might be seen and realized through intensive practice on an extended mindfulness meditation retreat. Retreats are of great and abiding value when we can arrange our lives to go off from time to time to practice in this way. But there are also many times when it may not be possible, necessary, or advisable to go off someplace else for an extended period, especially when we are juggling the responsibilities of parenting, family life, and work.

This is where the metaphor of seeing the whole experience of parenting as an extended meditation retreat may be useful. It is not that parenting is a retreat from the world, although to some extent, family life can buffer the stress of the outer world and create feelings of inner security and peace. Rather, it is that we are using the very circumstances of the world and of parenting as best we can, and usually under difficult conditions, to help us cultivate mindfulness, look deeply into our lives, and let our doing come out of our being, not just from time to time, but concertedly, as a way of life.

The daily schedule of family life, of course, is much more complex and chaotic than on retreat. It will change as our children change and grow, sometimes from day to day, sometimes moment by moment. But the essence of the practice of mindfulness is always the same: as best we can, to be fully present, discerning what is actually happening to whatever degree possible—not always so easy, as we have seen—and if action is needed, to act with intentionality, awareness, and kindness. Our interior work can be anchored by a daily period of formal practice at a convenient time, but the major commitment will of necessity be the cultivation of mindfulness in everyday life, responding to the ever-arising calls of parenting from moment to moment and from day to day, allowing each day and each moment to provide the arena for a deepening of mindfulness.

In this way, waking up in the morning is waking-up meditation. Brushing your teeth is brushing-your-teeth meditation. Not getting to brush your teeth because the baby is crying is not-getting-to-brush-your-teeth-and-taking-care-of-the-baby-first meditation, and so on. Getting the children dressed, getting food on the table, getting them off to school, going to work, diapering, shopping, making arrangements, cleaning up, cooking, everything becomes part of our practice of mindfulness. Everything.

The Importance of Practice

To affect the quality of the day, that is the highest of arts.

THOREAU, *Walden*

There is no doubt that just hearing about the importance of being more present, more aware, more empathic, and more accepting in one's life and, particularly, in one's parenting can be suggestive enough to some people to put them on a different track, to awaken them to their own capacity to, as Thoreau put it, "affect the quality of the day" intentionally, to inspire them to new openness and sensitivity in their lives and in their parenting.

But we also know that the human mind has its own particular way of operating, which makes it difficult for most of us to "just wake up" all of a sudden. To get in touch with the present moment usually requires effort and consistency. Seeing clearly is not something that easily sustains itself. For instance, we may catch only occasional glimpses or vague intimations of our own sovereignty and our capacity to embody it in everyday life. Insight and transformation do not, as a rule, come easily to us as human beings.

We have to *practice* learning to live in the present. We have to *practice* seeing with eyes of wholeness. Why? Because, perhaps due to the nature of the human mind, we spend much of our lives practicing the exact opposite of mindfulness. We *practice* not living in the present moment. We *practice* being carried away from ourself, from our sovereignty, from our interconnectedness by our thoughts and feelings, by our likes and dislikes. We *practice* anxiety. We *practice* getting angry. We *practice* grasping for what we most want. And the more we practice, through repeating these patterns in our lives, the "better" we get at them, and the harder they are to break out of.

This is why mindful parenting has to be understood as a practice, a discipline, and not simply a philosophy or a good idea. As a practice, it helps us liberate ourselves from the deep patterns in our minds and in our lives that keep us apart from ourselves and from the only moments we have in which to live and grow and affirm our interconnectedness.

We are using the word *practice* somewhat differently from the way it is ordinarily thought of. *Practice* here means "embodying presence and wakefulness right now." It is not like practicing the piano or a dance step. It is not an exercise or a rehearsal. It is not to get better at something by repeating it over and over again, although a deepening does happen the more you practice being mindful.

Every time you pick up your baby, if you do it with awareness, it is practice. It is a matter of being fully there. And what does "being fully there" mean? It means "being fully *here*." It means knowing that you are picking up your baby while you are picking up your baby. It means being in touch with feeling, smelling, touching, listening, holding, breathing, with whatever is happening, and embracing it all in awareness as you do whatever it is that your intuition, and your baby, and the moment tell you is what needs doing, whether it is feeding, diapering, dressing, singing, or something else. This something else can include nothing at all. It may be that nothing is called for other than just being as present as you can be in that moment.

You do not have to be "good" at this, and certainly judging yourself is not part of the spirit of being mindful. It's good enough to be present in this particular moment. Why? Because you already are. Why not be here completely? Then you might be able to taste wholeness in this very moment, because it is always here, now, to be seen, felt, and embraced. We are separate and yet not separate at the same time.

So practice simply means intentionally remembering to be fully present with whatever comes up so that you are not on automatic pilot or acting mechanically. When you are picking up the baby, you are picking up the baby. When you are hugging your child, you are there with hugging your child. When you are setting a limit or communicating an expectation, you are fully present for that. Your mind is not off someplace else, or if it is, you are aware of that, too, and so can bring it back. It is simple, but it is not so easy, because our minds are so readily carried off elsewhere.

There are many, many ways to practice. There is no aspect of life or of parenting that cannot become practice simply by bringing it intentionally into awareness and holding it in awareness as it unfolds. The more we are willing to pay attention, the more firmly grounded we become in mindfulness and in mindful parenting. Each one of us has all the equipment we need to do this inner and outer work. Each child, each circumstance, each breath, every moment, it is all here, waiting to be embraced right now. If we approach life in this way, then, as Thoreau was suggesting, affecting the quality of the day truly becomes an art form. It is an ongoing refining of how we live and are in the world, allowing ourselves to be refined by what each day provides.

Breathing

How then do we get started with mindful parenting in a way that feels comfortable and authentic? Do we wait for "the right moment," or do we take our moments as they come, such as they are? Do we have to begin in pregnancy or with the birth of our first child in order for this to "work," or can we begin anytime, wherever we are in our lives?

Habits of mind being what they are, we will probably be breaking healthy new ground for ourselves if we decide not to wait for a largely fictitious "opportune time" to begin, but rather seize the moments that we have, ragged and ratty and messy as they may be.

Resolving to begin where we are, and now, with the resources at hand, already puts us in the spirit of mindfulness practice. We can explore for ourselves the value of being fully present no matter what is happening and precisely where we are right now, whether we are just starting out as a parent, have grown children, or are a grandparent.

One way to get started on the practice of mindful parenting is to cultivate a certain intimacy with your own breathing in quiet moments and right through the day. Your breath is flowing constantly. It is always present. It is deeply connected to your life, to your body, and to your emotional states. Becoming aware of the breath brings mind and body into the present moment with wakefulness and clarity of perception.

You might try touching base with your breath right now, and see if you can keep it in the forefront of your awareness for a few minutes. The basic idea is to *feel* the breath as it moves in and out, knowing that the breath is coming in as it's coming in and that the breath is going out as it's going out. You can experiment with dropping in on the breath and "riding the waves" of inbreath and outbreath with full attention, feeling their rising and falling much as you would feel the movement if you were in a rubber raft, floating on gentle waves. Later on, in other moments, you can try bringing awareness of your breathing into whatever it is that you find yourself doing, and as you deal with whatever it is you are facing.

You may quickly discover as you do this that your mind, like all our minds, has a life of its own. It may not want to remember the breath and stay in touch with it. It isn't used to sustaining awareness. You will find that like all our minds, it goes here and there constantly, to the past, to the future, and invariably from one thought to another and one feeling to another, one desire to another. It is even more this way when we are feeling pressed for time, or dealing with problems, or conflicted in one way or another. Anybody who sits down to follow their breathing in stillness for the first time, for even a few minutes, discovers this state of affairs right away. It applies even when the outer conditions are peaceful.

Through ongoing practice, it is possible to develop an intimacy with the breath that extends your awareness into whatever else is happening in your world at that moment. Cultivating awareness in this way allows the deep potential in each moment to become available to you.

The value of cultivating an awareness of your own breathing

will grow on you as you work at it. It lights up the present moment and helps you hold it with greater calmness and clarity. But extending an awareness of the breath into any activity in any moment takes energy and commitment. It is a looking out for and a looking into, so it is a looking *and* a seeing, what might be called discernment, or wise attention. You can bring this awareness to any aspect of your life: the breath *and* diapering; the breath *and* shopping; the breath *and* eye contact; the breath *and* playing with your children, or reading to them, or being firm about something, or putting them to bed, or talking with an older child; the breath *and* cooking dinner; the breath *and* juggling ten things at once and feeling like you are about to lose it; the breath *and* having lost it and now having to somehow pick up the pieces and move on. This takes no extra time. Only remembering.

Diapering, cleaning up messes, breaking up fights, rushing here and there, sitting around worrying and feeling anxious, working or playing, "on" time or "off" time, are all appropriate occasions for using your own breathing to be more present.

Practice as Cultivation

You can cultivate mindfulness in your life and in your family just like you can cultivate tomatoes or corn in a garden, and this cultivating is what we mean when we speak of *practice*. The key role in any cultivation is tending that which has been planted, whether we are talking about our intention to be more mindful or about tending to the growth of our children. *Tending* means "attending," which comes from *attention*. These words all carry in them the quality of being present, wakeful, stretched toward, in readiness, conscious. The feeling extends to being tender, an *extending* of oneself through care and caring.

This tending or attending is the heart of mindfulness practice. Just as young plants require protection and support as part of their tending, so it is with children, and so it is, as well, with a nascent mindfulness practice. If you wish to undertake mindful parenting, the very intention, as well as your efforts to practice, need to be protected or they will be easily trampled by the chaotic circumstances and constant demands of our lives, and soon abandoned. Creating a supportive framework for our intentions and efforts to cultivate mindfulness in our lives can be extremely helpful.

This framework consists of specific formal and informal exercises and disciplines that together make up the practice of mindfulness. The formal practices take some time. Whether you want to practice in this way and how much is always up to you. As we have seen, the informal practices, such as being in touch with your breathing throughout the day, don't take any time. They just take attention, and remembering.

Although we are all mindful from time to time in a conventional sense, to sustain meditative, nonjudgmental, nonreactive awareness, it's very helpful to generate and regenerate the *intention* to be mindful. Part of it is learning how to get out of our own way, to not be so ruled by our thoughts and emotions. Usually we have to learn that lesson over and over again. It is done by observing our thoughts and feelings and practicing not getting carried away by them.

As with cultivating corn or tomatoes, discipline is necessary here, too. Not an outwardly imposed discipline, but the inner self-discipline of ongoing tending. As we have seen, mindfulness is a means for staying in touch, or touching base periodically with what T. S. Eliot called the "still point of the turning world."

Because mindfulness practice and raising children really demand the same basic grounding in attention and self-discipline, it is not that big a stretch to attempt to cultivate them together. In doing so, each feeds, deepens, and supports the other.

In the Zen tradition of meditation, people are fond of saying that the practice is nothing special. The practice is nothing special in the same way that being a mother or giving birth is nothing special, that being a father is nothing special, that being a farmer and bringing things forth from the land is nothing special, even that being alive is nothing special. That is all true in a way, but try telling that to a mother or a father or a farmer. "Nothing special" also means very special. The utterly ordinary is utterly extraordinary. It all depends on how you see things, and whether you are willing to look deeply, and live by what you see and feel and know.

Free Within Our Thinking

When we ask people who have gone through the MBSR program what the most important things were that they got from it, they invariably say two things. The first is "The breathing." The second is "Knowing that I am not my thoughts."

Of course, everybody was breathing before they came to the program, so what they mean by "the breathing" is a new awareness of their own breathing and the discovery of how powerful mindfulness of the breath can be when cultivated in periods of quiet and when brought to the activities of daily living.

The second statement points to the fact that most of us are at best only vaguely aware that we are thinking all the time. We may not experience this in a forceful way until we start systematically paying attention to our breathing and we begin observing, nonjudgmentally, what is on our minds, and how difficult it is to stabilize our attention, to keep our focus on anything, even on something as simple as the breath.

When we start paying attention to the breath and to what is on our minds that carries us away from the breath, we come to see almost immediately that thinking is going on all the time and that most of our thoughts are opinionated and either partially or wholly inaccurate. We see that much of our thinking is preoccupied with judging and evaluating our perceptions and generating ideas and opinions about things. We also see that our thinking is complex, chaotic, unpredictable, frequently inconsistent, and contradictory.

This stream of thinking is going on all the time, virtually unexamined and unknown by us. Our thoughts really do seem to have a life of their own. They are like clouds coming and going, events in the field of our consciousness. Yet from them, we are constantly creating models of reality in our minds in the form of ideas and opinions about ourselves and others and the world, and then believing them to be true and frequently denying evidence to the contrary.

Not knowing that thoughts are just thoughts can get us into trouble in virtually every aspect of our lives. Knowing it can help us stay out of the traps our own mind sets for us. This is especially true in parenting.

For instance, if you have the thought "Tom is lazy," you will easily believe that this is true about Tom, rather than see that it is just your opinion. Then, every time you see Tom, you will tend to see him as lazy and not see all the other aspects of who he is that are blocked or filtered out by your strong opinion, for which you may or may not have much evidence. As a consequence, you may only relate to him in a limited way, and his response to how you treat him may only confirm and reinforce your view. In reality, you have made Tom lazy in your mind. You are not able to see Tom as Tom, for who he is as a whole being, rather than just the one attribute you are fixated on, which may only be true to a degree, if at all, or may change depending on circumstances. This attitude on your part may make it impossible for you to connect with him in any meaningful way, because everything you say or do will be "loaded" in a way that he may feel, and feel uncomfortable about, and that you may not even recognize as coming from you.

Teachers sometimes do this. Parents do, too. For in truth, we are all doing this, not just with children and other people, but with ourselves. We tell ourselves that we are too this or not enough that. We label ourselves. We judge ourselves. Then we believe it. In believing it, we narrow our view of what is real and what is true, and our view takes on aspects of a self-fulfilling prophecy. It limits and confines us and our children. It can be a source of major suffering. And it blinds us to the possibilities for transformation in ourselves and in others, because we carry around a rigid view of things that tends to be fixed and does not see things in terms of multiple dimensions, complexity, wholeness, and constant change.

So when practicing mindfulness, it is important to see your thoughts as thoughts and not simply as "the truth." Feeling states can also be looked at in this way, since our feelings are intimately tied to our thoughts.

When we look at our thoughts and feelings in this way, we can sometimes experience a loosening of the grip of personal pronouns. In such moments, it may no longer be "my" thought, but just "a" thought; not "my" feeling, but simply "a" feeling. This can free us from a strong attachment to "our" thoughts and opinions and feeling states, and give us more perspective and latitude. Whether it is a feeling of annoyance or embarrassment, impatience or anger, recognizing its presence in awareness and knowing what it is ("annoyance, embarrassment, impatience, anger feels like this") opens up new choices for us so that we won't necessarily get lost or stuck in it or react mindlessly. It doesn't mean we won't take our feelings or our thoughts seriously, or that we won't act on them. But an awareness of thoughts as thoughts and feelings as feelings can help us to act more appropriately, and to be more in touch with ourselves and with the needs of the situation.

*

Be empty of worrying.
Think of who created thought!

Why do you stay in prison
When the door is so wide open?

Move outside the tangle of fear-thinking.
Live in silence.

Flow down and down in always
widening rings of being.

RUMI (TRANSLATED BY COLMAN BARKS)

Discernment versus Judging

We speak of mindfulness as the awareness that arises from paying attention on purpose, in the present moment, and nonjudgmentally—in the service of greater self-understanding and wisdom and, ultimately, freedom from our own usually unexamined mental habits and the ignorance and suffering they engender. The nonjudgmental part is crucial. If we spend any time noticing what is going on in our own minds, we will soon notice that we have something of an inner judge or critic at work almost all the time, judging not only everything around us, but ourselves and our experience, as well. Without knowing it, we can become virtual prisoners of all this judging. It uses up a great deal of energy and frequently prevents us from seeing clearly and from ongoing learning.

As we saw in the previous chapter, we often form opinions quickly and hold to them with utter conviction as if they were the truth, when actually, they are just thoughts, and the *content* of those particular thoughts are the conclusions that our minds have arrived at about things or people or ourselves. And just as with other thoughts in the mind, we can lock in to these conclusions, whether they are positive or negative, accurate or inaccurate, and lose the ability and freedom to see beyond them to anything else. To the extent that we get attached to our ideas and opinions, we become diminished and constricted. Our possibilities for growth narrow.

If we live in this way a great deal of the time, we may look back years later and see with deep regret that our opinions at a particular time in our lives were just that: opinions. We may come to see that they kept us from pursuing or even seeing other options and possibilities, and led us down paths that were not quite true to our innermost being. Our opinions can obscure our sovereignty as clouds obscure and filter the light of the sun. They also block our ability to recognize the sovereignty of others, including our own children.

What is called for in the cultivation of mindfulness, and in mindful parenting, rather than judging, is *discernment*, the ability to look deeply into something and perceive relevant distinctions keenly and with clarity. Discernment is the ability to see this *and* that, as opposed to this *or* that, to see the whole picture and its fine details, to see gradations. Being discerning is an inward sign of respect for reality, because we are taking note of subtleties as well as the gross outlines of things, aware of complexity and mystery. There is a fairness in it, a rightness in it, because it is truer to the whole of reality. In the story of the Loathely Lady, Sir Kay and the other knights judged Dame Ragnell narrowly, on the basis of her appearance, and in doing so, betrayed their own code of chivalry and decency. Gawain discerned something deeper and did not judge her.

When we speak of mindfulness as a nonjudgmental awareness, we are not suggesting that we aren't seeing what is occurring in the moment and making necessary and important distinctions. In fact, it is only through being nonjudgmental that it might be possible to see and feel what is actually happening, past surface appearances and the filters of our own limited opinions, our likes and dislikes, beliefs, fears, our unexamined and sometimes unconscious prejudices, and our deep longing for things to be a certain way.

Being nonjudgmental means that we are aware of those aspects of our own mind that are judging all the time and that we intentionally suspend judgment and bring the mind back to directly observing the actuality of things, with all their distinctions, and rest in that open awareness, a form of nonconceptual knowing. This orientation is not only important to the inner work of mindfulness and of parenting. It is also essential to other pursuits, such as scientific endeavors that seek to discern an underlying order at the boundary between the known and the unknown. The scientific method recognizes the critical importance for scientists to be acutely aware of their own biases and prejudices and the tendency of the mind to jump prematurely to conclusions or become too comfortable with what it thinks it knows. That can become an impediment to novel and breakthrough insights that go beyond the known to what is yet to be discovered or realized.

A discerning awareness can hold even our own judging in mind and know it for what it is. We can observe this ingrained habit with some degree of compassion and not judge ourselves for being so judgmental. In recognizing the significance of what we are perceiving, discernment can give rise to wisdom. It frees us to act more wisely with our children without getting so caught up in our own likes and dislikes and fears that we can no longer see clearly. If we look beneath the surface of many of our criticisms and judgments as parents, we will often find fearful thoughts. These can be treated like any other thoughts and simply held in awareness. In such moments, it can be helpful and illuminating to question how relevant or true they are.

It is in the nature of the mind to judge. But without discernment, seeing the gradations between black and white, this or that, all good and all bad, our judgments are more likely to lead to unwise action on our part. Discernment allows us to see and navigate wisely through emerging moments in which new openings are possible, whereas our quick-reaction judgments put us at risk for not seeing such openings. Without discernment, we can automatically and unwittingly limit our view just when we most need to stay open to imaginative options for responding mindfully rather than reacting reflexively.

If a mother is continually seeing danger in every situation with her five-year-old boy and hovers over him constantly, naming all the terrible things she is afraid are going to happen if her son does this or that, she is locked into a very narrow way of seeing that in all likelihood does not include an awareness of her own thinking and behavior, or the effect she may be having on her child. In this way, she may only add to the child's fears or put barriers in his way and constrict him unnecessarily.

If she were able to catch herself in that moment and look more deeply into and discern her own behavior and the mind-set from which it is emanating, she might modulate some of her fear-based impulses and be freer and less constricted within herself. She might perceive that she has a wider range of choices than she was able to see the moment before, and with this awareness, perhaps find a better balance between her fear—which has important elements of concern for her child's safety—and her child's need for autonomy. In this way, she might give freer rein to his curiosity and desire to explore. Fathers, of course, can fall into the same fear-driven behavior, and it can be directed as much to daughters as to sons.

It is helpful to bring a degree of generosity and self-compassion to our deeply ingrained habit of seeing things in terms of only this or that, good or bad, dangerous or safe, okay or not okay. For example, if you have done a number of things that you regret as a parent, it is also important to be able to see those things that you have done well, and vice versa. A rigid, black-and-white, either-or view is invariably inaccurate and only perpetuates illusions, delusions, and conflict between spouses and with children.

When we bring mindfulness and discernment to our parenting, we may come to realize how much we tend to judge our own children as well as ourselves as parents. We have opinions about them and who they are and how they should be, perhaps comparing them to some ideal that we have created in our minds. When we judge our children in this way, we cut ourselves off from them and them from us. By intentionally suspending judgment and cultivating greater discernment, we create the potential to reconnect with them and with ourselves.

Discernment includes seeing that even as we attempt to see our children for who they are, we also cannot fully know who they are or where their lives will take them. We can only do our best to love them and accept them, and honor the mystery of their being.

Formal Practice

Even if you choose not to practice formally or you only engage in it occasionally, it is helpful to become familiar with the instructions for formal meditation practice because they provide a clear map of how to cultivate mindfulness. They also serve as a useful guide for bringing greater mindfulness and heartfulness into all aspects of daily life, including our parenting. When you attend to your experience through the lens of mindfulness, as we have seen, your whole life becomes your meditation practice. All your moments become precious occasions to cultivate awareness and to wake up a bit more.

For those of us who are drawn to developing a formal meditation practice, whether primarily for parenting, for stress reduction, or simply to nourish ourselves in a profoundly healing and transformative way, we might make use of whatever quiet moments we have, even if they are rare, or even if they have to be arranged by, say, getting up earlier than usual, or by shutting off all our devices and screens at certain times.

Solitude, time by and for oneself, alone, is an important form of deep sustenance for human beings. It is rapidly becoming lost as the pace of life accelerates. For parents, finding time for formal practice when we are not exhausted may feel virtually impossible at certain stages. We can each make our own choices about whether and how and when we might make some time in our lives for stillness.

A quiet period of stopping does not have to be long...it could be for one or two minutes, if that is all the time you can find. It could be stretched out on the couch in the middle of the day, or in bed before you go to sleep, or five minutes during your lunch break, or in a parked car while the baby is sleeping. If the motivation is present, most of us can probably find or free up a few minutes, or even fifteen minutes or so, somewhere in the twenty-four hours of our day. But there does have to be a strong intention to make it happen, even if it is hard or boring at first. Otherwise, we will quickly fill up any "free" moments we find with e-mail, surfing the Web, texting, tweeting, reading the newspaper or a magazine, with television or the radio, or some other form of doing to "fill up" or "pass" the time. We live now in perpetually distracting and self-distracting times.

Sometimes it is hard to remember that quiet moments of wakefulness feed body and soul. Parents of young children may need it more than anyone else. Time for ourselves, time alone, is what many parents have least and desire most. Yet often we don't know what to do with it when we do have it, especially if it is only a few minutes here and there, not long enough to do anything special with, or if it comes at the "wrong time."

There is no question about it—formal mindfulness practice does unavoidably take some time. But it is a time worth taking if you are drawn to it. It does not have to be long to be of profound value. This is in part because when you are in the present moment and truly let go of the past and the future, and step out of the stream of thinking, the experience is of timelessness. Even a few minutes can be restorative because timeless moments are liberating moments. There is no place to go, nothing to do. You are momentarily released from the press of time and obligations and can enter into the experience of being whole and complete right in this moment, and part of a larger interconnected whole.

If you want to try to integrate formal meditation practice into your life, this is one way to get started: Find or make a few moments of quiet time by yourself. Then lie down, or sit in a dignified posture. Focus on your belly for a few moments and feel it moving with the breath; or place your attention at the nostrils and feel the flow of the air there. In either case, try not to push or pull the breath or the belly but just allow your breathing to flow and your belly to move however it does.

Paying attention to the breath and to your body doesn't mean interfering with it. It simply means attending to the feelings in your body and the sensations associated with the breath as it moves in and out of your body. Those sensations might be of the abdomen rising, expanding with each inbreath and falling, deflating with each outbreath, or of the feeling of the air passing back and forth at the nostrils. After experimenting for a while, it would be good to choose one of these to focus on and keep your attention there as best you can.

As we have discussed, you will soon discover that the mind is often turbulent, like the surface of the ocean, or a flag being blown first in this direction, then in that. The mind tends to be preoccupied. It gets carried away by thoughts and feelings. Your attention may wander off the breath or be pulled from it time and time again, often without any moments of seeming peace or continuity, even for one breath's worth of time. It may also seem anything but relaxing to try to stay with the feelings of the breath. You may experience mostly anxiety, or ceaseless distraction.

That is all fine. It's not supposed to feel relaxing, although it often can. In fact, there is no particular way you are supposed to feel.

Rather, the invitation is just to be aware of how things actually are with you from moment to moment. So if you are feeling tense, you note that you are feeling tense; if angry, then angry; if dull or sleepy, then dull or sleepy. That's all. You just watch your own mind and your own body. No judgment is necessary. In fact, we are attempting to cultivate a nonstriving, nonreactive, nonjudgmental orientation toward our experience of *any* moment, just perceiving and feeling what is here to be felt or perceived and, if possible, recognizing and letting go of any tendency to attach personal pronouns—in particular, *I, me,* and *mine*—to the feeling states.

The other crucial instruction to keep in mind when you are starting out with formal mindfulness practice is simply this: Whenever you notice that your attention is no longer on your breathing or in your body, note where it is. In other words, notice what is on your mind. This noting is very important, because it brings thoughts and feelings and images into awareness and deepens our familiarity and intimacy with our own mind states. Once you have allowed whatever is on your mind in this moment to be recognized in awareness, you purposefully let go of it—which means letting it be as it is—and come back to the breath itself, either at the belly or at the nostrils, and just pick up with the sensations and direct experience of this inbreath, this outbreath. If the mind wanders away from the breath a thousand times, you just bring it back in this way a thousand times, after first bringing mindfulness to the particulars of what is on your mind, no matter what it is. You neither pursue the content of your thoughts nor do you attempt to suppress any of the activity of your mind. You simply observe it, let it be, and let it go, returning to the breath. With time, you can expand your practice to include other objects of attention within and beyond the breath.

Formal and informal practice go hand in hand. The one

strengthens the other. Ultimately, meditation is no different from life itself. For the most part, you are not going to be parenting while sitting still, so it is important to allow all of our moments to matter. We have only to let our children, and everything else in our lives, become our teachers and keep our intention to be present as strong and as vibrant as possible.

There are many other ways in which to practice mindfulness meditation formally if you make the time for it. In MBSR (mindfulness-based stress reduction), people cultivate mindfulness on a daily basis using a number of different guided practices, including a lying-down meditation called the body scan, various sitting meditation practices, and mindful hatha yoga. More details about what these are and how to practice with them are given in *Full Catastrophe Living*; *Wherever You Go, There You Are*; *Coming to Our Senses*; *Mindfulness for Beginners*; and a number of other books. If you care to experiment with them, guided mindfulness practice CDs, digital downloads, and smartphone apps with meditations of varying lengths are also available from websites and are listed at the back of this book. These can be helpful in developing and deepening your own regular, if not daily, formal meditation practice.

Letters to a Young Girl Interested in Zen

One day, I (jkz) received a letter from Caitlin, the daughter of a friend. She had chosen to do a project for school on Zen Buddhism and wanted to go beyond what she could learn from the few written sources that were available to her. Her father had suggested she write to me. Her letter was so beautifully composed, her tone so self-possessed, her questions so filled with genuine interest, that I sat down on the spot and tried as best I could to convey to her a sense of the beauty and the depth of the Zen perspective on meditation practice. I realized later that my response touched on elements of meditation practice in ways that might be helpful to adults, and so I include it here.

In general, we believe that we have to be very careful in offering meditation to children, and that parents may not be the best people to teach it to their children. It is wonderful, of course, when they see you meditating. Sometimes, when our children were little, they would come and sit on my (jkz) lap as I was sitting. I would wrap them up in my blanket and arms, continuing to sit silently. When they were ready to go, I would open the blanket and they would emerge. If they said, "Daddy, I'm hungry," that was the end of my formal practice that morning. Still, in the spirit of bringing mindfulness to all aspects of our parenting, it is important to be sensitive to what is coming from our children, and what we may be forcing on them from our desire to have them value what we value. Now, there are several resources for parents who want to try to meditate with their young children, in the form of books such as *Sitting Still Like a Frog* and *Building Emotional Intelligence*, both of which have guided meditation CDs that approach practice with a very light and playful touch (see Suggested Reading).

In Caitlin's case, the impulse to learn about meditation came from her. You might say that my response was an attempt to provide her with some tools for cultivating her own garden. What I found out was that she was quite a gardener already. With her permission, I share parts of my letters to her and some of the poems she sent me.

✻

February 11, 1996

Dear Caitlin:

Thank you for your wonderful letter of January 31. I was happy to hear that you are excited about Zen and Buddhism, and I think it is great that you are taking your interest out beyond the usual sources from which we gather information when we have a project such as yours. Books can be very helpful, and I have enclosed a few of my favorites here, which I hope you will dip into every now and again, as what they say to you will change over time. But especially in Zen, you have to go beyond what the books say, to *EXPERIENCE* what they are pointing to, to really understand what it is about.

What Zen and Buddhism are really about is *KNOWING WHO YOU ARE*. You might say, "Well, that is silly. Of course I know who I am!" Then you might say, "I am Caitlin and I am 11 years old." But "Caitlin" is just a sound (we call it a name, and a very beautiful one) that your parents gave to you when you were born. And 11 years old is just the number of times the Earth has circled the Sun since you were born. Weren't you "you" before you got the name Caitlin? Also, are you the same "you" that you were when you were five, or when you were two? Of course you are; and also you're not, because you are always growing, and changing. What you thought then, or wanted then, or felt then may not be what you think or want or how you feel now. But the deep something that is "you" is still you and will always be you.

But can you see that this is also a little mysterious, the question of who you are? So Zen is about knowing yourself, understanding yourself, and knowing what that means. Part of what it means is knowing that some kinds of knowing and understanding are beyond words, and beyond thinking, and beyond anybody being able to tell you about. This knowing is very personal and intuitive. That is why much of Zen is in the form of poetry and impossible riddles. They cut through the thinking mind, and point to something beyond it, which is freer, and more fundamental. That doesn't mean that thinking is "bad." Thinking is great, and very important, and it is necessary to learn how to think well. But it is not all there is, and thinking, if you're not careful, can dominate your life and make you forget the deeper, more feeling, more intuitive, more artistic aspects of your being, of your true self (as the Buddhists call it…who you "really" are…beyond your name, your age, your opinions, your likes and dislikes).

Sound confusing? That is only because I have to use words to talk about what is beyond words. It is really very simple, and that is one of the beauties of Zen...its utter simplicity. But that also makes it seem mysterious on the surface when it's really not. You just have to understand what it is pointing toward.

So here are some traditional Zen pointers. A friend of mine once wrote a tiny book full of them, which she illustrated.

> When sitting, just sit.
> When eating, just eat.
> When walking, just walk.
> When talking, just talk.
> When listening, just listen.
> When looking, just look.
> When touching, just touch.
> When thinking, just think.
> When playing, just play,
> And enjoy the feeling of each moment and each day.

NARAYAN LIEBENSON,
When Singing Just Sing: Life as Meditation

You ask me if there are any Zen riddles (they are traditionally called koans in Japanese) that are meaningful to me and that really stay with me throughout the day. Yes, there are, and I have found them to be quite wonderful and helpful over the years. The key, as you suggest, is to be open to letting them visit you and revisit you throughout the day.

Here are a few:

- Does a dog have Buddha nature?
- What was your face before your parents were born?
- Who are you?
- Have you finished your breakfast? Then go wash your bowl!

Remember, you cannot answer these adequately or understand them by thinking about them and speaking in the usual way. One of my teachers, a Korean Zen Master, used to say, "Open your mouth and you're wrong." (This is sometimes the way Zen Masters speak.) They have a saying, "Don't mistake the finger pointing at the moon for the moon." So think about Zen riddles and stories as fingers pointing to something. The pointing is not the something. (You wouldn't climb on top of a sign saying "New York City" with an arrow, and think you had gotten to New York City, would you?) In the case of Zen koans, the "something" that is being pointed to is not even a "thing." So it's best to just keep the riddle or the question or the story in mind, to hold it, to cradle it in your mind and in your heart, whatever that means to you, and not try to answer it, or even understand it in the usual thinking way. This is what meditation is really about. It is keeping in the front of your mind the mystery and the beauty of living, of "having" a body, of being alive, of being connected to your family and friends and to nature, and to the planet, of not having all the answers, or even knowing where you are going all the time. It is all OK. What is important is to be *AWAKE*, to be present in this moment, with the whole of your experience, with your feelings, your intuition and imagination, your body and everything it feels and does, and with your thinking. It is all part of who you are, but you are more than all of it, being whole, and always growing as well, being and becoming, knowing and not knowing. Not only is it OK, it is absolutely wonderful. That means, *YOU* are absolutely wonderful already, and so you don't have to become wonderful, or better, you just have to let yourself be yourself, and learn not to get in your own way all the time (this is a problem you may not have, but a lot of people do, unfortunately, and that is why meditation can be so helpful to them). This was the Buddha's original discovery. It's both very special, and not so special, since everyone's mind is potentially the same as the Buddha's. It's just a matter of being awake and paying attention. That's why my friend Joko Beck's book, which I have enclosed, is called *Nothing Special*. By the way, she is a 78-year-old American grandmother Zen Master, and if you met her, you would think she was just a regular person, because she is. Just like you and me and your mom and dad. Nothing special, only very special.

So, this brings us to techniques, which is your third question. Yes, there are techniques to help cultivate this understanding of who you are, and of a full appreciation of being alive and sharing in life with all living things. But it is important, before I tell you a few of them, for me to say that you will have to remember that the techniques are also just fingers pointing at the moon. They are not the goal, they are merely signs pointing to your own experience, and helpful aids, like training wheels on a bike, to use formally until you get the "feeling" of what it is really about to be present from moment to moment (remember, "when walking, just walk…") for that, in a nutshell, is what it means to have "Zen Mind."

It turns out that "just walking" or "just sitting," in fact, *just* doing anything, isn't so easy. Take walking, for instance. If you try to "just walk," you may find that, in addition to walking, you are also thinking about where you are going, or worried about being late, or what will happen when you get there, so that you are not fully aware of your body, say, your feet, or your hands, or your spine, or your breathing. So just walking is not so easy. You have to work at it, and this working at it is called "practice" or "meditation practice." That's right. Meditation is simply working at being aware of each moment, no matter what you are doing, and not being carried away by your thoughts or feelings, whatever they are, whether they are interesting, happy, unhappy, or blah. It is not about trying to change anything. The point is just to be aware of this moment as you are experiencing it.

If you learn this when you are young and it becomes a way of life with you, it can have an incredible effect on your life for years and years and years, because it develops your deep inner capacity for being a wiser, happier, and more caring and playful person. We all have this capacity, especially when we are young, but age and life can sometimes weigh on people to such an extent that they forget that they are miraculous beings, and that they have tremendous capacities for wisdom and compassion and creativity. Meditation practice is a way to keep yourself from forgetting this, and a way to develop *WHO YOU ARE*, fully, across the entire lifespan. Then, it turns out, things will change in marvelous ways sometimes, and difficult ways other times, and you will be able to participate in those changes and contribute to them, and give direction to your life out of your own wisdom and awareness. Then your life choices will be healthier, and you will be better able to handle all manner of things, even very difficult times and lots of stress.

So, if you want to practice, there are lots of techniques. Paying attention to your breathing is probably the best one to start with, because you can't leave home without it. You are not always walking, or talking, or sitting, or eating, but you are always breathing. So you can pay attention to your breathing, and become friends with it at any moment. If you do, it will calm you down when you are upset, but more importantly, it will help keep you in touch with the present moment. This moment is it. You will never have it again. So Zen says, don't miss it. "Don't let an opportunity like this go by" (the great Sufi/Indian poet Kabir said that).

One more thing. Just as the techniques are not what it is really about, but just a systematic way to get more intimate with your own life, so the practice of meditation is not limited to just sitting or lying down and tuning into your breathing for a period of time each day. It is really about being present, awake, and aware in your life, moment by moment, and day by day, in everything you do. And since your breathing goes with you, wherever you are, you can always use it to bring you into your body and back into the present moment so that:

when you are walking, you are just walking,
when you are eating, you are just eating,

when you are helping your little brother, you are just
    helping your little brother,
(when you are teasing your little brother, you are just
    teasing him),
when you are talking on the phone, you are just talking
    on the phone,
when you are studying, you are just studying...

I think you get the idea.

One more thing: the idea is to practice moment-to-moment awareness of your breathing or anything else without judging, and without a lot of emotional reacting. It's not that these won't happen. Of course they will. But the idea is to be aware of your constantly judging mind, and try to suspend judgment and just let things be as they are, at least while you are practicing. If you are always judging everything and everybody, and have opinions about everything, your mind and your heart will already be filled up with thinking and judging, liking and disliking, and your opinions will cloud your ability to see clearly.

Here is a favorite Zen story: A university professor came to see a Zen Master to ask him what Zen was really all about. He had done a lot of reading, and was now following up to get the real story.

The Zen Master invited the professor to sit down across the table from him and proceeded to serve him tea. He poured the tea into his guest's cup, and when the cup was full, he just kept pouring and pouring, and the tea ran out of the cup and over the saucer and all over the table and floor.

The astonished professor yelled, "What are you doing? Can't you see the cup is already full?"

"Yes, I see," said the Zen Master. "Similarly with your mind. How can you expect me to put anything in it when it is already so full of ideas and opinions?"

So remember, try not to judge everything all the time and have a strong opinion about everything. I know this is difficult, because school and the whole of society is constantly trying to get us to have opinions. But you are not your opinions, and it's good to know that. In fact, you are not any of your thoughts. You might say, you are the thinker, the feeler, the seer. But, coming back to page one of this letter, who is that? That is the question to keep in mind. Trust awareness and wakefulness above all else. Trust your true self, your own heart, your own intuition. Another way to say this is that it is fine to have opinions, but if you are not aware of them, you will get so attached to them and closed-minded that you will not be able to learn anything new.

You asked me why I chose to start practicing these techniques and teachings. Because I knew in my heart that there had to be more to life than what I was experiencing when I was a graduate student studying molecular biology, and I didn't want to miss my own life as it went by. So I got into yoga and meditation and the martial arts because I found that they fed something deep in me that nothing else was feeding. And as a result, I became a lot less angry, and a happier person. Meditation helps me to be calmer and clearer and more loving and accepting, and to take more effective action in my life than I think I would have been able to do if I had not started practicing it, now some thirty years ago. And I still keep at it every day…not to get anywhere or even to feel good. I do it because it is one good way to love life and to be in touch with what is important. I love listening to silence.

You ask how Buddhism and Zen affect the world? I think they are pointing to something universal in life and in people that is important for our survival as a species, and for our happiness in society and as individuals. As the world gets more and more complicated, and as it goes faster and faster, and we feel more and more time pressure and stress, we will need to learn how to take better care of ourselves and our planet. Buddhist wisdom can help us out a lot here. There is such a thing as "Buddhist economics." Perhaps you have heard of the phrase "small is beautiful." That is part of it. Not causing harm to living creatures is another part of it that the world could learn from. I think that we need more awareness and more selflessness in politics and in business, and in the world in general. Nowadays, millions of Americans are practicing meditation. This is very different from even twenty years ago. This is a very positive change.

Finally, you ask about unusual beliefs or practices that I find interesting and insightful. I guess you might say that all of the above is somewhat unusual. I suppose that we should just come full circle here, to say that watching your own mind is what it is about. Beliefs are fine, but it's important not to get so attached to them that they blind us to other aspects of reality. In the end, it is just a matter of being yourself, and feeling comfortable in your own skin. The practices are all to help us to do that, and to remind us that we are already OK, and very precious. And unique.

There is a saying that goes, "I asked him what time it was, and he told me how a watch works." Maybe it's the same here, I don't know. All I know is that I loved your letter and the enthusiasm behind it, and so I find that I have written you seven pages in response. I hope you don't feel overwhelmed by this letter. Perhaps I have said too much, or made it too complicated. If that is the case, just take the parts that make the most sense to you and throw away the rest.

Feel free to write if you like. And good luck on your project.

With warm best wishes,

Jon

February 22, 1996

Dear Caitlin:

Thank you for your letter, and for your poems. What a wonderful project you have chosen (or did it choose you?). William Stafford, one of our great contemporary poets, wrote a poem every morning, before he did anything else, for thirty years. Quite a meditation practice!

And while you are right to think that your understanding of Zen and Buddhism will grow over the years, I can see from your letters and from your poetry that you have "soaked up a lot," as you put it.

Thank you for the pleasure of getting to know you in this way. Good luck with your project. Feel free to write any time.

With warm best wishes,

Jon

＊

A SAMPLING OF CAITLIN'S POEMS

Branches
Thin, intertwining
A silhouette no artist could cut
But nature.
Mara takes the many shapes
Of gold and jewels and satin drapes
Of diamond rings and plastic hearts
Of false I-love-you from Hallmark cards
It chases, tempts, and hooks you on
And entraps you with its phony song
To search for the Truths as Buddha told
You must listen to riches from days of old
The trees, the air, and NATURE'S song
Have been the *real* pleasures all along.

(Mara tempted the Buddha with worldly delights just prior to his enlightenment.)

＊

Zen
Still, distinct
Appreciating, being, watching
A single flower in the starlight
Awareness

The Stillness Between Two Waves

Mindfulness and the clarity that can come from it are very simple. It is truly nothing special, except that it is also very special. T. S. Eliot, in his *Four Quartets*, referred to this "nothing special" as

> A condition of complete simplicity
> (Costing not less than everything)

All children are unique, each a fathomless universe of possibilities and feelings. Can we learn to listen carefully enough to hear the texture and resonances of their voices, their songs, their lives? Can we hear, as Eliot put it, "the hidden laughter of children in the foliage"? For there is only right now in which to do this work.

> Quick now, here, now, always—
> A condition of complete simplicity
> (Costing not less than everything)

Quick now, only in *this* moment is anything, whether it is our children or the fluctuations of our own mind, to be seen or felt or heard. But that can happen only if we are willing to pay attention and be present and completely available, to look and listen and remain open. Otherwise very special opportunities for seeing and for relating to our children can remain opaque to us.

Not known, because not looked for

But if we do look, perhaps we will catch a glimmer; if we listen inwardly, perhaps we may hear our life, our deepest self calling to us:

But heard, half-heard, in the stillness
Between two waves of the sea.

That is, when our own awareness can hold the space between thoughts, in the stillness we can hear

The voice of the hidden waterfall
And the children in the apple-tree

Over and over again, the poet's deep insight reminds us of the calling, the yearning, the possibilities latent in the present moment. Eliot points to and names that very space, that very stillness that reveals our essence and our possibilities:

We shall not cease from exploration
And the end of all our exploring
Will be to arrive where we started
And know the place for the first time.
Through the unknown, remembered gate
When the last of earth left to discover
Is that which was the beginning;

At the source of the longest river
The voice of the hidden waterfall
And the children in the apple-tree
Not known, because not looked for
But heard, half-heard, in the stillness
Between two waves of the sea.
Quick now, here, now, always—
A condition of complete simplicity
(Costing not less than everything)
And all shall be well and
All manner of thing shall be well
When the tongues of flame are in-folded
Into the crowned knot of fire
And the fire and the rose are one.

This unceasing exploration is the great work of awareness. We can bring it to anything. But what better place to cultivate such a way of seeing, such a way of being, than in parenting?

PART FIVE

A Way of Being

Pregnancy

Pregnancy is a natural time to begin or deepen the practice of mindfulness. The increasingly dramatic changes that occur in our bodies and in our very perceptions, thoughts, and emotions invite new degrees of wakefulness, wonder, and appreciation. For some of us, being pregnant may be the first time we experience being fully in our body.

The changes in our body are of interest not only to ourselves, but also often to people around us. We are constantly reminded of our special state of being by the reactions we get from other people, ranging from warm inquiries, to unasked-for advice, to sudden pats on the belly.

The myriad physical and emotional changes we experience give us unique opportunities throughout pregnancy to work intimately with many aspects of mindfulness practice—paying attention to our experience; being fully present; being aware of our expectations; cultivating acceptance, kindness, and compassion, particularly toward ourself and our baby; experiencing feelings of deep interconnectedness.

Opportunities to bring mindfulness to this special time abound for fathers and partners as well. Pregnancy is a time of major shifts, physical, emotional, and relational. Partners can bring mindfulness to the full range of their own feelings, some of which may be new and uncomfortable, including their feelings about our changing bodies and the changes that the birth will inevitably bring to their lives. They have their own outer and inner work to do, participating in the planning and in the various choices that need to be made, as well as getting more in touch with their capacity to be giving and caring, perhaps in new ways.

Openhearted awareness and acceptance are themselves ways of recognizing and honoring this special state and the miracle and the mystery of the whole process of two becoming three, of three becoming four.... This awareness will be even more essential once the baby is born.

*

Prior to getting pregnant, we may have been living our lives in a state of constant doing, in a sort of hyperdrive: fast, relatively unconscious, focused on doing more and more. Then all of a sudden we may find ourselves in a slower, more receptive "being mode." The extreme fatigue we feel at times may force us to slow down as our body works hard to create, grow, and nourish our baby via the newly formed, miraculous placenta and our greatly increased blood supply. If we ignore these changes as we push on with life as usual, we can miss out on a rich and quickly passing opportunity to experience the world in a different, slower, more conscious and sensitive way. Even as the impending birth continually pulls our thoughts and imaginings toward the future, our ever-changing state also draws us more and more into the miracle of what is happening now.

The naturally inward focus of pregnancy gives us a chance to tune in to ourselves, using the breath to ground ourselves and deepen our connection to the present moment. We become more aware of our thoughts, our feelings, of our body and our baby. Allowing the breath to become slow and deep, acknowledging where we feel tension, we can begin to let the tension in our bodies flow out with each outbreath. The energy that we may have used in the past to cover up or ignore anger, fear, or anxiety will be freed up as we begin to observe our feelings with receptivity, watching them change from moment to moment.

Pregnancy can be a time of highly charged and rapidly changing emotions. No matter how much we have wanted to be pregnant, along with our happiness we may also experience moments of fear, ambivalence, regret, and uncertainty. How will our lives change? Are we ready to be parents? During pregnancy, women often feel more emotionally vulnerable, more open in general, and more sensitive to sights, sounds, and smells.

Every pregnancy is different, every woman is different, and every day is different. The range of experience is enormous, from feeling healthier than we have ever felt before, radiant, with a sense of total well-being, to feeling incredibly sick, miserable, and immobilized. We may find ourselves disappointed or angry or frustrated because what we are experiencing doesn't coincide at all with the expectations we had about what our pregnancy would be like and how we would be feeling.

Being mindful while pregnant doesn't mean that we are "supposed" to feel a certain way, or that there is some ideal state we have to achieve that will be best for our baby or for ourself. It means acknowledging and accepting the full range of how we are feeling and what we are experiencing and working with it as best we can. This orientation, grounded in awareness and acceptance, can often lead, paradoxically, to greater calmness, relaxation, and feelings of well-being.

We all carry with us, to varying degrees, painful experiences, difficult family relationships, and old wounds that may or may not have healed. It can be important, as we prepare to become a parent, to acknowledge the judgments, criticisms, and conditional love that may have been part of our own childhood. We might begin by bringing awareness to any moments in the day when we catch ourselves judging or belittling ourselves. Can we make room for whatever arises and hold it in awareness with some kindness toward ourselves, at least for brief moments?

Another way we can begin to heal is by making some time in the day to focus inwardly and bring some caring attention toward ourselves. For some, it may feel natural and easy to direct lovingkindness and acceptance to their innermost being and their baby. For others, generating this kind of energy and directing it toward themselves may be very difficult, or feel stilted or awkward. It might help to think of a person or an animal for whom we have felt love and acceptance, and then, as we get in touch with the feelings we have for them, allow those feelings to begin to flow toward ourselves as well.

As we focus inwardly, aware of the many changes we are experiencing, we can also direct our awareness to any deep-seated and emotionally laden beliefs that we may be carrying about pregnancy, labor, birth, and parenting. We all have such beliefs, conscious as well as unconscious, stemming from our own experiences, from what we see or hear from various media, and from stories we have heard from family, friends, and acquaintances. These deep-seated, frequently unexamined beliefs can color our hopes and our fears for the coming birth.

It is important for us to keep in mind that our beliefs about birthing, whatever they are, are not necessarily "true." They are just beliefs, or, as one of our children at the age of four put it, "believements." Becoming more intentionally aware of them as thoughts, examining them on purpose, trying to understand their origins and the context that originally fed them, is the beginning of defusing any negative influence they may exert on our psyche.

Toxic seeds, in the form of negative beliefs or attitudes toward pregnancy, birth, and parenting, can be planted unwittingly by seemingly casual comments made by friends and family. These comments can have even more of an effect on us when they come from those we consider powerful and knowledgeable authorities, whether they be our own parents, health-care providers, or friends.

One way to become more aware of our own beliefs about giving birth is by talking with our mothers and our grandmothers about their birth experiences and other family birthing stories, trying to elicit as much detail as possible. We might also seek out practitioners who have been present at many births that occurred without unnecessary medical intervention. We can ask them to interpret frightening birth stories we may have heard, from their base of knowledge, experience, and their own beliefs.

Although there are situations in which a Cesarean section is necessary, a recent study (*Health Affairs*, March 2013) showed that the rate of Cesarean sections performed has increased significantly, even for women with "low-risk" pregnancies. For all women, the range was 7.1 to 69.5 percent; and for the low-risk cohort, it was 2.4 to 36.5 percent, depending on the hospital and caregiver. With such a wide range of rates of C-sections, the study suggested that variations were based more on care patterns in different hospitals rather than actual medical risk factors.

Through educating ourselves about normal birthing, we may come to see and understand that while we cannot control everything, there is much we can do to create a positive birthing environment. An important part of this process will be choosing the team we want to support us during our labor and birth. Meeting with practitioners in preparation for the birth is a time to try to see with some clarity and be aware of any tendencies we may have to put blind faith in professionals and authority figures. Childbirth educators, doulas, midwives, and obstetricians are formed by their training and their own unique experiences. They, too, have their own various belief systems about the process of birth. Those who believe in the body's ability to give birth without unnecessary interventions and who have experience assisting at many such births are likely to have more confidence in the birthing process. Ideally this translates into their being better able to support women in ways that are respectful and empowering.

It is not enough that a practitioner seems like a nice person. If it is possible (and it may not be for various reasons), interviewing several prospective caregivers, asking them specific questions such as where they practice, who covers for them, their criteria for inducing labor, and what their Cesarean section rate is, can give you important indications about their attitudes toward birthing and how they practice. Speaking with other women who have used these caregivers and hearing the details of their experiences can be very helpful.

As we gather information, we can become increasingly aware of what we feel comfortable with and what is important to us. By listening closely to the language practitioners use, and asking about the parameters within which they feel comfortable working, we can begin to see their different points of view and can then choose caregivers whose views are most compatible with our own.

An important part of our preparation is deciding where we will feel most safe and most comfortable giving birth. Some people start out thinking they would feel safest in a hospital, only to find farther down the road that they want to have a home birth. Others may think they want a home birth at first, only to find themselves feeling more comfortable with giving birth in a hospital or a birthing center.

Depending on our health-care network and our particular health insurance, or lack of it, we may feel we have very few choices, if any. And this may be true. But being more open, finding ways to work creatively with the limitations we face, and working both inwardly and outwardly using a combination of information gathering, self-awareness, and intuition can help us make informed decisions and chart a course that will best meet our needs and the needs of our baby.

Birth

The power and intensity of labor pull us right into each moment. Each labor is unique. Like life itself, you never know how things will unfold. Every labor has its own rhythms, its own tempo. Sometimes labor and birth have a quiet, holy feeling. Each person does his or her part, and the labor steadily progresses and builds until the baby is born. But labor and birth can also feel a bit like a wild comedy when labor is progressing rapidly and the atmosphere is bustling and intense.

Birth is such an all-encompassing experience that it can force us to put aside our expectations and judgments and be open to whatever comes up in each moment. We may have had positive images of being massaged and stroked during our labor, only to find that when we are actually in labor, we don't want to be touched. We may have made plans to have beautiful music playing and many friends in the room, only to find that we want quiet and only a few people with us. We may have had an image of ourself as a serene madonna laboring quietly, only to find we are angry or frustrated, at times cursing or complaining, and making all sorts of outrageous sounds.

Labor gives us an opportunity to take off the quiet, kind, thoughtful, neat, taking-care-of-others, "good girl" mantle so often adopted by women in our society, and allow ourselves the freedom to be whoever and however we find ourselves, completely free to be inwardly focused and fully engaged in the work at hand. If those around us can accord us our own way, our own sovereignty in this miraculous process in which we play a central and critical role, birthing can be a powerful affirmation and a powerful healing of our own psyches, an initiation into a new domain of being.

If you have been using the breath to cultivate mindfulness during your pregnancy, by the time labor begins you will have some familiarity with how it can help you to be more present, relaxed, and focused. As labor becomes more intense, you can focus on the feeling of the breath moving in and out of your body to open to the pain and the demanding moment-to-moment work of birthing. Regardless of how your labor actually unfolds, and as intense and painful as it can sometimes be, a ferocious moment-to-moment awareness, conjured up as we face this huge and unknown process, can help bring the experience into the realm of full acceptance and ownership. The result is not only a new baby to welcome and nurture, but also a powerful experience we will carry with us our whole lives.

To cultivate mindfulness during labor, we can remind ourselves to keep the breath slow and deep as we feel the intensity of the contraction building, using the inbreath to stay with the intense sensations, and using each outbreath to release any tension or holding back that we feel in the body. The end of each contraction always brings a rest, no matter how short, giving us an opportunity to change position, have a drink, a hug, a laugh, or just stay focused on the breath. Being aware, being present, we are better able to see or sense what we need in each moment.

Using awareness of the breath to be fully present during labor, to breathe into any pain or discomfort, takes less energy than either trying to distract ourselves from it or fighting against it. The body has its own inner wisdom. Resisting and tightening up can make it harder for our bodies to do the work of opening and birthing. Breathing slowly and deeply, working with what we are feeling by changing our position, having a support person apply pressure or hot compresses, expressing our feelings, our frustrations, holding on to our partner or friend, all can help us to be more fully present as we labor.

Women often find that their fear of the pain of childbirth is worse than the pain itself, that if they intentionally experience each contraction without worrying about how long it is going to last, or thinking about the next one, then they have more positive energy to give to the work at hand in *this* moment. Being fully present from one moment to the next in this way during labor and birth requires courage, concentration, and the love and support of the people around you.

We are used to associating pain with pathology. The pain of labor and birth is the healthy pain of an intensely physical process, as the uterus contracts to first open the cervix and then push our baby out. Women can bring positive "believements" to labor by associating the power, the intensity, and even the pain they are feeling with images that we intentionally evoke in the mind, such as our cervix opening like a flower, or the baby slipping and sliding lower and lower down with each contraction. Making open *ooh* and *aah* sounds with each contraction, which allows our throats to open, and associating in our mind's eye the opening of the throat with the opening of the cervix and vagina, gives us another way of working intentionally inside the very intensity of our labor.

Birthing is a process in which, like parenting, each situation and, veritably, each moment brings a different challenge. At times we meet it fully. At other times we may retreat, close down, go on automatic pilot. There may be times when we completely lose it, or find ourselves complaining and cursing and rejecting what feels like a miserable and overwhelming experience.

When we find ourselves retreating and shutting down, it can help to gently bring our attention back to the breath. This brings our focus back into each moment and allows us to work with it as it is. Each moment truly is a new beginning, and new beginnings are exactly what is called for after each contraction, especially if one is feeling spent, anxious, or discouraged. Our willingness to embody new beginnings mirrors the biggest new beginning of all. After all the preparation and hard work, the child is born, and with it, the mother...and a new family constellation.

*

Sometimes in birthing, as in life, what occurs is unexpected. We cannot anticipate or control everything that may happen. Birthing is a time when it is important to be gentle with ourselves. When our expectations of ourselves and of the birth are not being met, for whatever reasons, our strong attachment to wanting things to be a certain way can cause us a great deal of suffering. We may be fiercely committed to having a "natural" birth, yet find ourselves asking for pain medication or in a situation that requires medical intervention. At those times, our expectations for the "perfect" birth or the "perfect" baby can get in the way of our ability to respond to what is actually happening to us. There is nothing passive about being mindful in the face of the unexpected. Even in very difficult circumstances, we can trust our feelings and our intuition and do the best we can to make the necessary, often spur-of-the-moment decisions.

Working with whatever arises and letting go of our strong expectations for things to be a certain way is not easy. It involves giving ourselves permission and time to fully experience all our feelings—frustration, anger, disappointment, fear, grief. Feeling compassion for ourselves, for our difficulties, for our efforts, for our limits, for our humanness, is an essential part of healing and restoring ourselves.

We spend most of our energy while we are pregnant focusing on the birth of our baby, and it is not until our baby is born that we truly understand that the birth is just the beginning. But the inner work we do during pregnancy and birthing is good training for mindful parenting, and as we give birth, the power and immediacy with which we are pulled into the present moment and are forced to let go of our preconceptions puts us in touch with the essence of mindfulness practice. In giving birth to our babies, we may find that we give birth to new possibilities within ourselves.

Well-Being

When we start to bring mindfulness into our lives and to our parenting, our new awareness may lead us to reexamine and question many basic assumptions that we usually take for granted.

For instance, new parents are often asked: "Is the baby sleeping through the night yet?" Behind this question is a natural concern for the parents' well-being. It is often predicated on the supposition that babies are supposed to sleep all night long. The underlying assumption may be that the parents' needs should take priority.

This assumption often surfaces in the form of unsolicited advice to new parents, such as: "Make sure you have time alone together." "Give attention to your relationship." "Leave the baby with a sitter and have a date." If we look closely at this, we may see that once again, the focus is predominantly on the parents' well-being rather than on the child's. Babies are seen as tough and resilient, while the parents are seen as vulnerable and in need of protection. Of course new parents do need to take care of themselves and each other, and they need the loving care and support of friends and family during this intense period of adjustment, when all sorts of new demands are being placed upon them. But it is important that in the process, the baby's needs are not minimized or lost sight of. If we can act with some degree of awareness, we can try to find ways to take care of ourselves that are not at the expense of our baby's well-being.

In deciding how we are going to parent and what our priorities are, we need to be aware of the paramount importance of building and maintaining trust and feelings of connectedness with our baby, both for his long-term well-being and for the long-term well-being of the family as a whole. As we noted in the chapter on empathy, scientists who study infants have found evidence that the most basic lessons of emotional life are laid down in the small, repeated exchanges that take place early on between parent and baby. Of all such intimate moments and exchanges, the most critical, according to attachment researcher Daniel Stern, seem to be those "that let the child know her emotions are being met with empathy, accepted, and reciprocated." This is part of the process of *attunement*. Knowing that attunement in infancy forms the basis of a child's later emotional competencies can motivate us to pay much greater attention, moment by moment, to how we actually interact with our children, especially when they are little, and to the choices that we make about their care.

Let's say a baby isn't sleeping through the night. The parents, tired and frustrated, decide to let the baby "cry it out" until she "gets the idea" and falls asleep. But consider for a moment what the baby's experience of this might be. The baby and the parents form an interconnected whole. When distressed, the baby cannot meet its own needs and depends on the parents to soothe her and stay in touch with her. If those needs are not met and the baby is left without human contact at such times, the feelings of distress may be overwhelming, and shutting down may be the baby's only option. Disconnecting and shutting down in the absence of human responsiveness is certainly something that adults experience as well. Why do we think it is okay for babies, who have far fewer resources?

Mindful parenting focuses on the mutual interrelatedness of the parents' and the baby's needs rather than seeing the baby's well-being as in some way competing with our own. According to William and Martha Sears, "There is a biological angle to mutual giving.... When a mother breast-feeds her baby, she gives nourishment and comfort. The baby's sucking, in turn, stimulates the release of hormones that further enhance mothering behavior.... The reason that you can breast-feed your baby to sleep is that your milk contains a sleep-inducing substance....Meanwhile, as you suckle your baby, you produce more of the hormone prolactin, which has a tranquilizing effect on you. It's as if the mommy puts the baby to sleep, and the baby puts the mommy to sleep." Having a greater awareness of the many ways in which we are so highly interconnected, we might look very differently on many aspects of parenting—including nursing and having our baby in bed with us.

To parent mindfully does not mean that we won't at times have strong feelings of frustration, or wish that a certain situation wasn't happening when we feel as if our needs are in direct conflict with our baby's. For example, there will inevitably be nights when our baby needs to be held or walked with at three in the morning. Our first impulse might be to resist what the situation requires of us. Intentionally bringing mindfulness and discernment to such moments, we can acknowledge our feelings of anger, resentment, and frustration, *and* also our feelings of empathy and understanding. In the spirit of seeing everything we face as part of the practice of mindful parenting, we can choose to see our resistance to meeting our child's need in that moment, drop down below our either-or thinking, no matter how rational and reasonable it seems, and respond with greater wisdom from our hearts. This way of holding the present moment allows us to find truly creative solutions that do not come at the expense of our child's well-being. Our well-being is nurtured as well, as we expand the envelope of what we perceive as our own limits.

Babies are not babies for very long. This formative stage in which they are completely dependent on us is relatively brief and very precious. During this time, their sense of well-being is intimately related to how attuned we are to what they are feeling and needing in each moment and the quality and constancy of our responses. So in parenting mindfully, we try as best we can to cultivate the kind of responsiveness that honors what our children most need from us.

Nourishment

Taking nourishment is a fundamental human activity to which we usually bring remarkably little moment-to-moment awareness, although it occupies enormous amounts of time, energy, and thought. A similar lack of awareness can cloud our ability to see and appreciate some of the most important aspects of providing nourishment for our babies, although it is something that parents engage in many times throughout the day and night. If we go into parenting with the understanding that human connection and relationality are of paramount importance, the seemingly ordinary but formative choices we make around feeding and, more importantly, the quality of the attention that we bring to it as we engage in it, will be more in tune with the full range of our infant's needs, and more likely to feed more aspects of our child's being than just his belly.

*

There is a kind of immersion, a soaking in bliss, that happens in those moments after the baby has been fed. At times, a mutual gazing arises, a wonderfully peaceful feeling and sense of palpable connectedness and devotion, captured in many Renaissance paintings in which the Madonna is gazing at her child.

The Ojibwa word for mirror, *wabimujichagwan*, means "looking at your soul," a concept that captures some of the mystery of image and substance. If it is true that we are mirrors to our infants and that looking forms the boundaries of a self, then perhaps we are also helping to form a spiritual soul self during these concentrated love gazes during which time stops, the air dims, the earth cools, and a sense of deep rightness takes hold of our being.

LOUISE ERDRICH,
The Blue Jay's Dance

Whether we choose to bottle-feed or breast-feed, we can feed our children in a way that is responsive to the cues they give us: feeding them when they need to be fed, holding them with sensitivity, close to the warmth and comfort of our bodies, making sure that there are plenty of times when we stay off the cell phone and the Internet, put down our book or newspaper, shut off the TV, give them our full attention, and cultivate the art of gazing. These are all meditations in and of themselves.

When a baby is fed on a schedule rather than in response to his cues, the food comes at an adult-determined "time for feeding," whether he is hungry or not. Instead of getting to experience hunger and then feeling the hunger satisfied as we respond to the myriad ways he subtly or not-so-subtly communicates with us, the experience can easily become one of disconnection from himself and the person feeding him. He is denied the ability to self-regulate and is placed in a more passive role. Being fed can become more of a dissociative experience rather than an enlivening one, in which feelings of trust and connectedness between parent and child are nourished and strengthened.

Whether babies are breast-fed or bottle-fed, feeding them in response to their cues reinforces and builds a sense of their own agency. They experience their ability to get what they need and to elicit an appropriate response from the world around them. This inner quality of confidence, built upon repeated experiences of successfully achieving a desired effect, is known as *self-efficacy*. Many studies show self-efficacy to be the single strongest factor predicting health and healing, an ability to handle stress, and the ability to make healthy lifestyle changes. The foundation for a robust and wide-ranging self-confidence begins in childhood with these kinds of intimate and mutually responsive interactions.

There are situations in which, for one reason or another, a mother may be unable to breast-feed her baby. This can bring up a range of afflictive emotions, including frustration, inadequacy, and guilt. Just as was said in relationship to our strong attachments to things being a certain way around the birth, here, too, we have an occasion to bring some kindness and acceptance to ourselves and the situation. How we hold and see and respond to our babies is in the end more important than whether we breast-feed or bottle-feed.

If you breast-feed your baby, it helps enormously to have support from experienced individuals or groups. The initial period can sometimes be frustrating and difficult, depending on the particular needs of both your baby and your own body. It is easy to feel over-whelmed as difficulties arise, but there are often very simple solutions to sometimes seemingly impossible or frustrating problems. With knowledgeable support and a willingness to work with the problems that come up, you can make it through the first few weeks and come through feeling a strong sense of confidence in yourself and your body, and what it is beautifully designed to do. At a certain point nursing can become effortless, the foundation of a child-centered way to parent that nourishes baby and mother at the deepest level.

There is now much more public awareness of the health benefits of breast-feeding and a growing understanding of its other important dimensions, such as emotional comfort, maternal-infant bonding, physical and psychological tuning of biological rhythms (how the bodies and minds of the mother and the baby interact), and long-term neurological and developmental effects.

Observing our children when they were babies and toddlers, I (mkz) could see the deep states of relaxation that they would immediately move into as they nursed. No matter what was going on in the moment, no matter what upset had just occurred, I could usually count on nursing to calm and rejuvenate my child. It provided a momentary withdrawal from the stimulation of the world into a quiet, peaceful place of comfort, nurturance, and renewal. As toddlers, they would move from playing and exploring at a distance back to me for refueling. By that time, they were eating lots of different foods. They weren't really nursing for food. They were nursing to renew other aspects of their being.

Another important and unique aspect of breast-feeding is the concentrated effort required of the infant to suck milk from the breast. With nursing, the milk doesn't come pouring down into their mouths; they have to work for it. The initial sucking may give them very little milk, and then at a certain point, if you watch closely, you can see them switching to the long, slow sucks that show you that your milk has let down and is flowing. The child relaxes into a satisfying rhythm—focused, working, but relaxed. When the breast is emptied, they often continue to nurse to meet their needs for comfort, calming, relaxation, and connection.

Years ago, I attended a conference sponsored by La Leche League, an organization devoted to informing women about breast-feeding and providing support. It was in a large auditorium full of women holding infants and toddlers in their laps, some nursing, some snuggling. It was remarkable to feel the babies centering on their mothers. The importance of this embodied relationship is discussed in sociologist Robbie Pfeufer Kahn's insightful book *Bearing Meaning: The Language of Birth*.

Breast-fed babies and toddlers see their mothers as the "source." Venturing out and exploring is balanced by a return to the source of their security and nurturance. They stay within an expanded maternal sphere, because they are strongly connected. They are able to come and go, grounded in their relationship to her and to her body.

In that auditorium full of small children, I was struck by the sustained quiet in the room, the feeling of contentment with being held or nursed, embraced by the aura of the mother.

Soul Food

When our children were little, people would frequently comment on how rosy their cheeks were. I (mkz) would smile to myself, knowing where those rosy cheeks came from. They came from nursing.

Once I had made it through the sometimes painful and frustrating first few weeks of nursing, in which my body was trying to find the right balance between too little milk and an overabundance of it, I found that nursing relaxed me and slowed me down. As I felt my milk let down, a wonderful haziness descended on me, and everything else became less important. I let go of the things I had planned to do, and instead let myself be pulled into the present moment, into being totally with my baby. It was a deeply meditative time for both of us.

Nursing was a huge cornerstone of my mothering. It gave me great confidence to know that I had what I needed to feed and comfort my babies anytime, anywhere. They often had a look of delight as I positioned them at the breast. First they would nurse for milk. Then, as the breast emptied, they would go on to suck for comfort, and from there, would move into a completely relaxed state of being. If they were at all tired, they would usually fall asleep. Getting them to sleep without a big fuss when they needed a nap was as easy as nursing them as they snuggled up to me. If they woke up at night, they would either already be sleeping next to me, or I would go and get them and bring them into our bed and nurse them, both of us never fully waking up, drifting back to sleep together.

As they got to be toddlers and were eating all sorts of foods, nursing remained a deep source of comfort. If their day had been wearing, overwhelming, or overstimulating, I could count on nursing to rejuvenate them. No matter where we were, a quiet space could be created just by their climbing onto my lap and nestling into my arms. Tensions were released by the quiet concentration of nursing, the warmth of my body, the rhythm of my breath. This ongoing connection to me through nursing gave them a deep sense of security and self-confidence. I could feel it in every aspect of their being. Their experience of the world was grounded in the body—in their relationship to me and my body, and in their experience of their own body nursing, being held. They knew the source of their satisfaction and renewal. It was visible, tangible, dependable. That grounding helped them to meet the world with curiosity and self-possession. Perhaps because nursing gave them a time to be snuggled, nurtured, and treated like a "baby" for brief periods, they felt secure enough to give up wearing diapers at a relatively early age.

When they started speaking, the nursing brought out an impish, playful side to them. When my son was one and a half, he made his first joke. He gave me a mischievous look, blew on my breast as if to cool it, and then said, "Hot!" smiling with delight. When he was about two and a half, we were nursing one morning and I said, "Let's go down and have breakfast." He responded with "Nurse!" Every time I tried to disengage he would say, "Nurse!" Finally I said, "You're a nut!" He looked at me and said, "No, I'm a raisin!" We laughed together and hugged, and proceeded to go down for breakfast.

My body was an essential and completely familiar part of their landscape. The children had their own unique words that stood for nursing, the breast, and breast milk. "Nuk" and "Noonie" were favorites. When I had a problem with a yeast infection on one breast and the skin was breaking down, my son matter-of-factly referred to one as "the booboo side" and called the other "the like-that side."

My youngest daughter loved to rhyme, and her creativity was particularly prolific around nursing. One morning she welcomed me with "Ooh, noonie is my best kind of juice, Myla Moose!"

She found lots of ways of expressing how valued "noonies" were to her. She could be very dramatic in her choice of words and her intonation. Getting out of the shower one morning, she held a towel around herself and said, "I won't let the gold fall out of my noonies." At another time, she said, in a tragic voice worthy of Shakespeare, "My noonie has been robbed!"

Nursing had such a powerful effect on my children that at times it could work its magic even without the presence of my body. When my older daughter was two, I was away all day assisting at a birth. When I called home in the afternoon, Jon said she very much wanted to talk to me. I was immediately filled with dread, knowing that as soon as she heard my voice, she would be overcome with sadness and tell me she wanted me. As soon as she got on the phone, she started to cry, telling me to come home right away. I told her I'd try to be home as soon as I could. Her response was a plaintive "Nukky me!" I said, "I'll nurse you when I get home." Her voice was insistent: "No, nukky me *now!*" Wanting to comfort her, I said very gently, "Okay, I'm nursing you right now. How is it?" She was silent, and Jon said she was sitting there with her eyes closed, relaxed and meditative, letting me "nurse" her over the phone.

Whether they were angry, frustrated, overwhelmed, or just ragged, nursing brought peace and contentment. They were their most loving selves when they were receiving love in this form. Nursing my daughter to sleep one night, she looked up at me and said in the lovingest tone of voice: "Mutha, you so sweet." We were both bathed in sweetness.

Even after the children stopped nursing, my body was still a source of comfort and well-being for them. There would be times as they were drifting off to sleep that they would rest their hand on my breast and get this wonderful, peaceful look on their faces. It was as if that was enough to bring them back to a blissful state of being that nourished them deeply. You might call it soul food.

The Family Bed

At the time we began having children, the dominant cultural view was that babies and children should sleep by themselves in their own rooms. This arrangement is very different from how most families in the world sleep, and from how most families in our country slept in earlier times. Yet our separate sleeping arrangements in early childhood may be one way in which the "advanced development" of a society deprives rather than nurtures. Parents and children alike may be the losers.

When our first child was born, our pediatrician told us to have him sleep in his own room, in his own bed, from the very beginning. But that just didn't feel right. We had an intuitive sense that our newborn baby belonged with us during the night. Sleeping next to us, he could relax into the softness and warmth of our bodies. He was bathed in the security and comfort of our presence. All was right with the world, for him and for us, when he was sleeping between us, usually snuggled right up against one or both of us.

Nothing can really describe the deep contentment we felt having our baby next to us, not needing to worry about being unable to hear him. Rather than wondering and worrying, "Is he covered, is he cold, will I hear him crying over the sound of wind and rain?"

there was no questioning how he might be, because he was right there with us.

When babies are born, their ability to self-regulate is not fully developed. Physical proximity to one or both parents helps them stabilize their physiology. Our breathing, for example, helps them to regulate their breathing. Our body's warmth keeps them warm. It is like a micro-ecosystem. Physical contact is an important part of this natural dynamic, as of course, is nursing.

For several years we slept together, breathed together. Even when he slept in his own bed, our bed was often where he started off the night or wound up by the morning. When we wanted to be alone, we would carry him into his room after he was asleep. More and more as he got older, he wanted to be in his own room, in his own bed. When the girls were born, being closer together in age, there was a time when we had both of them sleeping in bed with us. At some point, we got a larger bed.

We didn't get a whole lot of uninterrupted sleep during those early years. Our children woke up a number of times at night, not only to nurse but sometimes because they were teething, or sick. Children are very different. Some sleep for long stretches during the night early on. Many don't.

Were there times we thought that perhaps we were inadvertently encouraging them to wake up by being close by and letting them nurse when they wanted to? Yes, of course. But our moments of questioning and wondering didn't bring an end to sharing sleep with our little ones, because we continued to feel that there were so many benefits. We worked with the difficulties the way we worked with everything else, trying to find the right balance. When they were toddlers, there were definitely times that we were getting woken up too much and were tired and frustrated. What we tried to do at such times was to make waking up less inviting, sometimes by having Jon walk with them rather than letting them nurse.

A greater intention came into play here, one we valued more than uninterrupted sleep. We intuitively felt that the security and the peace that our physical presence gave our children was nourishing to their whole being. The effect was tangible. We could see it in their open, curious, lively, loving faces. We felt our presence at night helped to ground them in their bodies and in the world, and that grounding could be seen in the way they quietly observed the world around them during the day. They were curious without being frenetic, active without being out of control. The well-being and joyfulness emanating from them was wonderfully contagious. They were wholly present, whether it was in a laugh of delight, a shout of anger, or a loving embrace.

Of course there were many times when life in the form of teething, colds, or stomach upsets invariably interrupted our sleep. Sometimes it felt as if we were playing musical beds. One of us would sleep in an empty child's bed if we needed to get more sleep. Along the way we had to redefine for ourselves what felt normal in terms of how much sleep we needed.

We parented this way out of the conviction that deeper things were being fed than our need for sleep, or even time alone together, for which we found creative solutions when we wanted to. At the time we believed that when the children were ready to sleep through the night, they would; and when they were ready to sleep in their own beds, they would choose to do so; and with some encouragement, they did.

When children are toddlers, nursing at night in the family bed can sometimes become disruptive to everybody's sleep, and it can begin to feel that the negatives are outweighing the positives. It is different for every family and for every child. This is why the more we can step back and mindfully examine the effects of our nursing and co-sleeping choices on the well-being of each member of the family, the more we can adjust what we are doing for the benefit of all.

We share our own personal family experience around sleeping arrangements and our views of it when our children were young because we felt strongly, and still do, about the importance of nurturing children in this way when they are little. We also emphasize it precisely because it runs so counter to the dominant sleeping practices in our society today, although it is the norm in many Asian countries. We simply want young couples to know that it is an option, and that it is doable, and that it, too, can be incorporated into a view of parenting as a sometimes challenging as well as deeply satisfying practice. Like everything else, having young children sleep in your bed has its costs, but it can also have very tangible benefits, a feeling of trust and connectedness that can help through the difficult times. In fact, recent research shows that there are long-term positive benefits related to self-confidence and independence in children who experienced co-sleeping. The whole question of co-sleeping and ways to practice it safely is an active area of debate and research. Notre Dame researcher James McKenna offers a useful set of guidelines for safe co-sleeping; see http://cosleeping.nd.edu/safe-co-sleeping-guidelines/.

*

As parents, we all have our own particular histories and personal experiences of childhood. Being aware of our feelings and having some understanding of where they come from is an important aspect of making choices that are right for us and for our family. For instance, if we grew up without the experience of caring, nurturing touch, or if our boundaries were violated and our trust broken by inappropriate touching, it is natural that there might be a strong hesitation, even fear, regarding sharing a family bed. Holding such feelings and the thoughts that accompany them in awareness without automatically judging them—or ourselves—allows us to see them more clearly and experience perhaps a degree of freedom from having them automatically dictate our choices as parents. At the same time, we also have to be respectful of our discomfort and the reasons for it.

Finding ways to meet the needs of our babies and children that we also feel comfortable with requires openness, flexibility, and thoughtfulness, and a willingness to stretch and grow beyond our fixed and often unexamined assumptions. But it is not so easy, for the same reason that mindful parenting is not easy. It is often bringing us up against what we think are our limits, encouraging us to hold them in awareness with gentleness and find new ways to both work with them and honor them. And certainly, trying out any new approaches in parenting can be particularly difficult if both parents don't share the same viewpoints or values. Mindful communication becomes even more important in such situations.

There are many ways to parent with awareness. In no way does a commitment to parent mindfully mean that you have to sleep with your babies or you will not be a good or sensitive parent. Mindful parenting simply calls on us to pay attention to what we are doing, including the choices we make, and to examine in an ongoing way the effect our choices have on our children and ourselves. It involves a continual inquiry into what we are doing and why.

We believe that decisions about warmth and comfort, closeness and feeding, and what boundaries and limits might best promote health and happiness and well-being in our particular families are of paramount importance. Mindfulness brought to that very decision making is critical to making parenting a conscious endeavor that is sensitive to the changing needs of both the children and the parents.

There is no one "right way" to do this. There are many ways to promote healthy children and loving families.

Moreover, choices around sleep may work for a while in a family, and then suddenly something shifts and a change is needed. If we don't get to see a baby or young child that much during the day, we might find that sharing sleep is a wonderful way to reconnect and nurture her. This might work well with one child but perhaps not so well with another who is a restless sleeper. We may find ourselves too grumpy and short-tempered to be able to function, and will then have to try something else.

There are times when parents need their children to sleep more consistently through the night, and it becomes an urgent priority. It can become clear that the parents need uninterrupted sleep, and the children may benefit from it as well. With some awareness, we can make changes to our nighttime rituals and find ways to promote a sense of trust and security. Giving up the physical closeness of sleeping together can be balanced with times in the day when we intentionally hold them and snuggle with them. With a baby, even if he or she is sleeping in a separate bed in your room, your baby's physiology responds to the sound of your breathing and to your presence. No one parenting choice will make all the difference. What's important is the whole tapestry that we create through the myriad choices we make. So it is always a matter of balancing different needs in the family with awareness, firmness, and kindness as best we can. There is obviously no one solution to these nighttime dilemmas.

Fortunately, there are many options. If sharing sleep in the same bed does not work for you or for your spouse or your child, you could put a bed next to yours, or have your child sleep in an adjacent room. You can create rituals that your child can count on and look forward to, whether it's reading to him, or telling a story, playing some quiet music, lying down with him as he goes to sleep, or sitting with him. You can embody a sense of confidence that it's okay for him to be alone, that he is safe and can learn to sleep on his own. Far more important than the choice of sleeping arrangements is finding your own way to foster feelings of trust, security, connectedness, and inner resilience.

It's important for both parents to keep asking themselves and each other what is in their child's best interest, and work together to find solutions to bedtime problems that come up. Sharing insights, examining emotionally charged reactions, and trying to see things from the child's point of view and from each other's point of view are all useful when we take a fresh look at how we spend almost half our lives.

PART SIX

Resonances, Attunement, and Presence

Resonances

When a tuning fork vibrates, it will cause other tuning forks in the vicinity to vibrate as well, especially if they are related—that is, tuned to the same wavelength. This process, whereby the activity of one vibrating body brings another body into sympathetic resonance with it, is called *entrainment*. A piano's A strings will be entrained to vibrate when an A is played on a violin across the room.

Parents and children also constantly influence each other's resonances. Our lives orbit within each other's force fields, physically, emotionally, and psychically, and we are continually interacting and influencing each other in subtle and not-so-subtle ways, sometimes known, sometimes wholly unconscious.

Scientists have discovered that our brains also resonate with each other when we are in each other's presence. Particular cells in the cerebral cortex, known as mirror neurons, fire when they observe another person engaged in a particular movement, especially if emotion is involved. This may be the neurological basis for empathy, our ability to *feel with* another person. We are literally experiencing the same areas in our brains firing in similar patterns.

Breathing itself is a basic biological rhythm that has each one of us vibrating with life. Tuning to this rhythm presents a wonderful occasion to literally resonate with our baby. I (jkz) used to breathe with our babies as a way of bringing greater mindfulness into the present moment. I would feel the two of us breathing together, swinging in a hammock, as the baby slept in my arms, or when I walked back and forth with a child late at night. Swinging or walking, breathing together, sometimes singing and chanting softly as well, we were resonating with each other.

If we intentionally become aware of the resonances between us, our relationship with a baby can be a continual exchange of energy of all kinds, sometimes harmonious, sometimes not. Either way, it will never be any richer than right in this moment, even as we may have to also cook dinner or do the laundry, or are interrupted on occasion by one thing or another. This is a good reason to step into the dance of breathing in whatever moments we can manage it.

*

Entrainment happens on a lot of different levels in families. At times it can take us places we may not want to go and without us knowing how we got there. If we are not aware of the energy of the moment, it can easily ensnare us. It can pull us down emotionally, as when we fall into depression, or anger, or anxiety, or any number of other feeling states. In a family, aren't we all constantly caught up in an ever-changing exchange of energy, putting out vibrations at different frequencies and interacting with each other's energy in the form of thoughts, feelings, and their expressions, verbal and nonverbal, through our bodies, our actions, and our emotional reactions to events and other people's actions, even tiny ones? If we know we are resonating with each other in different ways, we can learn to move more skillfully in relationship to such rhythms without losing our balance.

Children can get into very strong energy states that can affect us in a number of different ways. If we can be aware of this, we can stay more in touch with ourselves and respond more consciously to them. If they hit a certain frequency, we do not automatically have to resonate on that same frequency and get caught up in ways that will not be helpful, either to them or to us.

At the same time, there are also many moments of integration and wonder that children experience, and that we can experience with them and resonate with...moments of pure pleasure.

✻

An outdoor restaurant in summer. A young couple with two children: one about three, the other about four months. The mother nurses the baby, snuggled in her lap. For the longest time, the baby's face is buried in the breast and under parts of her mother's blouse. But her hand is playing with her mother's the whole time. Later, her head surfaces, and she lies on her mother's lap, gazing at her. The mother makes cooing noises and tilts her head slightly. The baby opens her mouth, making a perfect circle, her blue eyes wide open, too, drinking in her mother's face. Her eyes are so open, her mouth is so open, her face so open, she is an incarnation in this moment of pure presence.

The mother puts her head down and touches it to her baby's forehead, then moves it back. The baby smiles. There is a complete force field connecting these two. This baby is in the orbit of her mother in this moment, and the two are speaking in a thousand ways, on a thousand wavelengths, across their bodies where they touch, across the air between them.

Later, the father holds the baby in such a way that she can look out over his shoulder. She is settled on his body. Her eyes are wide open, totally receptive. She sees my (jkz) face, and her gaze comes to rest. I smile. Her face registers it in some way I detect instantly but find impossible to describe. It is alert to novelty. She smiles. It is like a benediction from a purer world. Her older sister's face is open, too. As she sits at the table, I can feel that she, too, is at home in her body and in the force field of her family. It is not even that they interact that much. They don't. But they form an inseparable whole in which she is completely at home. It shows in her presence, too. As they are leaving, the mother tells us that they had just spent many hours in the car, and the kids needed out.

Just an ordinary meal, but it is clear that these children are experiencing that constant give-and-take with parents that forms the bonds of love and conveys the benevolence and receptivity of the world to young life.

Attunement

ATTUNE: To bring into a harmonious or responsive relationship.

Attuning to our children involves being aware of the messages they are giving us, not just with their words, but with every aspect of their being.

I (mkz) walk into our local coffee shop and see my neighbor sitting at a table, nursing her nine-month-old as she waits for a friend. I say hi, and her baby, curious, stops nursing, looks up, gives me a big smile, and then goes back to nursing. As I wait in line, she begins a game with me across the distance that separates us. She nurses, and then drops her head down so that she is looking at me upside down. She grins and goes back to nursing, and then drops down again, and stares at me. Her mother takes her cues from her, and lets her move her body as she chooses, laughing with pleasure at her daughter's pleasure. On this rainy Wednesday morning in a local coffee shop, one baby is in a state of bliss.

✼

I (mkz) am reminded of when our own children were babies as I take care of my friend's ten-month-old son. Holding him against me as I walk, I try out different things, aware of how he is responding, until

I find the right combination of gentle up-and-down movements while chanting softly and rhythmically. I slow my breathing down. I feel his body soften and relax into mine. He has no problem telling me without words what he wants. As I sit down with him, he lets me know with his whole body, "No, don't sit down, carry me, walk with me." Then he starts to make little sounds, and I pick up on them and we make them together. His head rests on my shoulder. I feel him softening and getting heavier and heavier until he is fast asleep. Slowly I lie down on the couch, feeling his warmth and softness, enjoying the sweet smell of his skin. This attuning is a wonderful gift to both of us. On this spring day, he is finding out once again that he can rely on the people around him. He feels a sympathetic responsiveness from me telling him that what he wants and needs is important and will be respected. When he gets what he needs, he feels satisfied, safe, and peaceful. All this from one small encounter.

*

When a mother sees her toddler becoming more and more active to the point of being wild and out of control, she decides to lie down on the rug and let him climb on her and play with her hair. She is literally letting him get back in touch with her. Gradually, he starts to quiet, to slow down, until after a while he is lying down on her, resting, settling into the soothing rhythm of her breath. She is helping him to attune to her calm energy. She understands her child's need for independence and separation, and at the same time his need to be close and connected. All are played out in this scene on the living room floor.

*

As children get older, attunement between parent and child becomes more complex. My (mkz) ten-year-old comes home from school and walks in the door with a scowl on her face. "I'm hungry!" she says in a fierce voice. I see in an instant that school has taken its toll on her. She's feeling overwhelmed. She's been with people all day. She's about to fall apart. I've learned to have a snack ready for her when she gets home. I've also learned the hard way not to ask her questions, to give her space. This is not the best time for objecting to her tone of voice or for teaching her manners. After this little respite, she usually looks at me in a somewhat more friendly manner and either comes up to me for a hug or disappears into her room to listen to music.

With older children, being attuned might mean being sensitive to their need to be left alone to concentrate on whatever they are doing, especially when they are in the same physical space with us. It may also mean sensing when to reach out and nurture them in small ways.

As I sit in my friend's kitchen, her sixteen-year-old comes in complaining of a pain in her neck. Her mother asks her to point to where it hurts. As we talk, she massages her daughter's neck, periodically stopping her conversation with me to quietly let her know when she feels the knots releasing under her touch. We continue to talk as she massages her, and after about fifteen minutes her daughter leaves the room. My friend tells me that this kind of moment together is a rare occurrence now. It probably helped to have another adult present, creating a bit more distance. It is wonderful to feel this mother's sensitivity, her willingness to be open to her daughter unexpectedly reaching out, and her ability to appreciate the preciousness of that moment.

Being in harmony with our children doesn't mean that things will always be harmonious. Being mindful in moments of disharmony and conflict often requires everything we have, every ounce of energy and insight, so that even in the midst of struggle, we have a chance to keep sight of who our children are and what they may need from us in that moment. In order to do this, we need to be willing to acknowledge to ourself our own fears, reactions, and concerns, and yet work at maintaining our equilibrium by staying in touch with our breath, our body, and the bigger picture as best we can. This sets the stage for us to recognize and meet their feeling state in more appropriate and imaginative ways. Of course, there will always be moments of struggle and disconnection—these can be opportunities for parents and children alike to learn that it is possible to recover and begin again.

Touch

The word *touch* has one of the longest entries in the *Oxford English Dictionary*, undoubtedly because it is so basic to the human experience. Ashley Montagu observed long ago that touch is fundamental to health and connectedness. Monkey babies don't thrive unless they have constant touching, warmth, and softness. Why think that we would be different? Touch is fundamental to life.

Touch involves being in touch. It can be a unifying experience. We cannot touch without being touched back. It is one way we know we are not alone. Depending on how we are touched, we can feel anything from loved, accepted, and valued to ignored, disrespected, and harmed.

Touch generates awareness and puts us in touch with the world. We touch and are touched through all our senses—seeing, hearing, smelling, tasting, as well as feeling through the skin—and also proprioception and interoception.

Being held with sensitivity grounds us in our bodies and awakens a sense of connectedness. It awakens us to ourselves and to the other. A child's whole being is honored when he is touched with awareness, sensitivity, and respect. Learning to be "in touch" with how you feel grows out of this experience of feeling safe and cared for. Through holding, hugging, cradling, snuggling, swinging, rocking, humming, singing, and gazing, parent and child experience themselves and each other—the magic of being in touch.

*

Waiting at the Registry of Motor Vehicles, I (mkz) watch a large, soft woman who is taking care of a redheaded three-year-old boy. She is sitting on a bench, waiting for her license. He is simultaneously using her body as bed, pillow, and jungle gym. He pushes constantly up against her with his body, his head, his arms. When he reaches out and plays with her fingers, she taps his hand, to his delight, with her long fingernails. She is totally accepting of him, never admonishing him to be still, or sit up, or stop what he is doing. There is a sweetness and peacefulness to the scene. The woman has an accent, and I wonder where she grew up, what her childhood was like, and what has influenced her to be so patient, so accepting, so comfortable with touch.

I don't see scenes like this often. Instead, it's not uncommon to see parents admonishing their children to "behave," and getting angry at them when they behave as the two- or three- or four- or five-year-olds that they are. I've seen tired toddler-age children following along behind a parent, crying, without the parent resorting to the simple solution of picking up the child. I don't often see adults relating to children affectionately and with tolerance for their energy and exuberance.

We seem to be increasingly turning into a touch-deprived and disembodied society. It is rare to see people being physically affectionate, friends holding hands or putting their arms around each other, or lovers embracing. Having some awareness of the importance of this essential form of nourishment and communication can motivate us to find ways to be more embodied and more in touch in our moments with our children.

Touch always happens at a boundary, and that boundary is itself important to hold in awareness. Otherwise, we may touch our children unconsciously and in doing so, risk being insensitive or disrespectful. The boundaries between us are changing from moment to moment. They cannot be assumed or taken for granted. Each moment is new and different. The child who yells "No!" when asked if she can be given a good-night kiss at another time wants to be comforted with a hug. When we are more attuned to our children, aware of their energy, their feeling state, we can better sense when they are in need of a loving touch or holding, and when they need to be left alone.

It may help at times to ask ourselves who the touching serves, as a check on our own mindless or invasive impulses. I (mkz) have vivid memories of relatives pinching my cheeks and kissing me. They had no awareness of how that might feel to me. How often are children asked for hugs and kisses to meet the adult's need for warmth and affection, regardless of the child's feelings or boundaries?

*

I (mkz) am moved, and somewhat astonished and grateful in those rare moments when my children come up to me and hug me. I am surprised not so much that they are hugging me, but by the way they hug me. They hug with a slow, relaxed, quiet, loving touch. As they hug me, I enjoy the nourishment that my children so naturally give in those moments. It feels like a circle of love completed.

Toddlers

Each age and stage, each child, and each moment provides many opportunities for exploring sympathetic resonances while being aware that a child's developmental and emotional needs are ever-changing. When our babies become toddlers, the challenge is to stay attuned as best we can as we give them some freedom to explore within a framework of clear boundaries and expectations that provide a feeling of containment and safety. We get this chance over and over again, because they are so active and their moods can change so rapidly. One moment our toddlers may be one way. The next moment, the picture can be entirely different. Toddlers don't yet have the language or the motor skills to do all the things they want to do, and so can get easily frustrated. If we can sense when these shifts and transitions are arising, we are more likely to come up with strategies for helping them through such moments.

This requires being aware of our own feelings as well, which can change almost as rapidly as our child's. It is all too easy to be entrained into our child's mood, as when we react with frustration to his or her frustration. Instead of constricting at such moments and automatically hardening in reaction, perhaps we can set ourselves the challenge of catching ourselves in such moments and respond with greater understanding and a kinder and more open presence.

One day, I (jkz) observed a young father in a restaurant trying to eat dinner with his three-year-old daughter. The food had taken too long to come. By the time it arrived, she was no longer able to sit still. She was frustrated, tired, demanding. He just couldn't eat. She was all over the place. It would have been so easy for him to become hard in that moment. To resent her or to be angry that the food had taken so long to come, or that he couldn't get to eat it even though he was hungry and probably tired himself. But he maintained his composure and saw what needed to happen. After one or two attempts to have a bite, he had the food packed up, paid the bill with her on his shoulders and pulling on his hair, and left. I smiled to him as he passed us and we talked briefly about the trials of parenting as I sat there with my girls, old enough now to wait patiently for the food to come, remembering with wistfulness the era when my own mind was tuned to "toddler mind" and my choices from moment to moment informed by their so strong and so rapidly changing needs. That period often feels like it will never end when you are in it. It can help to remind yourself that it is over all too soon, and surrendering to what is needed may present unexpected gifts.

Every age and stage has its own particular dramas. I found it uplifting to watch this father respond so skillfully and so generously with his daughter.

*

I (jkz) used to leave work early when I could and go on one-on-one "dates" with my toddlers. I would take them to the playground, or sledding, or for walks along the river, or to hang out in the city center, just watching people and cars and the activity of the world. On the weekend, it was fun to take them with their friends to fairs and farms and lakes. Any occasion with a toddler, even for just a few undivided minutes of play, or wrestling around on the floor, or rolling little cars back and forth, or a ball, is an opportunity for bonding.

When the children were little, we loved to play "squirm," a game that my son and I spontaneously invented one day. We would lie on the floor and I would wrap my arms around his waist. Then he would try to squirm out using his whole body. By adjusting the pressure of my arms, I could hold him more or less tightly, giving him just enough resistance so that he really had to work to overcome significant obstacles, and come up with various strategies for how he was going to do it in order to break free.

It seemed to me that being constrained in that playful way and having to use all their energy and cleverness to finally break free was a great metaphor for other life trials that the children would be facing sooner or later. This mostly nonverbal wrestling brought us closer in many ways, as we breathed together, squirming and struggling against each other, playing the edge of breakouts and breakthroughs and bursting into laughter from time to time. Attuning physically through this kind of game helped us to fall into quiet times afterward that felt full of resonance and delight.

On occasion, the children would join me on Sunday mornings, practicing yoga on the living room floor. Sometimes they would play "yoga teacher" and direct me in various postures that we would do side by side. We also did some "yoga for two," with the children rocking with me as I made my body into a rocking chair, or climbing on me in the shoulder stand, or flying in the air like a bird as they balanced horizontally on my feet as I lay on my back, or going underneath me when I became a bridge. It was endless fun.

As they got older, it became harder sometimes to find ways of sharing moments of concentrated activity and the stillness that comes from them. Even so, we found ways, through playing catch, or sometimes running together, even dancing on occasion. The resonances remain; the forms change.

Time

Parents can easily fall into feeling that there is never enough time. We are pressed for it and driven by the lack of it. One morning, I (jkz) heard myself telling one of our daughters when she was about four years old, "Hurry up. I don't have any time," as she was selecting which of three dresses to wear that day. What a message.

There are things we can do to give ourselves more time, and to make the best use of the time that we have. We can wake up early enough and get the children up early enough to have time in the morning without rushing. Sometimes it can help if they pick out their clothes the night before. We can work at keeping our own time urgency from coloring everything we do. We can do this by remembering to tune in to our breathing and to see that our fears about the future are just thoughts, while the present—what is happening now—is a precious occasion, not to be trampled on. The timeless quality of the present moment is captured in the little things, like remembering to make eye contact when saying good-bye, or taking a moment now and then for a hug. Of course the key here is not doing any of these things in an automatic way because they're "good" to do, but allowing them to arise out of our presence and openness.

It is also helpful to listen to the tone of our voice as we realize that we are going to be late. As an experiment, we might try lowering our voice and dropping more deeply into right now, into our body, into this breath.

Another thing we might do is to try not to over-schedule our children and be aware of our impulses to do so. They need time to just be. Downtime slows time down and makes room for imaginative play, alone and with friends. Our children need time to be bored and to find out how to go into boredom and through it, sometimes with guidance from us and sometimes not.

If we are not aware of the effects of time pressures on the family, we run the risk of living lives of ever increasing acceleration and nonstop doing, and passing this way of life on to our children. The trend in the world today, with all the various digital devices that are so ubiquitous and continually pull us out of the present moment by interrupting or distracting us or offering us a "better moment," is characterized by a former Microsoft researcher, Linda Stone, as a condition of "continuous partial attention." In the face of this societal disease of perpetual self-distraction, stillness and presence need to be cultivated and brought into the home to restore balance and to nurture those aspects of being that are best touched through nondoing.

Many people who have been through the MBSR program say that waking up early and spending time meditating in stillness sets the tone for their whole day, and is worth far more than the same amount of time spent sleeping longer. They are able to be calmer and more intentional in their approach to what they have to do that day, and what they really care about. They also observe that other people in the family feel the effects of their meditating. Stress levels in the whole family can be lower when one person is practicing mindfulness.

Sometimes, decisions to opt for more time together rather than for making more money can be extremely healthy for a family. It is not always possible to do, but sometimes it is more possible than our own mind would have us think. Otherwise, we may wind up, ironically and tragically, missing what may be most important in our lives as we work to "make a living" without examining what this "living" might be.

> Ridiculous the waste sad time,
> Stretching before and after.

T. S. ELIOT,
"BURNT NORTON," *Four Quartets*

Presence

"Mom, you're not listening!"

Despite my seeming presence, I've been caught with my mind elsewhere. I'm pulled back for a moment, only to wander off again into creative mental explorations or obsessive, mostly irrelevant thoughts about the past or the future. This happens to all of us, and it happens a lot. Mindfulness is most fundamentally about cultivating moment-to-moment wakeful presence in the face of our wandering minds and seemingly endless impulses to distract ourselves. It is difficult to show up fully, even for a moment, even for ourselves. As we cultivate mindfulness in our parenting, we are intentionally reminding ourselves to be more aware and tuned in rather than tuned out.

Of course, we get lots of opportunities to practice noticing when we're lost in thought and distracted in one way or another. It's part of being human. There are always going to be things we want or need to think about. The question is, is this the moment or time to do that? Can we be aware that we are being pulled away from the present moment, and aware of what in particular is pulling us away? Can we see what we might be missing by being so caught up in our thoughts? Awareness gives us a choice, and a chance to come back.

For example, when a child walks in, can we remember to

intentionally take a moment and really see her and acknowledge her presence? We do that with acquaintances but we often don't with those closest to us. It doesn't always have to be in words, either. Silence can be a profound manifestation of presence when it is embodied.

At the same time, it is important not to misinterpret "being present" to mean that parents should constantly pay attention to their children. This, of course, is neither possible nor desirable. It is essential for our children to have their own experiences. They need to sense from us that we are comfortable with their intrinsic autonomy. Mindful parenting and the cultivation of presence do not mean that we should hover over our children, continually commenting about what they are doing, encouraging them, praising them, or intervening and rescuing them from age-appropriate challenges. It is problematic for them and for us if we lose ourselves in becoming overly child focused.

There is no question that the quality of our presence with our children has a huge effect on the quality of our relationship with them. Cultivating presence requires intentional effort, over and over again coming back to this moment, attending to what is most salient and important, a willingness to be authentic, awake, and attuned.

Being authentic means that we are being genuine. We are not hiding or pretending. We are not discriminating against certain feelings that arise in ourselves or in our children. Rather, with awareness, we can recognize whatever feelings we have, even if they are uncomfortable for us, and metaphorically put out the welcome mat for them. However, if we've grown up having to hide our feelings or dissimilate in order to feel safe, being authentic can be extremely scary and difficult. It may be new and unknown territory.

We communicate so much through how we hold ourselves. When we are lost in thought, especially when we are worried, anxious, or stressed, all of that is carried in the body. Our children sense it when we are tense and contracted. It helps if we can remind ourselves to come back to the present moment and to be aware of what we are sensing and feeling, in other words, to ground our experience in awareness of the body. Our own breathing can be a trustworthy ally in this regard. Intentionally focusing on the sensations of breathing relaxes the body and allows us to soften and be a little more open in the face of whatever is going on. The more we learn to inhabit awareness itself, the more we come to embody authentic presence. In this way, we become more available to ourselves and to the people we love.

Even being a little more mindful can make a big difference in terms of how we are experienced by our children and in the quality of our own experience. Presence grows out of the practice of coming back to ourselves over and over again.

Jack and the Beanstalk

Children want total attention and engagement from adults at key times; at other times they want and need to be left to their own devices or with their friends.

For adults, it can be hard to give our full attention to anything, especially over a sustained period of time. Adult minds, as a rule, tend to be filled with conflicting impulses and thoughts that constantly compete for our attention. We have multiple responsibilities. We're very busy. A child may want us to play or to read, and we may do it, but we may do it with only a fraction of our mind, and they sense that easily. Many a time I (jkz) have caught myself reading to one of my children but thinking about the next telephone call I have to make as soon as the child is asleep. Or reading a story and realizing that I was getting through the story but that I had no idea what the story was about. I was thinking universes of thoughts in between each line, if not each word.

Once, when I was so tired I could hardly keep my eyes open, I was telling my daughter a story about a lion, making it up as I went along. But five minutes later, in my tiredness, the lion had become a rabbit. She noticed. We had a good laugh about that.

When our son was about four, "Jack and the Beanstalk" was a

favorite of his. He wouldn't just let me read it once or twice and then move on to another story. He wanted to hear it over and over again at the same sitting. I loved the story, too, but it was hard for me to read it for the seventh or eighth time. Then I realized that he was hearing it each time as if for the first time. The deep theme of the milk running out and having to sell the cow, the tension of hiding from the giant in his castle and observing his covetousness, the challenge of stealing the giant's gold and magic hen and singing harp, the thrill of being chased down the beanstalk, and of getting the ax from his mother just in time to cut it down and destroy the giant—these were real for him every time. His body would tense when the giant came in, and he would smile with delight as Jack tricked the giant each time.

Seeing the story through his eyes taught me that I, too, could be fully present each time I read it, even though part of my adult mind was resisting like crazy. Letting go of that, the story became like a piece of music, repetition of the essence. It is the same each time it is told or read, but it is also never the same. Realizing this expanded my world. "Jack and the Beanstalk" became part of my meditation practice for quite some time. It taught me to be present when I didn't want to be present anymore. Once again, the child becomes the parent's teacher. Fee Fi Fo Fum...we lumber about.

Bedtime

It helps to make space in the home for quiet moments, moments when "nothing" is happening. At those times, often just before children go to bed, or are in bed waiting for sleep, growth spurts, breakthroughs, creativity, sharing, connecting can emerge. The world has come to a stop. In the quiet, my (mkz) daughter reaches for her sketchpad, sits peacefully, concentrating and creating, completely absorbed in her work. On another night, I might read her a simple story that absorbs her imagination, looking into her eyes in moments when the story touches us or makes us smile. Sometimes I just sit with her, and after a while, she may bring up something that happened in school, or something that is bothering her. In the silence of the night, things have a chance to surface.

When our children were little we sang to them, told them stories, or read to them. As teenagers, some of them still liked to be read to at times. They also listened to music before drifting off to sleep. By bedtime, many different currents from the day are coming together.

Each child is different. Some children find it easy to fall asleep. For others, the transition is very difficult. At times, when our children were little, we tried everything possible to make bedtime a peaceful ending to the day. Sometimes, especially when we were tired ourselves, no matter what we did, it was anything but peaceful.

As hard as we both tried to protect this time, many things got in our way. Work to be done, phone calls to make arrangements for the next day, more than one child needing us, or children of different ages having different needs, often pulling us in different directions. Older children's needs can get shortchanged, taking a backseat to the younger ones. It's an ongoing juggling act. Sometimes a peaceful bedtime gets lost in all this. But the nights when we made the space to be fully present and somehow it came about, sharing a child's concern or feeling her drift into sleep reminded us how precious this time can be.

*

Now, by the small body of my sleeping son
the hidden river in my chest flows with my son's
and I time my speech to the rhythm of his breath

joining my night with his, singing his night song
as if those waters underground
were secret rivers washing through the soul

bringing out the untold life
which is the stream he'll join in growing old,
in silent hours when his sureness

of his self recedes. There he'll find
the rest between the solid notes
that makes the song worthwhile.

DAVID WHYTE,
from "Looking Back at Night," *Where Many Rivers Meet*

Gathas and Blessings

Sometimes short poems or sayings are used in meditation retreats or as part of a daily mindfulness practice to remind us of what we already know but so easily forget or take for granted. These poems or sayings are called *gathas* in the Buddhist tradition. There are gathas for waking in the morning, for saying over a meal, for having tea, for remembering to appreciate this inbreath and this outbreath, for almost every occasion in everyday life, all so that we can stay in touch with what is real and not lose ourselves in thought.

If they are repeated mindlessly, by rote and habit, these verses are virtually of no value. But if they are held, like precious birds, and invited to visit, and used judiciously, they can have enormous power. They are very simple, just reminders, but they have a wonderful directional energy. They heal and they soothe. They also point to what we need to remember. Our children learned this little gatha in school:

> The sun is in my heart
> It warms me with its power
> And wakens life and love
> In bird

And beast
And flower.

The whole class recited it aloud at the beginning of each day in kindergarten and the first few grades of elementary school. The words were accompanied by a series of arm movements that painted a flowing picture: making a sweeping circle over the head for the sun; the hands then tracing lines from over the head back to the heart, palms open to the sky; arms extending out with warmth; the hands then being brought back to the chest, closed around each other, and, finally, opening with the life of bird and beast, and completing the movement as the fingers and palms form the petaled cup of a flower.

We very much liked that the children were visiting this little gatha of the heart on a regular basis. We thought it good food for their minds and bodies and as important, if not more so, as anything else they might be learning. It felt like the daily repetition of this verse was protecting and nurturing something precious in them, and reminding them each day of the power and the preciousness of life and of the central empowering energy of the heart, which we call love. A little morning meditation for the class, to call the heart to awaken and remind the children of interconnectedness...sun, heart, life, power, bird, beast, flower, children, love, all one inseparable whole.

We learned many such gathas from our children. They said one before lunch in school that became our way of moving from the busyness of the day to a moment of silent connection as we sat down to dinner as a family, holding hands around the table:

Earth who gives to us this food,
Sun who makes it ripe and good,

Dear Earth, dear Sun,
By you we live,
Our loving thanks
To you we give.

Then we would keep silent for a moment or two, look at each other around the circle, look at our food and at the whole table set for dinner, and then say, "Blessings on our meal and blessings on our family." If guests were present, we might say, "Blessings on our guests."

We never said any blessings or grace in our families when we were growing up, and we sometimes felt uncomfortable when we ran into situations in which saying grace was the rule of the house. But as we got older, we both understood more and more the importance of intentionally and mindfully blessing what is wholesome and good in life so that it doesn't go unnoticed and uncelebrated.

Perhaps that is why we found these gathas of awareness and gratitude so congenial when our children brought them home and taught them to us. They were mindfulness blessings. They seemed so inclusive, so appreciative, so embracing. We like to think that during all the years we spoke these little verses and took the time to linger in the feelings they evoked, they were watering seeds within our hearts that continue to flower in our family and in the children, wherever they go. It is good to know that the sun is in your heart.

And these gathas may have also planted seeds in the children for loving what is behind the veil of appearance, what great poets know and celebrate so uncannily with words....

So great a sweetness flows into the breast
We must laugh and we must sing,

We are blest by everything,
Everything we look upon is blest.

WILLIAM BUTLER YEATS,
from "A Dialogue of Self and Soul"

PART SEVEN

Choices

Healing Moments

Most of what I (mkz) have learned in my life, I have learned from being a parent. My children are continually teaching me what I need to know, when I need to know it. Over the years I have had to remind myself to see things from each child's point of view, and in doing so, often my eyes have been opened to old patterns of relating from my own childhood that were limiting or damaging. What has been harder for me to see are the ways in which I can sometimes overcompensate for things that were lacking in my own childhood by going to the other extreme. Parenting decisions are often influenced by our experiences growing up within the particular dynamic of our family of origin. It can be useful to remind ourselves that there are significant differences between the family dynamic our child is experiencing and the one we grew up with. With some awareness that the context within which everything is happening is different, our choices as parents can be more balanced and appropriate to what is actually called for in the present.

Each time we are able to see and understand something about our own experience as a child, it can act as a guide for us in our parenting and liberate us in some small way from the grip of the past. When we sense the arising of an old and destructive pattern, whether it is in the tone of our voice (for instance, belittling or minimizing a child's feelings), a look on our face (disdain or contempt), or in our words (for example, "What's the matter with *you?*" or calling them some kind of hurtful name), we have a precious opportunity to make a choice. We can continue with our automatic and sometimes cruel behavior, which in some ways may feel familiar and comfortable because we may have experienced being treated this way ourselves growing up, or we can stop in that moment and try to see more clearly behind our own intense reactions. We can try, in spite of the strength of these highly conditioned emotional habits of mind, to see with fresh eyes, and to ask, "What am I doing right now? Why am I reacting so strongly in this situation? Where will this take me if I keep going in this direction? What does my child really need from me in this moment? What choices do I have here?"

Clearly it is a lot to ask of ourselves in such moments to consider the possibility of opening our hearts right there and then—especially when we are already being carried away by the inner momentum of it all and our own deeply ingrained habits of a lifetime. Is it possible for us to stop ourselves at such times and hold the present moment in awareness, as it is, and observe our impulses without having to automatically act on them?

As our children move through different developmental stages, our own demons from similar periods in our lives can come back to haunt us in particular situations. They can make themselves known with a sudden jolt of recognition, or they may simply be floating around, cloudlike, at the edges of our consciousness. Certain familiar situations can trigger intense reactions on our part that have more to do with us than with our children. The reaction might be a harshness in our response to something a child does, or a pattern of tuning out at particular times, or feelings of fear, anxiety, or discomfort.

When one of those disquieting feelings is triggered, it can be helpful to pause inwardly, if just for a moment, and listen closely to it. The more upsetting it is, the harder it may be to bring into focus. A clue to how disturbing it really is is how quickly the feeling gets pushed aside. Such moments may be very difficult to capture in awareness at first, especially if our feelings as children weren't accorded much value in our family. We may be used to sweeping them under the proverbial rug.

If we can bring such a feeling back into awareness, it becomes a clue pointing to something deeper. Its significance may not come to us until later, perhaps after repeated experiences that bring up similar feelings. Taking the time to stop, to breathe, to locate and feel the emotion and accompanying tension in the body gives us at least a chance to recognize that in some way we are under an old spell, and perhaps to wake from it with a more mindful and imaginative response.

In the moments when we are able to catch ourselves and change course, when we choose to act differently and in a way that is more aligned with what our child may need from us, a transformation and a healing can take place within ourselves. It becomes a healing moment.

When we choose to honor our children's needs in this way, there is also a potential honoring of our own unfulfilled childhood needs. When we choose to be kind rather than cruel, we get to experience kindness. It becomes real for us. If we were hit as a child, there can be a deep feeling of satisfaction if we are able to choose a better way to resolve conflict when the impulse to lash out comes up in us. If we were unprotected as children, when we care for and protect our children, we may find ourselves experiencing feeling safer and more secure as well.

In any moment, we can choose to set aside the emotional armor that may have been useful to us in the past, and give our children the gift of a more open, compassionate, and understanding parent.

In the process, we get a taste of the way it might have been in our own childhood, and more importantly, we get to share the intrinsic freedom and connectedness of this moment not only with our child, but also with ourself. In choosing to break out of a negative cycle, the magic of a love that is unconditional touches us as well. Each time we are able to do this, we take another step toward wholeness and our own liberation.

*

A young mother recounted the following story:

> I remember a moment of vivid clarity and recognition following the birth of my second child. My parents came over to visit, and my three-year-old was having a hard time and was acting out because the new baby was getting so much attention. I remember my parents' disapproval, their reprimanding her and chiding her to behave better, and I saw clearly in that moment that as long as my children or I were acting "nice," or "good," we were wonderful in their eyes, but as soon as we strayed from what they considered "acceptable" behaviors and expressed any "negative" emotions, we were met with judgment. Realizing this, I defended her in their presence. That was a healing moment for me and for her. I was empathic, I was on her side. I didn't betray her. How things "appeared," keeping things "nice," was not as important as my daughter's well-being in that moment.

Perhaps you can recall moments when your feelings were dismissed, disregarded, made fun of, or belittled as a child. Each interaction taken by itself may seem trivial and insignificant ("What's the big deal?" "Why are you so sensitive?"). But they are not insignificant, and when they are repeated over and over again, they can have a damaging effect on a child's self-confidence and trust.

Bringing awareness to our own tendencies to act or react in such ways gives us the possibility of breaking this harmful pattern. Such a moment occurred when a mother was driving her nine-year-old son and his friend to her home after school so that the boys could have some time to play together. In the car, the friend was talking to her son nonstop. Her son was uncharacteristically quiet, and occasionally said something back in a grumpy, taciturn way. She reprimanded him for this unfriendliness and reminded him how lucky he was to have his friend coming home with him. After about an hour of playing together, her son completely fell apart, yelling and kicking and crying, and she found herself exasperated and angry with him. It was only later, in thinking about what transpired, that she had the realization that being well-behaved and polite were of paramount importance in her own family of origin. In telling her son how lucky he was in response to his grumpiness, she was basically telling him to stuff his feelings and make his friend feel welcome. She was taking care of the friend's feelings and her own feelings, but not his.

She realized as well that she could have done any number of things that would have taken into account her son's feeling state. She could have named what she was seeing in a matter-of-fact way, acknowledging how he seemed to be feeling in that moment, suggested a quiet time in the car for both of them, and let her awareness of the situation inform the choices she gave the boys when they got to her home. Instead, she saw that she had adopted an automatic mode of behavior that was repeating an old and familiar pattern of denying feelings when those feelings were not "positive," polite, and friendly.

At another time, this same mother had taken her son to visit her mother, who hadn't seen him more than two or three times in his life. The grandmother decided to invite one of her friends over at the same time and proceeded to ignore her grandson and engage in a lively chat with her friend. Meanwhile, trapped in an environment that had little to interest him, he became bored and restless, and proceeded to run around the room and knock into the furniture. Embarrassed by her inability to control her son's unruly behavior, the mother angrily dragged him out and took him home. She was furious and admonished him for behaving rudely and not listening to her when she told him to stop. He looked at her with a pleading look and said, "But, Mom, Grandma didn't even *talk* to me!"

Suddenly, a veil fell from her eyes and she saw that she had put her son in the same situation she had always been put in when she was a child. No matter how much her mother had ignored her feelings and needs, she was always expected to be polite, friendly, and thoughtful. Now, as a mother herself, she was able to see that her mother had not made any effort to reach out to her grandson, to engage him in any way or to think about what would be fun for him. Instead of being able to feel angry or upset with her mother, she became angry with her son and replayed the familiar scene from her own childhood. Her son knew that his grandmother was ignoring him, but she had been unable to see it until he pointed it out: another example of how we learn from our children.

In thinking about all this later, the mother said she felt that it would be unrealistic to expect her mother to change, but that the next time they visited, she would bring some things for her son to do, or meet in a park, or insist that her mother come to *her* house. She also did something that was very important in rebuilding trust. She apologized to her son for getting angry with him when he was having a difficult time in a difficult situation. In being able to communicate her understanding and acceptance of his experience, she was strengthening his trust in her and also supporting him in trusting his own feelings.

No matter how much we love our children and want to be the best parents we can be, at times our automatic reactions can lead to moments of discord and disconnection. Such moments are inevitable, a natural part of life, since it is virtually impossible for us to be mindful all the time, or even most of the time, nor is it desirable. What is important is that we discover that we can navigate the interpersonal difficulties we encounter or even generate ourselves. At the same time, our children get to see that these kinds of temporary and painful ruptures can be acknowledged, worked with, and repaired. Mindfulness is not an ideal or an end state. Rather it is always a process, a way of being in relationship to what is actually unfolding, including or especially in moments of mindlessness. Self-judgment and remorse often follow. Each moment affords us a new opportunity to work with some degree of kindness with our own automaticity, fears, and expectations and the very real effects they can have, and learn from them.

At times, we may need to apologize and acknowledge how hurtful our behavior was, although the impulse to apologize can itself become too facile and automatic. It may be more helpful to simply acknowledge what happened silently to ourself and inwardly renew our commitment to be more mindful and more open to the complexities of the present moment. We can also, if we catch ourselves, stop and bring awareness to our breathing, grounding ourselves once again in the body, and perhaps say to our child, "Let's start over."

Becoming aware of limiting or destructive patterns of behavior in our own family as we grew up, becoming aware of our own childhood experiences of sadness, anger, and alienation is both a painful learning process and a tremendously useful one. We can use this awareness to help us make wiser choices in our parenting.

Who's the Parent, Who's the Child?

There is a certain amount of suffering that is just a part of the human condition. And then there is suffering that we make for ourselves and others, not intending to, but out of our own unconsciousness, ignorance, and unmet emotional needs, often stemming from our family of origin and how we ourselves were seen and treated in childhood. There is certainly enough anguish in families to not compound it by creating unnecessary emotional burdens and prisons for those we love out of the unexamined habits of a lifetime. To bring this domain into greater focus, we might reflect on the unwritten and unspoken emotional rules in our family of origin and how they might have influenced us.

A friend once described only being visible to her father when she spoke with him about his work, which was in science. Only when she failed her premed courses did she realize that she had been following a path that wasn't really her own, and she began to focus full-time on her artwork, incurring strong disapproval from her father. The tacit rule was, "I am happy to approve of you as long as you do something that I value."

Such tacit emotional frameworks are different in different families. In some, the parents' emotional needs dominate. In others, emotional needs are ignored completely. Unspoken patterns of relating are often set up for the benefit of the people with the most power, usually one or both parents. Appeals based on guilt, shame, devotion, duty, and responsibility can all be used to manipulate and coerce children to maintain such insidious patterns, leaving little room for the child to have and express his or her own feelings and needs.

Some parents only know how to feel close and connected through their wounds and their pain. They unconsciously want their children to feel their pain with them and, sometimes, to carry it for them. A subtle entraining may take place between parent and child—wholly beneath the conscious awareness and intention of the parent—in which the child learns to tune into the emotional needs of the parent, often without anything being said. Rather than the parent being empathic and compassionate, the child takes on that role and is expected to empathize with the parent's feelings, troubles, and stresses. The child becomes predominantly "other-oriented," acting as the parent's confidant, a sympathetic ear. The child's own feelings, needs, desires get buried. The son may become a "good boy," the daughter a "good girl," at the expense of their own feelings, their own inner selves. They may feel that in order to hold on to who they are, they have to do something extreme, such as get into self-destructive behaviors, run away, or become emotionally isolated and remote.

For our children's innate capacity for emotional intelligence to develop, it is important that over time they come to some awareness and acceptance of their feelings, whatever they may be, and what they might be needing. When they are little, they can learn from our naming what we are sensing and seeing—"You seem really frustrated right now [or tired, angry, or impatient]"; "Joey looks really sad. Why do you think he feels that way?"—and by communicating awareness of our own feelings and needs. Through this process, they slowly learn how to more effectively communicate their feelings and recognize for themselves what they might be needing. They also benefit greatly from a sympathetic emotional responsiveness from those around them. When this happens, over time children naturally learn to be more aware of other people. They begin to experience what it means to engage in dialogue and have a sense of "the other." They speak, the other listens; the other speaks, they listen. Hopefully, they begin to have direct experiences of reciprocity. Through having their feelings and needs heard and responded to, and through being able to put their trust in others, they are better able to develop the skills needed to have full, reciprocal relationships of their own. This takes time. For most of us, it is a lifetime's work.

When children feel the latitude and safety to say how they feel and how they see things, it is only natural that they will challenge their parents at times. It can take a long time for children to be able to acknowledge their part in things and take responsibility for their actions. This requires a lot of patience on our part. In fact, we may notice that sometimes we don't find this so easy to do ourselves.

A man wrote to his father telling him about some of the things that pained and troubled him in their relationship. The father wrote back, "I forgive you for that terrible letter." He completely disavowed that there might be any truth in what his son wrote. Instead of asking his son to forgive him, he was dispensing forgiveness as if his son had committed a crime by telling him his feelings. How much less damaging, to say nothing of healing, it would have been if he could have heard his son's pain and felt some compassion for him even though he was unable to understand it. Then he might have replied, "I feel for you deeply and regret any pain I might have caused you. I am willing to get together if you would like to and try to understand what happened and my part in it."

*

A woman who turned her back on a "perfect marriage" and came out as a lesbian said: "I didn't want to lose my mother, but my choice was to lose her or to lose myself, and I couldn't do that."

*

One of two grown sisters, speaking of their mother, said, "We don't think of her as our 'real' mother because she doesn't act like a mother. It feels more like we're *her* mother. She is constantly letting us know that we are not doing enough, that we can't love and appreciate her enough."

*

What did your parents expect of you? What were you responsible for emotionally in your family? In what ways were your parents child oriented? What basic needs were met and in what ways? How much room were you given to act in different ways? Who in the family was responsible for the quality of the relationships? Who had to make things better? Who nurtured whom?

Sometimes as adults we find ourselves carrying a heavy emotional pack on our backs. This pack holds all sorts of things that may not really belong to us, but that over the years we have been in the habit of carrying—our parents' pain, their expectations, their disappointments, their secrets, their anger, their wounds. Sometimes, even thinking about putting down this load can fill us with such feelings of inadequacy and guilt that we are paralyzed emotionally, unable to make a move. If we put down the burden, we will be a "bad" son or daughter. How could we do that?

When we finally do try to put it down, when we try to step out of a role that was imposed upon us a long time ago and that we have been playing primarily through force of habit, guilt, and fear, when we refuse to play by the old, unspoken emotional rules of the family, all hell can break loose.

Disengaging from the old, comfortable familial patterns of relating and moving toward greater emotional independence may be seen as a major betrayal. We may be met with ferocious resistance and criticism. Creating new emotional patterns in our lives takes tremendous courage and persistence.

It's never too late to put down the load we are carrying and try to create new patterns of relating that are more appropriate and balanced. This process in turn may help us to see more clearly the unspoken patterns and expectations that we have with our own children. We have the potential to free ourselves and our children from some of these unnecessary emotional burdens. Everyone can become lighter, more spacious, and more authentic.

So, perhaps it's a good idea from time to time to ask ourselves whether our children are here to meet our needs, or whether it is the other way around. When our children are little, it is obviously our job as parents to meet their needs, which change over time. In addition, as they get older, with some awareness on our part, we can support them in their own ongoing process of identifying and learning how to meet their own needs. This capacity is key to developing into a healthy and emotionally integrated adult. The other aspect of this is that as parents, we have our own needs. Cultivating greater self-awareness and learning when and how to effectively communicate our needs is an essential aspect of having a healthy relationship with our children.

Even with grown children, there are times when they need us to give them support, understanding, and, to the degree that we can, assistance. If there is a disagreement or a rift between us, can we find the courage, with all the pain and the gulf of time and hurt, to reach out to our grown child, to find ways to heal, to reconnect? It may not be possible in all cases. We can only try, and perhaps never give up our willingness to reconnect in healthier ways. But sometimes, we have to wait for our children to want to again.

If we didn't get our emotional needs met by our parents, as much work in psychology has shown, we may find it particularly difficult to give to our children or to ourselves, and the cycle may be repeated over and over again, from generation to generation. Working with awareness, moment to moment, we have a chance to end this vicious cycle.

As our children get older, there will be ways in which they will continue to need our support. And as we age, there will be times when we will need their support. A circle of life, an ongoing giving and receiving, changing over time, can nourish us all.

✳

My hands reach down, trembling with anger, reach toward the needy child, but instead of roughly managing her they close gently as a whisper on her body. As though I am somehow physically enlarged, I draw her to me, breathing deeply. The tension drops away. At this moment, I am invested not with my own thin, worn endurance, but with my mother's patience. This is a gift she has given to me from far away. Her hands have poured it into me. The hours she soothed me and the deep quiet in which I watched her rock, nurse, and comfort my younger brothers and sisters have passed invisibly into me. This gift has lain within me all my life, like a bird in a nest, waiting until the moment my hands need the soft strength of wings.

LOUISE ERDRICH,
The Blue Jay's Dance

Family Values

What we value in our own family changes over time, but in general, it includes a sense of connectedness, of being part of a larger, loving whole that shelters and nurtures and allows each person to be known and accepted for who he or she is, and in which there is a fundamental commitment to being honest and respectful along with a willingness to work through the difficult moments.

This doesn't just magically happen. It takes a certain kind of inner work and a complementary outer work to build and maintain a family culture within the home that reflects what we value. The form constantly changes as the family changes in size, as children grow, as we grow and change as parents and as people, and as changes take place in the society that have a profound impact on us. And at some point, the children leave the family culture to create their own.

Every family develops its own unique culture whether it is aware of it or not. The challenge of mindful parenting in part involves bringing the qualities of one's family culture into awareness and trying to make conscious choices that reflect and embody one's values as parents.

Much has been made of the whole question of "family values." Often this is done in a highly politicized or moralistic framework that holds a narrow view of what constitutes a "good" family. The word *value* literally means "that which is accorded priority." What we make a priority will set the tone for the family culture. So "family values" is not just a theoretical concept. It doesn't matter what we think or believe, or what our principles are, if none of it is being actualized in practice.

Our individual and collective values speak volumes through how we conduct ourselves in the ordinary, everyday unfolding of our lives. We embody our priorities whether we know it or not. So it can be very helpful to bring awareness to the whole domain of what we are already embodying, in a spirit of inquiry and acceptance rather than judgment. If we don't feel comfortable with particular aspects of what we see in our own behavior or in our priorities within the family, perhaps, in the spirit of mindfulness practice and of mindful parenting, we might look at the whole question of what it would take to incrementally establish different priorities that reflect more deeply what we care about. We might ask ourselves, "What *is* most important to us? What *do* we value most as parents? Are there basic principles we can point to that are priorities for our family, that we actually put first in our choices and in our actions?"

In our own family, we value sovereignty, empathy, acceptance, and awareness as fundamental avenues for expressing love and caring. Out of these come other values, such as respect, kindness, truthfulness, responsibility, flexibility, autonomy, and privacy. We try to live in accordance with these values as best we can. Of course, there are times when we find ourselves acting in ways that are not at all in accordance with these values. When we become aware of this, the practice is to see what is happening, as painful as that can be, and renew our commitment to act in ways that are more in alignment with our core values. This is what we mean by the *embodied* practice of mindfulness.

We also value peace and harmony, but sometimes family life is anything but peaceful and harmonious. Our experience is that peace and harmony cannot be imposed on children any more than other values. They can only be encouraged, cultivated, and nurtured by example. This requires some patience and trust on our part that these qualities will take root and grow over time. This is not about our being exemplary people or "perfect parents." What is most important here is our commitment to the *process* of working with our own awareness. When our children see that we are human and can make mistakes and acknowledge them, in our view they are learning important lessons about values and about life.

*

The emotional and physical atmosphere parents create within the family sets the stage on which the ongoing development of that family's values unfolds. The more that mindfulness can be brought to this dimension of family life, the more likely it is that the deep inner values of the family will be reflected in parenting decisions.

One aspect of family atmosphere and culture that we value is a sense of the home as a haven, a refuge from the bombardment of outside stimuli, a place in which our own values set the tone and can have a tempering effect on the sometimes superficial, frenetic, and materialistic values of the broader culture.

Family rituals can be an important part of the fabric of a home culture. Rituals can create a comforting atmosphere that grounds the family members in space and time and strengthens the feeling bonds between family members. It is the quality of our intentionality and the consciousness that we bring to them moment to moment that give family rituals their meaning.

Anything can be made into a family ritual, from waking up the children in the morning, to tying their shoes, to brushing or braiding their hair, to having a bath, to having dinner together as often as possible, to lighting candles at the dinner table, to saying a blessing, or singing a song together, or sitting around the fire in winter, or telling stories before bedtime. All can serve to enrich family life. However, they may require the added ritual of intentionally shutting down the Internet at particular times so we can experience these kinds of profoundly human analog moments.

We can also bring mindful awareness to creating rituals around maintaining the physical environment in the home. While a clean and orderly home may not always feel like the highest of priorities, when the home is dirty and in chaos everyone's energy can be affected. This goes beyond keeping the house orderly merely for appearance's sake. Mindfulness can be brought to sharing in the work of maintaining the home. The various tasks of daily life can become rituals that give children a sense of feeling needed and useful. Even small children can be given simple jobs that allow them to work alongside their parents and siblings. Cooking together, cleaning up together, or folding the laundry can all be occasions in which the children, depending on their ages, can participate. Communicating clear and consistent expectations, we can make organizing and cleaning the house a family ritual so that the work is shared by everyone. The home is made ready for new beginnings.

As parents, we find we need to cultivate an overarching awareness of the family as a whole. The family is nourished by being held in our consciousness and having its needs considered in much the same way that we ponder the needs of our individual children. There are times when the family itself needs attention. We bring everyone together, sometimes to identify and solve particular problems, sometimes just to check in with each other, sometimes just to have fun. Over time, a collective sense of being part of a larger whole develops in the children.

Children naturally form their own broader societal values out of the atmosphere and culture of the family and from their expanding interfaces with the world. As we have said, just as we cannot impose values of peace and harmony in the family, we cannot inculcate qualities such as generosity, compassion, nonharming, equality, and appreciation for diversity through moralizing or coercion. It is through observing these qualities in others, and through our embodying such values ourselves, that our children have a direct lived experience of them.

*

A friend shared with us the following story:

> My son had grown up in the outer boroughs of New York City. His father and I having divorced when he was rather young, I felt it was up to me to instill in him the values which I believed were important in life. Among them was respect for all people regardless of their heritage or life circumstance.
>
> Since his childhood, much had changed in New York City. Many areas, including the neighborhood he now lived in, were inhabited by homeless men and women—sometimes aggressively begging and sometimes more passively sitting or sleeping in doorways.
>
> One cold winter evening I was eager to meet my twenty-three-year-old son at his apartment to take him out to dinner in his new neighborhood. My visits with him were precious moments to me—all too infrequent, as far as I was concerned, but at the frequency that suited him. I knew that

it had to be that way in order for him to be successful in establishing his adult life on his own terms.

As I approached his building, I noticed a woman sitting on the sidewalk, begging, just to the right of the doorway. I felt tension building in my body as I averted my eyes from her, pretending not to see her as I entered the building. I didn't want any awareness of human suffering to interfere with my intention of spending an evening enjoying the company of my son.

Soon my son and I were on our way, down the elevator and out the door, to choose from among the wide variety of local restaurants. We would visit with each other that night over a leisurely meal.

As we stepped out of the doorway of his building, he walked over to the woman sitting on the sidewalk—in the same spot where I had made a concerted effort to avoid seeing her just a short while before. As he gave her the change from his pocket, to my surprise he said to her—in introduction—"This is my mother." As I looked in her direction I was greeted by a warm, open smile—and we acknowledged each other with "Hello."

He knew it was okay to see her as just another person— in a terrible situation—to whom to be kind.

I had wanted him to learn to see the common humanity in all people without exception—and so he had. I felt deeply moved as I realized that now he was reteaching me a value that on that evening I had lost track of. It was a value that I had taught to him so many years before.

Consuming Choices

In the intensely consumer-oriented culture of today, we can easily find ourselves as parents acquiring products that may lead to our babies and toddlers experiencing the world more through their contact with objects than through sustained contact with living, breathing human beings. Even a little awareness can provide a much-needed compass for navigating the sometimes overwhelming choices we have as parents. The huge array of products, some of which are meant to entertain and enhance learning at an early age, and many of which are supposed to make parenting easier, can readily become a replacement for the essential human interactions a growing child needs.

For example, a baby might be carried briefly and then put in a car seat, then carried from the car in the car seat into a store, then back home where she may be placed in a crib or a baby seat, and later put into a stroller for a walk. Most of the baby's day could be spent passively contained and touching lifeless objects. The ambient sounds that dominate her world may very well come from the TV or radio or from wind-up toys. Without some awareness on the part of parents, a child's environment can easily become overly utilitarian, chaotic, and disembodied, oriented primarily around the parents' needs rather than the child's.

If we are continually relying on objects to hold them or entertain them while we are getting things done—such as winding up the swing, playing a recorded story, turning on the TV, or putting them in front of other screens—we may inadvertently be encouraging them to be passive rather than active participants in their world. These "child-occupiers" can have the effect of putting our children in a disempowered, disconnected mode that is inherently defined and limited by the objects themselves.

Of course there are times in the day when we have to take care of other things while we are also taking care of our children. It is a natural part of life and important that our children experience us doing what needs to be done. If we bring mindful awareness to the particulars of our situation—including a child's age and temperament, as well as the home environment and what we need to get done—we can usually find creative ways to engage them and keep them safe while we work, at least for some stretch of time.

For infants and babies, we might wear them in a carrier as we take care of things. For older babies and toddlers, it could involve creating an enclosed space within sight of us, in which children can move safely on their own, crawling or pulling themselves up, or rolling over, thereby being free to express their agency through initiating activities with more open-ended possibilities. By putting pads on the floor to cushion falls, having balls and soft blocks available and simple structures to climb, a space can readily become a kind of safe home exploratorium. This also gives our babies and toddlers important opportunities to experience frustration at times and, by our not jumping in to "fix" things, they can learn to overcome developmentally appropriate challenges. This is a difficult but worthy practice for us as parents.

As we have seen, the quality of our presence is felt by our children whether we are directly interacting with them or not. While parents can become very good at doing more than one thing at a time, the key is developing a flexibility of attention and a broader field of awareness that includes not only our children but also our own state of body and mind. Our children can feel it when we are rigid and resentful or open, flexible, and kind. In every moment, we have the capacity to be aware of and modulate the quality of our being. When we are stressed, we can always remind ourselves to come back to the breath, to the sensations in the body, and to the richness inherent in all of our moments.

*

As for the consumer choices that we face as parents, sometimes little by little, with seemingly minor and innocuous decisions, we run the risk of precluding precious interactions with our children and they, as a consequence, of losing a certain kind of nourishment from us. In making these choices, we can bring a degree of mindfulness to how the products we acquire to support our parenting might affect our child's experience of the world and her relationship with us.

For instance, we may put an infant in a stroller without giving it much thought. But if we consider what it might be like for her, we might see that in some strollers, she will be facing out to the world with no protection from all the stimuli, bodies, noise, and energy that are coming directly toward her. We might also see that while all these unpredictable stimuli are coming, unfiltered, at this very new being, she is physically removed from what she knows best and from what helps ground her in her world—namely her parents. Each baby is different, and as parents, we can sense when our baby is ready to interface more with the world.

We can also carry our baby in a sling or a cloth carrier close to our body. Here, she can be in the world and yet protected from it at the same time. Depending on the child's temperament and age, even front-facing cloth baby carriers may provide too much visual stimulation at times, and may overwhelm a sensitive nervous system. There's no one right choice. Mindful parenting is an ongoing process of noticing and adjusting what we do based on what we see and sense and feel.

In some families, when the distance is not too great, toddlers are encouraged to walk, and it soon becomes the norm for them. A child can also be worn at times on the parent's back in a child carrier. In that way, she gets to feel the movement and warmth of her parent's body, and can reach out and touch his face and hair. In this position, other people's faces are right at eye level, allowing her to communicate with them over her parent's shoulder or lean into his body if she is feeling shy. All the while, her feet ride on the foot bar, pushing against it, moving her whole body up and down, stretching. A sense of security and a whole world of sensory stimulation and responding come just from being carried in this way.

Making these kinds of choices may require somewhat more thought and work for us in the short run. However, there are wonderful gifts and pleasures for both parents and children that result from doing so. We can be closer, more in touch, and more in tune with them. We are also less likely to miss a child's subtle communications, whether a smile or a sound, or the light touch of a hand…moments of pure pleasure and connection.

⁂

Many child-care products are designed to free us up so that we can do other things. We acquire them with the expectation that they will make our lives easier. But if we are not paying attention, we may find they can become substitutes for essential human interaction and presence. They can end up isolating and depriving our children or overwhelming their nervous systems. We may find ourselves paying many times over for the time that was freed up, when we are faced with children who are acting out because they are hungry for attention, physical contact, and human warmth, or who crave constant stimulation. Children in this needy state are tremendously demanding, as they should be. Repairing the damage from both neglect and overstimulation is much more difficult and much less satisfying than meeting a child's needs in the first place.

There are certainly times when objects of convenience are both useful for parents and fun for children. But as parents, we have to keep looking at the whole of our child's daily experience. The key is to find the right balance. We might use a carriage or baby seat when we need to, and yet make sure there are other times in the day when we hold or carry our baby or toddler. We might play a story in the car at times, and also find other times to read or tell them stories. Soft cloth dolls and animals, teething toys, and baby blankets can be comforting, and babies and toddlers can use them to self-soothe. But we might ask ourselves whether we want these objects to become the main source of comfort in our child's life.

Each object that takes the place of a human interaction has the potential of robbing us and our children of the richness of shared moments. Since relationships are built on shared moments, these are important choices to keep in mind.

Media Madness

We live in a time when things are changing more rapidly than ever before in history. We have infinitely more information available to us, but perhaps much of it is not what we most need. We have moved across an invisible and irreversible threshold, from the analog world of all of human history, nature itself, and evolution, into a brave, new digital era in which our lives are interfaced with ever-increasing computing power in an interconnected web of virtual global communication. From a time when parents were concerned about the effects of television watching, we now face the ubiquitous presence of ever-smaller and more mobile digital devices that connect children to the Internet and the World Wide Web, the world of texting and other forms of social networking, Facebook, Twitter, Instagram, YouTube, video, graphics, music, games, as well as countless cable channels, and movies…a Pandora's box of infinite access to unlimited content. What are parents to do in the face of our children being exposed to worlds we may know little or nothing about, or feel may be unhealthy, even toxic in some cases? How do we protect our children from these kinds of unfiltered exposures? And how do we identify and regulate, depending on their ages, whatever aspects of the technology we think may be positive and growth enhancing?

Between smartphones and tablets, parents now have access to anything and everything digital, and also infinite occasions to distract ourselves and be so absorbed in the digital world that we are out of touch with the present moment and the natural world. Not only do we need to consider our children's exposure and use of the various media available to them, but we also need to be aware of and perhaps regulate our own use and possible addiction to it in order to be present at all in our lives and with our children. More and more, children are having to compete with these devices to get their parents' attention. What is more, parents are handing them to small children to keep them occupied. Smartphone apps are increasingly being developed for this very purpose. Our children may be at risk for developing a primary attachment to electronic devices rather than to human beings. And so may we.

There's no question that the world we live in is transforming before our very eyes. These technological inventions and those yet to come, both in hardware and software, are making a new world. By the time they are adults, our children will be immersed and well versed in it. All the more reason for them to be strong and balanced in body, mind, heart, and spirit, and develop a deep connection to and appreciation for the analog world.

There is no question that the ubiquity of the Internet as well as of social media adds new dimensions to childhood and to parenting that need continual adjusting to and monitoring. This relatively new and ever-changing world requires us to be aware of it up close and, if necessary, regulate its use and the kinds of content our children are potentially being exposed to. Hopefully, with awareness of its looming availability and its seductive pulls, we can find ways to promote balance with other activities—new and uncharted territory for those attempting to parent with some degree of mindfulness in the digital age. If we are addicted to these devices ourselves, it may convey the message that our children are not as important as our e-mails, texts, and tweets.

Fully embodied human beings cannot be nurtured through technology, no matter how clever or engaging the technology may be. We need embodied experiences and the nurturance of the human heart by human beings who feel and who care. Devices, overused as electronic babysitters when parents are busy, or as a convenience when children are bored, can too easily displace important childhood experiences and face-to-face human interaction and activities.

What may on the face of it seem like helpful additions to our lives can have ramifications we may not have fully anticipated. For example, many children now have their own cell phones. Although this can be incredibly useful at times, and certainly in an emergency, the unanticipated downside may be that any time something difficult arises, it is all too easy for a child to immediately seek help or advice from a parent rather than having to rely on his or her own ability to problem-solve. This is one of an increasing number of issues that parents face. Another is the question of whether we allow our children unlimited access to the Internet just because it exists. To what degree are we examining and thinking about its potential positive and negative aspects? Are there ways to tilt things toward the positive and minimize the negative? In this domain, we often have far more questions than answers. But the questioning itself is very important. It is one way of bringing greater mindfulness to the effects these technologies are having on our children and on the family.

Another avenue might be for us to notice the effects of these various devices and technologies on our children while they are engaged with them. What state are their bodies in? Do you see any signs of tension? What kind of movements are they making? What images are they absorbing? How much violence is there? What might the cognitive, emotional, and social effects be on children who more and more inhabit this virtual world? What messages are they getting from engaging in this way? What values might they be absorbing? How many real-life social interactions are they not having by being perpetually absorbed in their devices, even on social media sites?

When children are watching TV shows, we think it is important for us as their parents to ponder similar questions. Studies have shown that on average, the American child watches twenty-five thousand hours of television before reaching the age of eighteen and witnesses more than two hundred thousand acts of violence, including sixteen thousand murders. In its 1996 *Physician's Guide to Media Violence*, the American Medical Association reported that the amount of time spent in front of a television or video screen is "the single biggest chunk of time in the waking life of an American child." The average family in America has the television set turned on for seven hours each day. Sixty percent of families have the TV set on during mealtime. That has not decreased over time. A 2009 Nielsen Company survey showed that children ages two to five spend more than thirty-two hours a week in front of a TV screen.

Again, as parents, we need to be mindful of the effects of such exposure on our children and observe our family's relationship to this powerful force. Questions we might ask ourselves include: What are we observing in our children when they watch television and in the aftermath of watching? What messages are they absorbing? How passive are they? To what degree are they mesmerized, in a hypnotic trance of sorts? How many hours do they do this each day, each week? What are they not doing while they are doing this? How much cruelty are they witnessing? Do fights start when the TV goes off? How is all this affecting their attitudes and behaviors at home and in school, and their views of themselves and of society? Just observing carefully and asking ourselves such questions can help us to make choices that may significantly increase the quality of family life and enhance the lives of our children. We can also foster more self-awareness in our children by suggesting they pay attention to how they feel when they are engaged in such activities, and afterward.

In many homes, the television is on almost all the time. The images that come from the news bombard even very young children with all the horrible things that are happening in the world each day. Whether they are actively watching the news or not, young people are growing up immersed in a particular, highly skewed view of reality, synthesized out of what corporate network executives decide is newsworthy. This process tends to focus on the most violent and terrible things that are happening locally and throughout the world. Conversely, huge areas of human generativity and creativity, which are equally or more important and actually new, and thus newsworthy, are virtually ignored.

Similar attention needs to be brought to other avenues through which our children are affected by the media and entertainment industry. Sometimes young children are exposed to movies with grotesque and terrifying images that sear themselves into their minds and their memories, when they have no way to filter them, put them in perspective, or understand them. It is hard enough for adults to do that with such mind-numbing and frightening images. The sound track alone can be a total assault on the nervous system, designed to elicit intense physiological distress reactions. Many of the images in violent movies are unthinkable, and it is unthinkable that children would see such things. It is unthinkable, and yet exposure to violent images has become the norm, and as a culture we have become inured to it.

Both movies and television can promote paranoia and distrust, giving the impression that the world is a terribly dangerous place full of crazy and violent people. So much good happens every day in the world but, as we've said, it doesn't make the news. So the view both parents and children have of the world gets very skewed. We find we have to keep reminding our children and ourselves that in spite of the violence in our society, it is still a relatively small percentage of people who commit crimes and cause harm. They need to know that even in the most dangerous neighborhoods, there are many people who are good and caring. Helping our children to feel safe and to see the world in a realistic way that allows them to feel hopeful is a difficult, ongoing challenge. The more violence they witness in the media, the more difficult this is.

There are neighborhoods where violence is more prevalent in children's lives, whether it is violence they are experiencing in the home or on the streets. Teachers report that children come to school having witnessed violent acts and knowing people who are harmed by them. Some teachers are now bringing mindfulness practices into their classrooms in inner-city neighborhoods to teach children self-awareness, calming skills, emotion regulation, and lovingkindness toward themselves and others. The basic practices of mindfulness, which have to do with being aware of thoughts and feelings, accepting and understanding the ever-changing nature of things, and cultivating an ability to be grounded in one's own body and breath can be helpful for children in stressful and emotionally challenging situations.

To come back to the example of television, a steady diet of cartoons and sitcoms does not benefit a child's development, no matter how engaging or clever these programs may be. The presence of television dramatically alters the atmosphere in the home. It looms as a constant and seductive offering, against which all the other activities children might engage in are measured. In this way, it subtly or not so subtly interferes with their experiencing the natural unfolding rhythms of the day, which include periods of quiet, even boredom, that can lead to both physically active and imaginative play, immersion in the natural world, time for musing and introspection, creative time, time playing with friends, time with the family, and time spent connecting with the larger community. Children are developing greater familiarity with characters on TV than they are with real people, and they can get attached to them. Real-life experience may be put on hold so that they won't have to miss an episode with their TV friends.

Media can easily wind up taking the place of all sorts of developmentally essential experiences that are relational, embodied, and hands-on and that further social and emotional learning and the maturation of pathways within the brain that are critical for effective functioning in adolescence and adulthood. While certain technologies may have some role to play in learning in childhood, it is important for us as parents to be aware of what might be lost, and of the need for balance and oversight.

When our son was five, he had a monarch caterpillar one summer that he put in a jar with some milkweed. He fed it and watched it day after day as it ate the leaves, then miraculously spun itself into a chrysalis and then, after a long latent period, emerged as a butterfly, which he then set free. It is from integrated, participatory experiences such as this that children learn about the world. They are also living metaphors that point to meaning and order and interconnectedness underlying the world and living things. Such experiences stimulate the imagination and delight children with their magic and mystery.

We often noticed that after our children had been engaged in a creative process such as drawing or painting or singing, or listening to us read from books that transport and elevate and excite—creating and populating whole worlds in their minds with beautiful language and finely developed characters and relationships—books such as *Ronia, the Robber's Daughter*, *The Adventures of Tom Sawyer*, *The Hobbit*, *Lord of the Rings*, the Arthurian legends, and fairy tales and myths from different countries and cultures, there was a sense of the children being enlivened, their eyes shining, their faces awash with pleasure.

We didn't see that look on our children's faces after they had been watching TV or movies. The process is too passive. No imagination is required. All the images are created for them, a strange combination of numbing and overstimulating the nervous system in an attempt to keep them engaged. There is no time for introspection or reflection, for pauses in which to connect the story to other meaningful experiences in their lives, or to share moments of deep feeling when something touches them.

We found that not having a television when our children were little, although a radical step given their ubiquity in American life, was a viable option—in fact, a wonderful one. Sometimes it takes getting rid of things to see the actual effect that they are having on the family. It is not until they are out of the home that their most pervasive and insidious effects on family life can actually be seen in the contrasting peace and creative uses of time that become options and a way of being only in their absence. What is lost in terms of entertainment for both children and parents is more than compensated for by a resurgence in aliveness that can emerge within the family.

The more difficult path of setting boundaries around the various screen technologies and media-laden devices that are now such a large part of our lives and an ever-more ubiquitous presence in our homes and in our pockets will of necessity take different forms at different ages and stages of our children's lives. Our understanding and clarity as parents is critical to setting limits. When children are little, they are not going to understand and they don't have to understand the decisions we make. When we are clear that a change needs to be made, we can respond to their feelings of anger, upset, and frustration simply and matter-of-factly, with some understanding and kindness, and also convey the unwavering message that we are setting a limit. Of course, over time things change, and with it our awareness of what is needed. As our children get older, the need for family agreements and limits can be discussed, with everyone contributing to the decisions that are arrived at.

A friend told us that his teenage daughter's schoolwork was suffering because of all the time she was spending on social media in the evening. They agreed that for several weeks, she would have a media-free trial period for a number of hours in the evening. At the end of that trial period, they had a conversation about the positives and negatives of limiting her access to social media. His daughter expressed the feeling that it was actually a big relief for her to have a clear boundary and wanted it to continue.

*

The practice of mindful parenting in large measure involves each of us discovering our own ways of navigating the various situations and conditions that arise within the family. These of course are continually changing with the times and with changing circumstances. How we hold and respond to the specific challenges we face in our lives and to the needs and demands of our children is the actual inner work itself. There are no absolute or enduring "right" answers or "perfect" solutions. The process that each of us goes through in doing this interior work, much of which involves uncertainty and at times some degree of confusion, tension, and pain, is an inevitable part of being a parent, and an inevitable part of bringing mindfulness into parenting.

It is important for us to remind ourselves that mindfulness is not simply about awareness or acceptance. It is also about taking action, hopefully wise action, in the face of complex situations. Any prescription that we might give for a specific situation would of necessity be inadequate from the start. Only you know yourself and your family and your children. What is more, when it comes to media issues, the technologies are changing incredibly rapidly. What we might recommend today may not even be relevant in a year or two. But your own willingness to work with things as they are and with sometimes not knowing how to proceed is the essence of the practice.

✻

One very hopeful sign in terms of the new media comes, ironically, from within the world of Silicon Valley itself. Many of the hugely successful founders of the biggest Internet start-ups are presently in their thirties and forties. It is encouraging and moving to see how many of these entrepreneurs in the digital world are being drawn to the cultivation of mindfulness. They do this both for their own life satisfaction and for modulating the stress of success at an early age, and the never-ending challenges of needing to keep the momentum going forward with continuous innovation in their businesses. Many of these young innovators seem to harbor a yearning for meaning and for a more grounded life experience in and out of work. After all, some are also parents of young children and face the same challenges the digital world presents to all of us. They seem to have a growing awareness of our human interconnectedness and of the importance of working to change the world for the better—not only through new technologies but also through how those technologies are used.

Balance

Seeking a degree of balance in our parenting is an ongoing process. It turns out to be quite a personal matter. What feels balanced to us may feel completely unbalanced to you, and vice versa, and what feels balanced to you may feel out of balance to someone else. Moreover, what feels balanced to us now may not feel that way at some other time. It's an ongoing process, because the balance point keeps changing.

It takes some reflection to define what balance or equilibrium means for us and to make choices that promote it for ourselves, for our children, and for the family as a whole. Working with balance is a dynamic, ever-changing process, not a fixed endpoint; for in truth, balance is always a matter of losing one's balance and regaining it. We can learn a great deal from losing our balance if we can hold the experience in awareness.

When our children were babies, the struggle for balance took the form of continually drawing on whatever inner and outer resources we had as we went through a period of intensive giving. With so much energy pouring out, both physically and emotionally, we needed infusions of energy and support from family, from friends, and from each other.

Our infants' inner balance was intimately linked to our

responsiveness to their needs. When they fussed, or cried, or seemed uncomfortable, we responded, and balance was restored sooner or later. When we were dealing with colic, there were times when nothing we did worked, but we kept at it, meaning we continued to work at being present, even in this very trying situation.

When our children were toddlers, balance took the form of providing them with freedom to explore within a safe container and maintaining a watchful eye on them. When they were having a hard time, we tried to help them restore a modicum of equilibrium by being sensitive to the cues they were giving us, whether it was that they were hungry, or tired, or overstimulated. There were times when balance could be restored by giving them a chance to release some of their energy in active and noisy play, and times when they needed to be held, soothed, rocked, and comforted. These kinds of responsive interactions can help children, over time, to develop their own ability to self-regulate.

When we sense that a child is stressed and out of balance in some way, a thoughtful reexamination of his or her daily routine may prove insightful. What is the relationship between activity and quiet time? What foods is he or she eating? Are they stabilizing (that is, protein, healthy fats, complex carbohydrates, fresh fruits and vegetables) or destabilizing (that is, too much sugar, junk food)? How much sleep is he or she getting? Young children thrive on consistent daily rhythms and rituals and need plenty of time to do things and adequate time to make transitions from one thing to another. In bringing awareness to these aspects of daily life, we can try to make decisions that reduce unnecessary stressors and promote greater balance in the child's day.

At times, especially with younger children, it can be helpful to follow the principle of "less is more." Simplifying their day as much as possible, giving them more of a routine, and having some quiet alone time with them may be just what is required. In the busyness of our scheduled lives, quiet moments can be squeezed out and lost without our even noticing.

Nourishing, restoring moments can take many forms. It may be a quiet, dreamy time in the bath, or playing a game with a child while remembering to be fully present. Or it may be telling a story, or singing a song, or doing something together like drawing or baking muffins, or skipping stones on the water. Renewal can come from something as simple as the quiet reassurance of being held in our arms, or on our laps. Putting aside our agendas and our impulses for self-distraction, we might bring our awareness to our breathing, keeping it slow and deep, feeling our child relax, his breath naturally slowing down, finding its rhythm, in harmony with our own.

> We can make our mind so like still water that beings gather about us that they may see, it may be, their own images, and so live for a moment with a clearer, perhaps even with a fiercer life because of our quiet.

> W. B. YEATS,
> *The Celtic Twilight*

Every situation we find ourselves in is different. Each moment is new. What was needed yesterday may not be helpful today. Discovering what our children need involves being sensitive to them, picking up on their cues, and responding intuitively and creatively. Our own stillness and patience clears the mirror in which such reflections can be seen.

✻

As they get older, school-age children experience their autonomy and their individuality in part through their friendships, their activities, and how they dress. They experience their power and agency as they discover their own unique interests and talents. They need privacy and lots of psychic space, but they still need support and guidance as their world begins to expand. They are better able to self-regulate at this age, but at times we may still need to help them restore equilibrium by stepping in and setting limits either for them or with them. Finding balance during this time often involves working to maintain meaningful connections with them as they strive for more freedom and separateness.

*

Some friends told us the following story: Their eleven-year-old daughter was invited to a birthday party at which the children were going to have cake and ice cream and then go out to a movie. Our friends learned that the movie they planned to see had scenes with violence and cruelty that they didn't want their daughter to see. A crisis ensued. "But everyone is going, why can't I?" The parents felt strongly that they did not want their child to see the movie. In speaking with some of the other parents, they found one for whom the pickup time at the end of the movie was difficult. Together, they came up with a plan to have both their daughters go to the party, skip the movie, and have an overnight together. This solution satisfied the girls and the parents as well. A happy ending, but only after some creative and sensitive negotiating.

"All my friends get to watch as much TV as they want!" "Why do we have to eat so healthy?" "Lauren gets to stay up and text with her friends as long as she wants, why can't I?" "All my friends have their own TVs." It takes a great deal of inner strength to stand up to what can feel like relentless pressure. It can be tempting to give in, especially when we're feeling tired or overwhelmed. But giving our children mixed messages around issues we feel are important just encourages them to push more to get what they want, and it does not serve either them or us.

Possessions are imbued with power in our society. A child who feels lost or powerless can fixate on material possessions, thinking that they will make him feel better or improve his status with his peers. The development of a child's inner life, his sense of himself and his own unique being, requires something more complex than the latest cool sneakers. Helping our children find enlivening activities, whether martial arts, dance, sports, playing a musical instrument, theater, backpacking, drawing, fixing or building things, journal writing, singing or rapping, or whatever it is that speaks to who they are can provide satisfying alternatives to the quick fixes of our consumer-oriented culture.

In doing this we are challenged to find the right balance between on the one hand overscheduling our children's lives, giving them too many choices and too many activities, and on the other hand, ignoring our children's needs and not putting in the time and energy to find outlets for their creativity and their unique gifts. Overscheduling can be a form of neglect, if setting them up with nonstop activities takes the place of spending time with them ourselves, or contributes to severe imbalance or stress in their lives in other ways.

Some children find their own balance easily, naturally seeking activities that interest them as well as knowing how to take time alone to be quiet and introspective. Other children need a push, sometimes a strong one, to get them to do things, to try new things, or to be active at all. Some need help in slowing down, in redirecting their energy into more quiet activities. Assisting children in creating some balance in their lives can take sustained effort, encouragement, and action on our part.

My youngest daughter, at the age of eleven, comes back from an art class with a sketch of a model's face. It looks like a person in her thirties and conveys a sense of her uniqueness as an individual, using colors that I would never have thought to use to give form to her face—yellow, blue, and olive green. She has always been very matter-of-fact about her drawing ability, but I can see that she is proud of this particular sketch, and she actually tells me that she feels proud of herself. Later on I see her looking at it as she walks by. She has gone from the nonthinking mode of pure looking and sketching to seeing the result with more distance. At one point she is troubled that the eyes look so different from each other, and she asks me what I think of them. I tell her that that is what makes the face so real, so interesting. People rarely have perfectly symmetrical faces. She seems satisfied. All the storms and disruptions, the struggles and difficulties of the past few days and weeks are swept aside. There is a natural feeling of balance and well-being in her and between us in this moment.

*

As our children go through adolescence, it can feel like the threads of our connection with them are stretched, stressed, and sometimes frayed compared to when they were younger. Maintaining those threads, seeing that they endure, doing what we can to strengthen them, can be a monumental undertaking. At times, those connections can be strengthened when we are able to accord our children more freedom to discover their own unique selves in spite of our anxieties, reservations, doubts, dislikes, and even our grieving for a perhaps more idyllic time now seemingly gone.

At the same time, we often need to balance their increasing

freedom by setting appropriate limits that take into account the realities of the moment. The questions of how much freedom, and what is harmful and what is harmless are ones parents continually wrestle with as we try to strike the right balance between freedom and limits.

When we sense that a teenager is suffering from a lack of balance, we might first want to encourage him to examine for himself what is working and what is not working in his life, and try to come up with his own creative solutions. If it seems that he needs our support in this process, we might help him identify possible strategies for making minor or major changes. These may take the form of modifying his school program, finding healthy outlets for his energy and creativity outside of school, and finding meaningful ways to connect with the broader community so that he can feel a greater sense of belonging and purpose. To do this in ways that do not diminish our teenager's confidence in his own strength and inner resources takes some skill and sensitivity. It is important that we be aware of our own impulses to take control or be intrusive, dominating, all-knowing, or disempowering.

In some circumstances, there may be nothing that can be done by either our child or us. Then we as parents have to take the long view while being sympathetic to his or her feelings, whatever they are. Being patient in such moments, anchored in the realization there are some things we as parents cannot change for our child's sake, and other things we shouldn't try to change no matter how much we may want to, can be a source of strength for us and ultimately for our child as well. Our understanding that our children can learn and grow from coming up against the inevitable limits that life itself presents may be what is most helpful. Our holding this view conveys the message that we have confidence in their ability to adapt to, endure, and ultimately accept adversity. We will visit this topic in more detail in the chapter on limits and openings.

During these years, we may find it harder to maintain our own emotional equilibrium and clarity at times. When our children are teenagers, we obviously have a lot less control and often a lot more to worry about. Communication can frequently go awry despite our best efforts and intentions. We can wind up feeling confused, scared, and despairing. The challenge of parenting teenagers sometimes requires us to stand inside such feelings, difficult as they are, and accept them without judging ourselves for having them or trying to do anything about them other than recognize them. Holding our afflictive emotions in awareness and with acceptance is a way to restore a degree of balance and perspective within ourselves. Such a shift can support us in dark moments and sometimes gives rise to unexpected openings or insights.

*

It's late at night when I pick up my older daughter from school. Almost fifteen, she's had a full day of classes, rowed hard for crew, and has just been to Boston with her English class to see a play they have just read. She wakes up early and is usually tired and grumpy by ten o'clock. Tonight, though, she's full of energy and in good spirits. Dark days of emptiness and boredom seem far away. She's fully engaged now—blisters on her hands from rowing, appreciating the quality of the acting she just saw, planning her strategy for getting done what is due the next day, asking my opinion about her course selection for next year. As we talk about what she wants to do next year, I cherish this feeling of balance in her life…this moment in spring, almost midnight, this quiet give and take.

*

At times, parents feel the need to try to counteract and attenuate as best we can the negative influences of the broader culture on the family. In doing so, we sometimes have to make decisions that are in conflict with what our children want and what their peers are allowed to do. School-age children can benefit from consistent but reasonable limits on their exposure to the potentially deadening, destructive, and addictive aspects of the culture—from malls to movies to the Internet. Our position may make them angry, but there can also be a sense of security at the same time in knowing that your parents care enough about you to stick to what they feel is important, even if you temporarily "hate" them for it.

Arriving at such decisions and working to help our children identify alternative activities and outlets for their energies in such moments takes time and energy on our part. It can be hard work to come up with solutions that we can live with and that are not totally depriving or punitive. We are always operating within the force field of peer conformity, which often exerts an extremely strong pull on our children. Working with it wherever possible rather than against it, we can understand and respect their need to fit in and be accepted and be "like everybody else," while at the same time encouraging them to find their own ways to both belong and express their individuality. As they struggle to define themselves, we can provide a reassuring framework that they can bump up against. Finding the right balance requires us to provide healthy limits while not being so rigid and restrictive that we create forbidden fruit and, in the process, push our children away.

*

Childhood is a time of innocence and naïveté, and that innocence needs to be protected. As children get older and engage more with the wider world, we need to help them balance their natural openness and trust with an awareness of potential dangers in that world. At appropriate ages and in appropriate ways, we can encourage them to be aware of how other people are behaving toward them and to trust their own feelings and intuition. We can embody this in our own behavior, letting them know when we see people acting in ways that seem disrespectful, deceitful, or strange. We can ask them how they felt in certain situations, and support them in their feelings. Naming troubling behaviors as we see them is an important life lesson, and developing a discerning eye that is able to see how others are behaving toward us is a learned skill. In being more aware in this way, our children may be appropriately cautious and wary, even distrusting, in certain situations. This is more than balanced out by the loving relationships they have with family and friends, bonds that have been built over time on a foundation of trust, respect, honesty, and acceptance.

✳

It can be a particular struggle for mothers to find a balance between being nurturing when it is appropriate and necessary and knowing when it is important for us not to be so giving and nurturing. This involves bringing mindfulness to our own needs and not letting them get lost in the force field of everyone else's needs in the family. This is especially difficult to do when we feel we are at the end of our rope, exhausted and overwhelmed. Ironically, it is in such moments that our children often want more from us.

We might begin by acknowledging what a child may be needing from us—"It sounds like you…" or "I can hear that you…"—responding in a matter-of-fact way, but also letting our child know what we need in that moment: "I can help you with this later, but right now I need to finish what I am doing." Or, "I need you to take care of this yourself." Or, "I need to lie down for fifteen minutes; then I'll be ready to discuss this with you." It helps to be mindful of our tone of voice. Being quietly firm is key here. All of this takes practice.

On another front, parents may find themselves conflicted as they try to balance their need to be engaged in meaningful ways in the world and support the family financially, with their childrens' needs and desires to have them at home and available. It is a continual process of striving for inner and outer balance. Sometimes we have to purposefully stop, step back, and take stock of what is happening in the family. In doing this, we may be able to see creative solutions that were not visible to us before.

When we ourselves are more balanced, we can be aware of our children without being child-obsessed. There is a big difference between having an ongoing appreciation of a child's unique qualities and being overinvolved and overinvested. When we feel balanced, we are more able to appreciate what is positive without needing it to always be in evidence. We are able to relate to our children from our own strong center, in touch with our own wholeness, connected in our own ways to the world, experiencing our own pleasures and meaningful connections.

We are always moved and encouraged when we see parents who have been able to transcend the limits of their own childhoods and the era and mores of the time in which they were raised, and create, sometimes out of nothing, a different way of parenting. Somehow they have managed to bring greater balance into their own parenting. They have found ways to provide nurturance and softness where, for them, there was only hardness, or to provide some protection and boundaries where there were none, or are able to give support and encouragement when they themselves were neglected and ignored. Seeing this gives us hope that if we can begin to pay attention and see the choices we have in each moment, a new way of parenting is possible, one that is more conscious and balanced.

As parents, we are continually walking the tightrope between freedom and limits, trust and distrust, activity and stillness, junk and substance, connection and separation. It's a worthwhile balancing act, a practice just like any balance pose in yoga, but much more challenging.

PART EIGHT

Realities

Boys*

The elemental exuberance of boys, their endless fascination and wonder at the world, and the thousands of ways their energy expresses itself in exploration, in play, in times of quiet and stillness, and in moments of anger or despondency offer endless challenges and opportunities for fathers to reconnect with these same elemental energies in ourselves as we nurture our sons emotionally as well as in other ways, and hopefully provide them with examples of embodied male presence as they grow to manhood. We would do well as fathers to remain open to getting to know our sons for who they are, unique beings who may or may not share our temperamental qualities, abilities, and interests. Most important is to be a presence in their lives and to see and accept them for who they actually are, and find imaginative ways to meet them where they are over the expanse of childhood, adolescence, and beyond. This is not easy to do. It requires ongoing caring, commitment, and discernment, as well as a willingness at times to step outside our own comfort zones as they grow and change and come to inhabit their lives more fully. It also requires our physical

* This chapter is written from my (jkz) personal perspective and experience as a father. It does not mean to suggest by any stretch of the imagination that mothers cannot engage fully with their boys in analogous ways, as many mothers, single and not single, do.

presence and, even more importantly, our emotional availability and our own willingness to learn and grow.

As a father, a special joy came from the times I spent with my son at different ages, encountering the world together and watching him express the unique qualities of his emerging being day by day. His natural exuberance made everything an adventure. Sharing the world through his eyes opened mine time and again.

When he was fascinated by dinosaurs, we would go to the science museum and stare at the huge tyrannosaurus, so ferocious looking, first at eye level from the second floor, then from the bottom, looking up. Then we would explore the rest of the museum. When I went running, I would sometimes take him along with me when he was little, holding the handle of his small plastic motorcycle as he rode alongside around the big pond where everybody went to run or walk their dogs. Later, on occasion, we ran together. I loved to read to him in the evenings, or on camping trips we took, and to tell him stories that involved him, which I made up as I went along.

We wrestled a lot, rolling around on the living room floor grappling like lions until we were exhausted. We did that for years, until he became a wrestler in high school and the risk of an injury to me got significantly higher.

When he was very young, I trained regularly in Korean Zen sword fighting (Shim Gum Do—the "Mind Sword Path") and would bring him to the dojo on occasion so he could watch us practice. He loved it, and so did I. I stopped training formally when he was around three, but for years afterward, every once in a while he and I would engage in stylized fighting forms with wooden swords, bowing to each other in appreciation before and after each bout. He had a short sword that he could wield easily. It was exhilarating to block each other's strikes with our swords, to see that we could protect ourselves from scary blows coming from different directions, and remain calm and stable, grounded in the movement, the rhythm, and the sound of the sticks clashing. He started training in various martial arts when he was seven. He never stopped.

On rare occasions, we clashed in anger, not with swords, but when our strong wills pushed or pulled in different directions. Gradually I learned to recognize and soften my fiery temper and make more room for him, lessons I learned with great difficulty as I struggled to grow beyond the vestiges of my own childhood. It was important to me to be as present as possible when I was with him.

It was made easier by the fact that we loved so many of the same things. Still, it required conscious effort at times, especially when I had a lot on my mind, an occupational hazard of parenting, with the never-ending pull of all the other things in our lives that can so easily subvert presence. The children always notice. Being distracted too much of the time conveys a sense that everything else is always more important.

Depending on their temperaments and interests, different boys will of course have different needs as they are growing up. But one thing they all need a good dose of is psychic space to grow on their own, to find things out away from their parents. As a boy growing up on the streets of New York City, I learned incomparable lessons I could never have learned from my parents by spending countless hours in the streets playing ball, or just hanging out, which we developed into a fine art, watching the underbelly of city life. I was lucky that my family's life was stable and that I could go home for dinner every night, get off the street, and learn other things from my parents and brothers.

In addition to all their various activities and pursuits, solitary and with their friends, boys have an abiding need for their fathers, their grandfathers, and other men to be present, to put them first, to care about them, to mentor them, show interest and share time with them, to tell them stories and listen to theirs. This is true whether they live with their fathers or not.

Boys can benefit greatly from male guidance in exploring their interests and skills and their power and its limits, and from being encouraged and shown how to use it in positive ways, both for themselves and for the good of others. We can support them in their efforts to explore and come to know their own strength without exaggerating or flaunting it. In a similar way, as fathers we can encourage their play, their creativity, and their sense of belonging, a sense of responsibility and of being needed.

Discoveries of this kind can come about by fathers and sons doing things together, or by spending time together in nondoing, which sometimes looks like fishing, or playing catch, or hanging out in a field looking at the clouds, or going for a walk, or riding the subway, or going to the ballpark or a museum.

Is it possible for us as fathers to commit ourselves, inadequate as we may sometimes feel in the face of such a challenge—hampered as we might be by our jobs, our professional obligations, our various treadmills, distractions, ambitions, and outright addictions—to spend such time with our sons? That nondoing—what in *The Wind in the Willows* is referred to as "messing around in boats," but is far more than that—can be a support to our sons in finding meaningful expressions for their agency and interests, and in helping them develop their strengths and a sense of mastery. Equally important, can we nurture an emotional landscape in which feeling things deeply is not only acceptable but also seen as essential to being fully human? Such an orientation is not fundamentally different from what girls need from their fathers as well. The energies may sometimes look different depending on their temperament, but the need for presence and for being seen and met with kindness and recognition are the same.

*

Our culture can be quite polarizing around the question of what it means to be a man nowadays. Norms are changing rapidly and becoming more inclusive and diverse in this era. Yet huge stereotypes still abound in the media equating fun and being cool with being macho, drinking, risk taking, and womanizing—just watch the beer commercials on TV or the truck ads, or follow in the press the trials of certain high school and college athletes, and of military personnel, and the horrific demeaning and violent behaviors that are often so graphically described. "Boys being boys" no longer has the infallibility it once had to excuse and exonerate harmful behavior, but there are many lessons still to be learned about honoring the sovereignty of others in terms of gender and sexual orientation in so many domains of society. Fathers can help their sons become aware of and interpret the various subtle and not-so-subtle messages and images the culture puts out, many of them demeaning to women and girls—and actually of men as well, when you stop and think about it. Perhaps then our sons will be less likely to get caught up in such stereotypic images and thinking, and the often hurtful behaviors that follow from them. Part of their education as males in this society is to come to understand in the deepest of ways that women and girls are human beings and not objects to be used. This is an enormous and endemic societal issue that is hugely important for us to be cognizant of as fathers and mothers of both boys and girls, and address head-on with awareness when it emerges in their experiences in school, within their social networks, and in their interactions with the broader society. It may require us as fathers to take a look at and acknowledge, challenging as it may be, how we ourselves may harbor and manifest deeply engrained and often unconscious habits in this regard.

Many of the dominant social images of men and women in the United States are products of what Robert Bly rightfully called, decades ago, the "sibling society," a world in which the father, and increasingly the mother as well, are absent physically or emotionally or both, and where the prevalent role models for both boys and girls are by default provided by the media, by the entertainment industry, and by peers. This phenomenon is increasingly being driven by the Internet and social networking. In today's world, it is hard for boys to find real-life mentors, and some kind of ceremonial initiation into adulthood and into the collective recognition, knowledge, and wisdom of those who came before. It is a world in which the past is often rejected without even being known. Deep, mutual alienation between the generations can lead teenage boys to attempt to raise and socialize themselves, and in the process, become increasingly at risk and vulnerable. Many aspects of the dominant culture are exploitative and predatory, even as some societal efforts are being made to promote and protect the rights of both children and women.

*

We might ask ourselves what a boy today will need in order to live wisely in a world that is changing so rapidly that we, the parents, cannot possibly know the challenges he will face in ten or twenty years, or even five. Absent a culture that honors, values, and prioritizes the needs of all its children and takes some societal responsibility for their development and their entry into the world of adults, parents are going to have to do yeoman's and yeowoman's work to serve as guides for their children. We know from extensive research that emotional intelligence and emotional balance, an ability to be in relationship with others under a wide range of circumstances, is certainly one capacity that will be needed for a happy and productive life in the future. Mindfulness is another life skill that will prove essential. As fathers, we can value the cultivation of inner strengths of our own for the sake of our boys, qualities such as lovingkindness, compassion, constancy, emotional reliability, flexibility, clear seeing, even wisdom. All these come out of moment-by-moment awareness of relationality, both inner and outer. We can value and draw upon our sovereignty, our truest nature, and the best of our own lineage or lineages, whether Native American, or African, Asian, European, Christian, Jewish, Muslim, Buddhist, Hindu, "none of the above," or "other." The alternative is a kind of rootlessness, that of not knowing who we are, and perhaps not caring, of having no "people," no community to which we belong and within which we are known and accepted as we are and to which we feel responsible and connected.

This is not to suggest some romantic ideal of fatherhood. Rather, we are talking about a process that we can and need to commit ourselves to because of our love and our caring, and out of our desire to be our best selves for our sons. Part of this process includes our own ongoing growth. Can we pay attention enough to our moment-to-moment experience, both inwardly and outwardly, to learn how to be more comfortable in our own skins, to be comfortable with *not knowing* at times, to work with our fear when it arises and our impulses to become emotionally closed off or numb? Can we practice bringing a degree of awareness to how we actually feel at moments throughout the day? Can we practice being more empathic, accepting, and playful? Can we be mindful of how totally consumed we may be by our work, and then work at finding a better balance? In essence, these approaches are simply creative applications of mindfulness in our lives and in our parenting.

The presence of a strong, empathic man in the role of father, grandfather, or mentor is always important for young boys, but it is increasingly important as boys move into adolescence. Adolescents desperately need to be seen, listened to, and heard, met and accepted, and encouraged to take responsibility for their own actions. For many boys, it is one of the biggest and most confusing, uncertain, and awkward transitions they will ever make in their lives. The transition from boy to man requires a vision, a new way of seeing, and a new way of being. Adolescent boys can be encouraged to recognize and appreciate mystery and the unknown, including other people and customs. They can be encouraged to learn the dangers of being swept up in a tribal mentality that makes absolute distinctions between us and them, and then, out of fear and prejudice, plunges into war and violence to vanquish "the other," not realizing that "them is us." This is the slow development of maturity, of adolescent boys learning to take their places, in Zen teacher Norman Fischer's phrase, to enter over time with increasing awareness into an ever-evolving and deepening secure relationship with themselves as well as with others.

*

Of course, boys receive essential sustenance from a loving, nurturing relationship with their mothers as well. Being held in the aura of a mother's love, without being controlled or having to take care of her emotional needs, creates a foundation of inner security and emotional grounding needed for the separations and adventures into the world that have to come as a boy gets older. But boys need their fathers from their earliest moments, too, as do girls. And the fathers need their sons. If we are not present at key moments in our sons' lives, we may not know them. If we see them born, hold them when they are little, dream dreams with them as they sleep on our shoulders, walk with them in the world and speak with them of what they see, offer them tools to work with and projects to put their arms and their minds to, get down on the floor with them and play and invent games, tell stories, watch the sun go down and the rain fall, dig in the mud and build castles at the beach, throw rocks in the water and carve sticks, climb mountains and sit by waterfalls, mess around in rowboats and canoes, sing songs, watch them sleeping and wake them gently... we will know them and they will know us in ways that further their flourishing and ours.

Fathers and sons can help each other grow and find beauty and meaning, through the easy times and, as we have been intimating, also through the darkest and most rending periods. Our boys need us to be honest and unwavering in our love and commitment to them. We also need to accord them the space to find their own ways through pain and suffering while being there for them as best we can. At times they will need us to establish certain boundaries in an attempt to keep them safe. At other times, we may have to establish limits just for our own peace of mind and well-being as parents. There is no script for this, but this is what love is all about; we are changed by it, and we learn hard lessons for ourselves, just as our boys learn their own lessons.

For us dads, this is also where mindfulness becomes invaluable. For how things unfold depends to an important degree on our own willingness to become more intimate with the unwanted and learn that, like it or not, at times it is all we are going to have to work with. We can be open to the possibility that the unwanted is itself *workable*, if we are willing to do a certain kind of interior work of our own. For instance, mindfulness may allow us to see in some moments just how fixated we can be on our own view of things; how attached we can be to thinking that we are right, when in actuality, we may not be; and allow us to see things we may have been unable to see before. It can reveal how easily we at times abandon our own hearts and common sense when we react out of fear or anger in those moments in which we feel frustrated or thwarted by whatever arises that we don't like and don't feel is "tolerable." When we find ourselves contracting in that way, it is an opportunity to catch ourselves and recognize our attachment to the story in our head about what is going on. We can then remind ourselves that it is not the truth—that it cannot be the whole truth, even though we may be convinced that it is. We can remind ourselves that if we can free ourselves from that too small view of things and our own tacit assumptions that remain mostly unexamined but don't have to be, we can be present and relate and act in far wiser ways. Most of our reactivity comes from the thinking mind, which is usually colored by something left over from our own past or by fear of the future. Reacting mindlessly causes us to lose touch with what might be required in the present moment, especially in the most difficult and trying ones, just when we most need to be in touch and respond rather than react.

As our sons grow into themselves, of course they will find other sons who share their passions and with whom they can form friendships, some of which may be enduring and deeply sustaining. Music and dancing, wilderness and woods and fields, city life, sports, literature and the arts, all beckon through periods of both light and darkness, offering worlds of meaning and value, serving as mirrors in which boys can see themselves and continue discovering who they are and what they love, coming to live their moments fully, trusting in their own power, grounded in their bodies, and becoming full-fledged planetary adults as they participate in the mysteries of generativity and of their new generation, and of assuming their own places in the world.

Growing up in this rapidly changing world, exploring what one's authentic place in it might be, is a nonlinear process that can be confusing and frightening, even dangerous at times. Ultimately, coming to adulthood is a developmental odyssey. When boys are met on a regular basis with some acceptance and kindness by their fathers and other men, they will resonate with it at some level or other, even if it doesn't feel that way to us at the time. They will be sustained in ways that will increasingly allow them to find or make their own place in this world. It may take a short time, or it may take a long time, relatively speaking, but that does not matter. The more familiar and confident boys can be with the workings of their own minds and bodies, their thoughts and emotions, desires and longings, the more they can come to trust that capacity for awareness within themselves, the more they can live with an increasingly larger understanding of who they are and be open to the vast range of possibilities and actualities before them.

*

When they [his boys, Kai and Gen] were four and five we would go over to Bald Mountain on foot and we could look back and see our place. When they were seven and eight, we went up to Grouse Ridge on foot and we could look down from Grouse Ridge and see Bald Mountain from which you can see our place. A few years later we went on up to the High Sierra and got up on 8,000 foot English Mountain from which you can see Grouse Ridge. And then we went on over to Castle Peak which is the highest peak in that range which is 10,000 feet high and climbed that and you can see English Mountain from there. Then we went on north and we climbed Sierra Buttes and Mount Lassen—Mount

Lassen is the farthest we've been out now. So from Mount Lassen, you can see Castle Peak, you can see English Peak, you can see Grouse Ridge, you can see Bald Mountain and you can see our place. That is the way the world should be learned. It's an intense geography that is never far removed from your body.

GARY SNYDER

Pond Hockey

When the temperature rises for a day or two and then freezes again without a snowstorm, the winter ponds in New England beckon for a good
game of ice hockey. When times like these occurred on the weekend or
over vacation, my son and I (jkz) would put on layers of warm clothing,
grab our sticks and pucks and skates, and head down to the pond below
the hill. There we would don our skates, struggling with the long laces
with freezing fingers until they were pulled tight enough, waddle over
the remaining feet of snow, and touch new freedom at the ice edge.

We would skate around for a while, inspecting the ice all over the
pond, adjusting to the feeling of being on skates once again. Then we
would carefully select a spot and set up a goal with a pair of boots set
a few feet apart.

We played one on one…one of us defending the goal while the
other came at it with the puck. The defender had broad latitude to
come out of the goal and try to take the puck away from his opponent,
so there was lots of fast skating all over the pond, clashing of sticks,
racing to get to the puck first. There were fakes and lots of shoot-
ing, chases, and bumps as we maneuvered around each other with
exhilarating swiftness and laughter. And of course, there was lots of
scoring, and the sheer joy of sensing the puck sail past the defender and

through the boots, sometimes on highly improbable trajectories that made us laugh.

As we played, we generated heat. No matter how cold the day, how biting the wind, after a time the hats would come off, and the gloves, then the coats and sweaters. Sometimes we would be down to just shirts on top. As long as we kept skating, we stayed warm.

We played for hours. There was never a time that wasn't the best time. Every time was just now, beyond thought, caught up in the joy of sharing what always felt like a particularly male energy in going up against each other time and time again, coming in with the puck, chasing one another, blocking shots, protecting the goal.

Sometimes we played at night, in the orange gloom of one tall flood-light put up by the town, hardly able to see the puck in the shadows. But most of the time, we played in the afternoon, on and on, as the winter sun moved toward its early exit. At times, we had to stop and catch our breath. Lying on our coats spread open on the snow at the edge of the pond and watching the clouds against the deep blue of the sky, or the strands of pinks and golds beginning to show themselves in the west, our breath visible in the air above us, we would revel in silence and perfection.

I would like to say we did this every weekend for years and years, but we didn't, and those days now seem long past. And I would like to say that my girls and I had similar feelings when we played pond hockey, and we did on rare occasions. The girls were drawn to other things. They loved to skate, and they skated better than we did, but they lacked interest in the game of stick, puck, goal, and pursuit.

Most of the time, the pond was covered with snow or rough ice and was unskatable. Some winters, it wasn't frozen enough when we wanted it to be. And we had other things calling us as well, and other chances to be together. But none was ever better than playing hockey on the winter pond.

Wilderness Camping

On occasion, when our children were young, we tried to take time with them individually, one parent alone with one child, rather than always doing things together as an entire family. Children need a dose of full attention from a parent from time to time, and to do special things without having to compete with siblings or the other parent. Such outings can be precious adventures, whether they last a few hours or a few days, whether in the wilderness or in the city, whether we are alone together or at some event with lots of other people. They afford new opportunities for closeness and seeing each other in a new light.

*

One of the things I (jkz) most enjoyed doing with my children was to take them camping in the wilderness, one on one. In a day or two, we would have experiences that gave new shape to our relationship, and memories that could last a lifetime. There is nothing like being in the wilderness for a few days to remind us of what is important and to get down to the essentials of living.

I took one of my daughters when she was nine years old to the Wild River in the White Mountains. We parked at the head of a trail and walked along the river for about five miles. She was missing her mom from the start. The stultifying heat didn't make our going any easier. At a certain point, in response to her unhappiness, I suggested we get into our bathing suits and soak in the river to cool down. She loved being in the cool river in the heat, but she still cried a good deal as we walked on. I carried her pack as well as mine. She alternated between wanting to be home, wanting to get where we were going, and not knowing what she wanted...just feeling miserable.

At one magical point, we ran into a train of llamas going the other way. That added an exotic touch to our adventure, if only briefly.

It was the usual story. We had to keep going so that we would get to the place I had planned to make camp before the sun went down behind the mountains. Of course, she didn't understand that, and she didn't see why one place wasn't as good as another. But I had a special place in mind, a large, flat place perfect for pitching the tent and close to a small waterfall, which I knew would delight her.

Missing home and unhappy, she walked along, while I tried to maintain my composure, struggling with feeling inadequate, worrying that maybe this was going to be a disaster, feeling like a failure for not being able to allay her fears or "make" her happy.

Finally, we got to the place I had in mind, a place I had passed through with her brother several years before on one of our adventures, which had taken us over South Baldface and down into this valley. The shadows were already long. As soon as we arrived, her mood changed. She enjoyed pitching camp, setting up the tent, stowing our sleeping gear, getting a fire going, and cooking dinner. The little waterfall was our companion, singing to us as we worked and cooked and ate while sitting on logs by the fire. The sky was full of stars as you never see them in or near the city, their shimmering light filtering down on our heads through the dark openings in the treetops surrounding our cozy clearing.

We got into our sleeping bags early and fell asleep to the singing of the river. She fell asleep first. I lay on my back looking out at the sky, breathing with my whole body, so happy to be with my daughter, listening to her breathing, feeling the joy of adventuring together.

We awoke to a crisp blue morning light, the mountaintops just turning golden. We got warm, had breakfast, and sat around the fire, making plans for the day. My idea was to hike to the top of the ridge. But that was not her idea at all. She wanted to stay put. She had no interest in going to the top of anything, view or no view. She didn't want to walk, hike, or climb, especially with a pack. She had her home now. So stay put we did, as I stowed away my own strong expectations and desires, realizing that under the circumstances, it was important that the choice be hers.

So we explored along the river, and when it got warmer and the sunlight descended into the valley, we explored *in* the river. Noontime found us sitting on a high rock with the river streaming around us on all sides, boiling and roaring. There, I read *Ronia, the Robber's Daughter* to her, Astrid Lindgren's wonderful story of a strong girl in olden days living in the forest with her young friend, Birk, as they try to sort out the craziness of their feuding families' lives. It was good to be in the woods together, alone, far from civilization. We were happy with very little. Sun, water, forest, each other, the timelessness of the moment.

Softball Breaks through the Gloom

Sunday of a three-day weekend—the start of school vacation week—I
(jkz) have been away so much of late that when I'm home, I feel like a
stranger. Myla and the girls develop their own rhythms in my absence.
To reconnect, I sometimes ask dumb questions, like "What are you
talking about?" when they are speaking together.

They don't like this. It feels intrusive. I stand in the doorway to
my daughter's room while Myla is having a conversation with her. I'm
seeking closeness, but it feels off to them, like I'm wanting something
to happen, filled with unvoiced expectations. In such moments, I feel
like a stranger in my own home.

My practice in such moments is to be present without imposing
myself and my needs. It is not easy. In fact, it's quite a struggle. Just being
present, doing what I need to do, but not succumbing to resentment or
isolating myself further by leaving the breakfast table early, or working,
or being on the phone—these are my challenges. If I do these things, it
feels like I'm still fundamentally away, even though my body is around.

*

The morning is gloomy with low clouds, a mid-April chill, communications with distant family, and the need to catch up on work.

But rather than isolate myself in my study, I come in and out of the kitchen, making sure that I am around and not giving in to the impulse to pick up the Sunday paper.

Trying to get my daughter out of the house to do something with me is not easy, but I try again today, in the late afternoon. At this age, she usually rejects anything I propose we do together. But her softball coach had called a few days earlier and told her she should play catch to prepare for the team's first practice. After dinner, she agrees to play catch with me. We go outside. The setting sun is shining now beneath the clouds, which had kept the day gray and gloomy, matching my mood. Now low evening light from the west floods the sideyard, setting everything aglow.

We start throwing the ball back and forth. At first we can't find a left-handed glove for her, so she throws rightie, claiming to be ambidextrous. And she is. She can throw accurately with her right arm and catch beautifully with her left hand. We play with intensity, the ball rocketing back and forth. I direct my throws first to one side of her, then to the other so she will have to backhand a fair number of balls. Then we expand to include pop-ups and low line drives, mixing up everything.

She catches about ninety percent of everything I throw, this after a year of not playing at all. We are in sync. I can feel her enjoyment of this, and her recognition of her own grace and mastery. She is good, a natural. But I know she should have the one left-handed glove we have somewhere. We take a break and I look for it in the one place I haven't looked yet, and find it.

Now her catching is shakier for a time, as she adjusts to the new glove and the opposite positioning. But her throwing, competent with her right arm, is three times more powerful and accurate with her left. Back and forth, back and forth, high, low, catching backhand, catching on the open side. I haven't done this in ages. I am fast revisiting ancient rhythms from my own childhood. The pattern hasn't entirely disappeared in forty years. It amazes me that the glove knows where the ball is so much of the time.

She is warming to this. Her cheeks turn red. She is fine in the chill air without a coat. She is also warming to me. I feel it. Finally, finally, we are doing something together out of doors, something we can both enjoy and talk easily around.

I have waited months for such a moment. I have invited her to bike ride together. "No." To Rollerblade. "No." To go for a walk. "No!" To drive someplace nice and sit by a pond. "No way." Yet right now, it is happening, and I feel that the effects of my having been absent are being washed away. Right now we are together, doing something that is rare for us and that we can come back to all spring if she likes. Now that we are on daylight savings time, we can play after I come home from work.

We are also rediscovering that it is still possible for us to have fun together. I feel her strength as the ball goes back and forth, and see her experiencing her own strength in the most natural of ways. I am enjoying this playing catch immensely and feel the same from her. We dwell so much apart and in such different worlds that we can become estranged from each other. But here is at least one way, at least in this moment, where we are being shown that we are still deeply connected and can enjoy doing something together. As we throw the ball back and forth and listen to the thud in the gloves and the sharp crack when it goes over my head and hits the wooden fence behind me, it feels as if we've been doing this forever. Time falls away.

I am careful not to find ways to stop or interrupt these moments for anything. I know they will not last. The light is fading. She is expecting a phone call from her friend about when she and her mom will be coming by to pick her up for a sleepover. The phone call comes. She needs to get ready. But we have met once again, she and I, and that counts for a lot with both of us.

Afterward, we sit around waiting for the doorbell to ring. We are alone in the house. Out of the blue, she offers (this never happens, I can hardly believe that it is now) to tell me how she made the larger-than-life sketch of herself in her art class. She explains that the exercise was to do the whole thing without lifting the pencil from the paper, looking in the mirror, and only rarely at the drawing. I could have asked her a hundred probing questions and never gotten her to talk about something like this. She doesn't answer probing questions. But she sometimes responds to presence. I see that it is my job to know this and to be accessible, even when it seems like there are light-years between us.

Girls

When our girls were little, I (mkz) took great pleasure in the wide variety of qualities that surfaced in them at different times. They showed enthusiasm and delight in the simplest of activities: picking strawberries and carefully tasting each ripe berry before putting it into their baskets; dressing up in old clothes of mine and remnants of cloth, and transforming themselves into queens and princesses; pretending to be baby dolphins as they swam around me in the bay. When they saw deeply into things and shared a sudden insight with me, or showed kindness or compassion in some way, I would delight in those wondrous and warmhearted aspects of their being. There were also times when they were fierce, angry, and completely unmovable. Even as I felt thwarted by their indomitable wills, I would find myself cherishing their strength, their power, their one-pointedness.

In those years, both home and school were, for the most part, havens from the broader culture. Their world was simple, with few pressures, expectations, or external distractions. As they got older, of course, things changed. Slowly I became more and more aware of the numerous messages they were getting from the prevailing culture, messages that were ubiquitous and limiting and that put all sorts of expectations and pressures on them just because they were girls.

Everywhere girls turn, at every checkout counter, in newspapers, in magazines, on TV, and in movies, they are exposed to images of women that can deeply affect how they view themselves. These images subtly or not so subtly suggest that the greatest power they have is related to being consumers and sexualized objects. These messages are tremendously limiting and potentially damaging to girls, particularly as they approach adolescence.

Such images are used to sell all manner of products. Not only is the focus constantly on buying and consuming, but also whole industries are devoted to convincing women and girls that they need to make their bodies more beautiful and more "perfect." Yet most of the images are of bodies that few women naturally have, or only have for a brief time. This "ideal" look, synthesized by the worlds of advertising, fashion, and celebrity, can foster in girls a strong dissatisfaction with their own bodies, their hair, their clothes, their skin, virtually every aspect of their physical being.

Appearance is accorded supreme importance. As a result, many girls spend an inordinate amount of time and energy preoccupied with how they look, or don't look. This can happen at the expense of developing their physical prowess and strength, their creativity, and their inner selves. Parents face a constant struggle to provide an authentic, supportive, balanced perspective on being a girl or young woman in the face of this very alluring, ever-present, enticing media barrage. As difficult as this may be, there are some things we can do.

We can start by becoming aware of the pervasive influence of this industry, so that it is not missed entirely or taken for granted as an inevitable part of the cultural landscape. Awareness is a first step. Once we start to pay attention to potentially negative influences on our girls, we can begin to see the effects they may be having on their self-image, their self-esteem, their self-confidence, their interests, and their goals. Rather than just continually attempting to repair damage that is done, we can be proactive and, when they are little, try to limit their exposure and consumption in whatever ways we can. As they get older, more and more we can talk with them about what we are seeing, in a hopefully non-heavy-handed way, so that they can see what lies behind these images of women. They can begin to recognize for themselves such implicit messages and how the desire for buying is fueled in the minds of viewers, readers, and consumers.

A girl who grows up immersed in various media is going to be saturated with many more narrow and demeaning images of women than a girl whose exposure to the media is more limited. Limiting exposure has the added benefit of freeing up time and space for real-life experiences that hopefully will broaden her view of herself as a whole person with many valuable strengths and skills and unique qualities. Girls often have such experiences playing sports or engaging in activities or projects, whether they be artistic, intellectual, or community oriented, that challenge and develop their creative powers.

At the same time that we try to create some sanctuary from the potentially negative cultural influences and encourage an awareness of the power of the media, we of necessity have to balance our restrictions and even the expression of our views, or we may end up creating a gulf between us. After all, girls are drawn not only by the surface allure of this world of advertising, TV, movies, and music videos, but also by its artistic and entrepreneurial creativity.

This is one reason why parenting with greater awareness can be so difficult. As parents, we have to continually work with our fears, our own limitations, and our feelings of powerlessness at times as we try to understand and relate to these cultural forces. The fine line we tried to walk in our family was to educate and limit at the same time that we tried to stay open and flexible. As the girls got older, this involved more and more negotiation and compromise and, ultimately, encouraging them to make their own thoughtful choices.

Children want so much to feel normal in what they can do and see, and they compare themselves, naturally enough, to what their friends are allowed to do and watch, and how they behave. What is considered normal in our society is often violent, cruel, and demeaning in various ways to women. It is so ever-present that we can become inured to it and hardly see it at all. In the face of this deluge of imagery—so much of which connects sex to violence, objectifies girls, and ignores or makes fun of women who don't fit in with the classic, light-skinned, vulnerable, thin-bodied "ideal"—anger would be an appropriate response. But of course women are not supposed to get angry. When we do, we are often labeled all sorts of unpleasant and degrading things. We are met with, "What's the matter with *you*?" "Why do you take things so seriously?" "Where's your sense of humor?" "Is it that time of the month?"

In parenting girls, we need to try as best we can to counter this narrow view of women. When we silently accept the dominant view, we are basically colluding in our society's denigration of women. As their mothers, we need to embody an alternative for them, a different way of being and a different way of viewing the culture they live in. Our girls need us as allies in a culture where their particular interests and ways of seeing things may not be acknowledged or valued, and are even scorned.

Girls need their fathers to be allies as well. Daughters need their fathers to embody a more respectful view of women and to feel valued by them for who they are rather than for how they look. As our daughters experience all the different and sometimes difficult physical and emotional transformations of preadolescence through the teen years, fathers need to be particularly mindful of unconscious or habitual ways they may have of relating to women. These patterns can also show up in their relationship to their daughters and take different forms such as being disrespectful or controlling or flirtatious or putting their own needs first. A father's need to be loved and adored by his daughter can keep him from seeing what it is that she really needs from him. Inevitably, stereotypic patterns will surface, and when they do, bringing awareness to them gives fathers a chance to act in ways that are less automatic, disregarding, and harmful. It's a process of noticing such habitual impulses when they arise and modulating their behavior in response.

It can be helpful for us as parents to examine how our expectations of our daughters may unwittingly limit their range of expression and their autonomy. We can ask ourselves if we might not be attached to their always acting in a certain way, for example, friendly, thoughtful, sensitive, kind, quiet. Do we expect them to smile a lot? Are we taking into account their temperaments at the same time that we are open to changes in them? Has a sanguine, shy daughter become a fiery, energetic, outgoing, vocal teenager? Can we allow our girls to be angry, loud, and boisterous at times in ways we would not find objectionable in boys? Are we supporting them in finding ways to express their unique abilities, creativity, and strengths? Our responses to these questions and others like them may change from day to day, or even from moment to moment. But asking them is an essential part of our own work as parents.

A large part of this process is working with other people's expectations of our girls. When we or our daughters become aware of messages that feel inappropriate or limiting or denigrating on the

part of an authority figure or their peers, including sexual harass-
ment or sexual stereotyping, can we help them identify and name the
troubling attitude or behavior and support them in their feelings? By
doing so, rather than minimizing the problem or denying the validity
of their feelings, we are letting them know we are their allies and that
when they are unjustly treated or subtly demeaned, feeling angry or
hurt is not only okay, but also a healthy response.

A disturbing trend among adolescent boys, as we noted in the Boys
chapter, is that they increasingly seem to have expectations of girls that
are objectifying and demeaning. This trend is driven by the ubiquity of
sexualized and violent Web-based images and video, amplified by social
media and their peer culture. In turn, many adolescent girls seem to
feel that they have to meet those expectations—even when they may be
harmful or traumatic to them—in part because these unhealthy power
dynamics become normalized. Unfortunately, girls get the message
that if they object, it is *their* problem and that there is something the
matter with them for having the feelings they have. Our challenge as
parents is to do our best to be aware of these dynamics and what may be
going on in our children's social sphere, and to support our daughters in
recognizing unacceptable behaviors on the part of others, standing up
for themselves, and setting healthy boundaries.

*

To keep my mouth shut. To turn away my face. To walk
back down the aisle. To slap the bishop back when he
slapped me during Confirmation. To hold the word *no* in
my mouth like a gold coin, something valued, something
possible. To teach the *no* to our daughters. To value their *no*
more than their compliant yes. To celebrate *no*. To grasp the

word *no* in your fist and refuse to give it up. To support the
boy who says *no* to violence, the girl who will not be violated,
the woman who says *no, no, I will not*. To love the *no*, to cherish
the *no*, which is so often our first word. *No*—the means to
transformation.

LOUISE ERDRICH,
The Blue Jay's Dance

*

When one of my daughters was eleven, for months she related incidents to me in which she felt her teacher was being disrespectful to
her or her classmates. I was glad that she felt she could tell me what
was happening in school, and I tried to be supportive of her as best I
could. One day she told me the following story. She was talking and
laughing exuberantly with her friends at an evening school event when
her teacher came up to her, called her by name, and said in a chiding
voice, "Be a *lady!*" She told me that she looked her teacher straight in
the eye and said, "I *am* being a lady, just a *strong* one!"

*

Through the experience of having their feelings validated, slowly, over
time, girls are better able to see and name attitudes and behaviors that
are troubling to them and can more readily be in touch with what
they are feeling, trust those feelings, and express them effectively. In
this way, they can begin to learn to empower themselves and build a
repertoire of emotional competencies that will be critical to their further development. Such strengths will be particularly important when
they are living on their own in a society that can be so disempowering
and exploitative of women.

I was in a small store that sells oriental rugs with my then eleven-year-old daughter. The storekeeper was from another country, and he related to us with what seemed like an exaggerated smile on his face. It made me uneasy, but I quickly proceeded with the business at hand, which was to look at a few rugs. When we got outside, my daughter told me that she felt really uncomfortable because whenever I looked away from him, she noticed he was looking at her in a "weird" way. I made some comment to her about cultural differences. Later I realized how inadequate my response was and how my focus had been to explain away and excuse his behavior rather than validate her feelings of discomfort.

That evening, as I was saying good night, I told her that I had been thinking about what happened in the store and that I didn't want something like that to happen again without our having a signal we could use so that she could let me know when something was making her uncomfortable. I suggested that if it happened again, she take my hand and give it a squeeze and I would know that something wasn't right and we should leave right away. Her eyes lit up and she smiled as she thought about this.

✻

Hard as it may be, and as inadequate as we may feel at times, our daughters need our support and encouragement to stay in touch with what is strongest and most vital in themselves, given that between the ages of nine and fourteen, girls are often socialized to surrender their voices and their sovereignty. In the following chapter, we share with you a Norwegian folk tale about a girl who remains true to her own nature.

Tatterhood—"I Will Go as I Am"

Once upon a time there was a king and queen who had no children, and this grieved the queen very much. She was always bewailing their lack of a family and saying how lonesome it was in the palace with no young ones about.

The king remarked that if it were young ones she wanted running about, they could invite the children of their kinswoman to stay with them. The queen thought this a good idea, and soon she had two little nieces romping through the rooms and playing in the palace courtyard.

One day as the queen watched fondly from the window, she saw her two lassies playing ball with a stranger, a little girl clad in tattered clothes. The queen hurried down the stairs.

"Little girl," said the queen sharply, "this is the palace courtyard. You cannot play in here!"

"We asked her in to play with us," cried the lassies, and they ran over to the ragged little girl and took her by the hand.

"You would not chase me away if you knew the powers my mother has," said the strange little girl.

"Who is your mother?" asked the queen. "And what powers does she have?"

The child pointed to a woman selling eggs in the marketplace outside the palace gates. "If she wants to, my mother can tell people how to have children when all else has failed."

Now this caught the queen's interest at once. She said, "Tell your mother I wish to speak to her in the palace."

The little girl ran out to the marketplace, and it was not long before a tall, strong market woman strode into the queen's sitting room.

"Your daughter says you have powers, and that you could tell me how I may have children of my own," said the queen.

"The queen should not listen to a child's chatter," answered the woman.

"Sit down," said the queen, and she ordered fine food and drinks to be served. Then she told the egg woman she wanted children of her own more than anything in the world. The woman finished her ale, then said cautiously that perhaps she did know a spell it would do no harm to try.

"Tonight I want you to put your bed out on the grass. After it is dark have two pails of water brought to you. In each of them you must wash yourself, and afterward, pour away the water under the bed. When you awake in the morning two flowers will have sprung up, one fair and one rare. The fair one you must eat, but the rare one you must let stand. Mind you, don't forget that."

The queen followed this advice, and the next morning under the bed stood two flowers. One was green and oddly shaped; the other was pink and fragrant. The pink flower she ate at once. It tasted so sweet that she promptly ate the other one as well, saying to herself, "I don't think it can help or hurt either way!"

Not long afterward the queen realized she was with child and some time later she had the birthing. First was born a girl who had a wooden spoon in her hand and rode upon a goat. A queer looking little creature she was, and the moment she came into the world, she bawled out, "Mamma!"

"If I'm your mamma," said the queen, "God give me grace to mend my ways!"

"Oh, don't be sorry," said the girl, riding about on the goat, "the next one born will be much fairer looking." And so it was. The second twin was born fair and sweet, which pleased the queen very much.

The twin sisters were as different as they could be, but they grew up to be very fond of each other. Where one was, the other must be. But the elder twin soon had the nickname "Tatterhood," for she was strong, raucous, and careless, and was always racing about on her goat. Her clothes were always torn and mud-spattered, her hood in tatters. No one could keep her in clean, pretty dresses. She insisted on wearing old clothes, and the queen finally gave up and let her dress as she pleased.

One Christmas Eve, when the twin sisters were almost grown, there arose a terrific noise and clatter in the gallery outside the queen's rooms. Tatterhood asked what it was that dashed and crashed about in the passage. The queen told her it was a pack of trolls who had invaded the palace.

The queen explained that this happened in the palace every seven years. There was nothing to be done about the evil creatures; the palace must all ignore the trolls and endure their mischief.

Tatterhood said, "Nonsense! I will go out and drive them away."

Everyone protested—she must leave the trolls alone; they were too dangerous. But Tatterhood insisted she was not afraid of the trolls. She could and would drive them away. She warned the queen that all doors must be kept tight shut. Then she went out into the gallery to chase them. She laid about with the wooden spoon, whacking trolls on the head or shoulders, rounding them up to drive them out. The whole palace shook with the crashes and shrieking, until it seemed the place would fall apart.

Just then her twin sister, who was worried about Tatterhood, opened a door and stuck out her head to see how things were going. Pop! Up came a troll, whipped off her head, and stuck a calf's head on her shoulders instead. The poor princess ran back into the room on all fours and began to moo like a calf.

When Tatterhood came back and saw her sister, she was very angry that the queen's attendants had not kept better watch. She scolded them all around, and asked what they thought of their care-lessness now that her sister had a calf's head.

"I'll see if I can get her free from the troll's spell," said Tatter-hood. "But I'll need a good ship in full trim and well fitted with stores."

Now the king realized his daughter Tatterhood was quite extraordinary despite her wild ways, so he agreed to this but said they must have a captain and crew. Tatterhood was firm—she would have no captain or crew. She would sail the ship alone. At last they let her have her way, and Tatterhood sailed off with her sister.

With a good wind behind them, she sailed right to the land of the trolls and tied up at the landing place. She told her sister to stay quite still on board the ship, but she herself rode her goat right up to the trolls' house. Through an open window she could see her sister's head on the wall. In a trice, she leaped the goat through the window and into the house, snatched the head, and leapt back outside again. She set off with it, and after her came the trolls. They shrieked and swarmed about her like angry bees. But the goat snorted and butted with his horns, and Tatterhood smacked them with her magic wooden spoon until they gave up and let her escape.

When Tatterhood got safely back to their ship, she took off the calf's head and put her sister's own bonny head back on again. Now her sister was once more human.

"Let's sail on and see something of the world," said Tatterhood. Her sister was of the same mind, so they sailed along the coast, stopping at this place and that, until at last they reached a distant kingdom.

Tatterhood tied up the ship at the landing place. When the people of the castle saw the strange sail, they sent down messengers to find out who sailed the ship and whence it came. The messengers were startled to find no one on board but Tatterhood, and she was riding around the deck on her goat.

When they asked if there was anyone else on board, Tatterhood answered that, yes, she had her sister with her. The messengers asked to see her, but Tatterhood said no. They then asked, would the sisters come up to the castle for an audience with the king and his two sons?

"No," said Tatterhood. "Let them come down to the ship if they wish to see us." And she began to gallop about on her goat until the deck thundered.

The elder prince became curious about the strangers and hastened down to the shore the very next day. When he saw the fair younger twin, he promptly fell in love with her and wanted to marry her.

"No indeed," she declared. "I will not leave my sister Tatterhood. I will not marry until she is married."

The prince went glumly back to the castle, for in his opinion no one would want to marry the odd creature who rode a goat and looked like a ragged beggar. But hospitality must be given to strangers, so the two sisters were invited to a feast at the castle, and the prince begged his younger brother to escort Tatterhood.

The younger twin brushed her hair and put on her finest kirtle for the event, but Tatterhood refused to change.

"You could wear one of my dresses," said her sister, "instead of that raggedy cloak and old boots." Tatterhood just laughed.

"You might take off that tattered hood and the soot streaks from your face," said her sister crossly, for she wanted her beloved Tatterhood to look her best.

"No," said Tatterhood, "I will go as I am."

All the people of the town turned out to see the strangers riding up to the castle, and a fine procession it was! At the head rode the prince and Tatterhood's sister on fine white horses draped with cloth of gold. Next came the prince's brother on a splendid horse with silver trappings. Beside him rode Tatterhood on her goat.

"You're not much for conversation," said Tatterhood. "Haven't you anything to say?"

"What is there to talk about?" he retorted. They rode on in silence until finally he burst out, "Why do you ride on that goat instead of a horse?"

"Since you happened to ask," said Tatterhood, "I can ride on a horse if I choose." At once the goat turned into a fine steed.

Well! The young man's eyes popped open wide, and he turned to look at her with great interest.

"Why do you hide your head beneath that ragged hood?" he asked.

"Is it a ragged hood? I can change it if I choose," she said. And there, on long dark hair, was a circlet of gold and tiny pearls.

"What an unusual girl you are!" he exclaimed. "But that wooden spoon—why do you choose to carry that?"

"Is it a spoon?" and in her hand the spoon turned into a gold-tipped wand of rowan wood.

"I see!" said the prince. He smiled and hummed a little tune as they rode on.

At last Tatterhood said, "Aren't you going to ask me why I wear these ragged clothes?"

"No," said the prince. "It's clear you wear them because you choose to, and when you want to change them, you will." At that, Tatterhood's ragged cloak disappeared, and she was clad in a velvet green mantle and kirtle. But the prince just smiled and said, "The color becomes you very well."

When the castle loomed up ahead, Tatterhood said to him, "And will you not ask to see my face beneath the streaks of soot?"

"That, too, shall be as you choose."

As they rode through the castle gates, Tatterhood touched the rowan wand to her face, and the soot streaks disappeared. And whether her face now was lovely or plain we shall never know, because it didn't matter in the least to the prince or to Tatterhood.

But this I can tell you: the feast at the castle was a merry one, with the games, and the singing, and the dancing lasting for many days.

*

Sovereignty and authenticity are the key to every ounce of Tatterhood's life energy and everything—on the surface so strange, even repulsive—that she did or said. Tatterhood is not afraid to be herself. She was born raucous and unusual—you might even say "ugly" from a conventional point of view. She is loud, dirty, fearless, and strong. She knows her own way and goes her own way, regardless of what others think. There is not a passive bone in her body. She has sailed her ship as both captain and crew, stolen her sister's head back, and seen something of the world to boot. She is a wild woman who is also capable of love and devotion to her "perfect" sister, a sister who has all the outward, conventional attributes that society adores in women. Tatterhood is as dark as her sister is light. Her appearance, perhaps not so pleasing, requires, even demands acceptance on its own terms, an honoring of the underlying essence of her being, deeply and always beautiful, although hidden to the unseeing eye.

Out of her love for her, Tatterhood's sister tries to get her to change her ragged clothes and wash her dirty face. She wants her to look her best. How many of us as parents have struggled with wanting to protect our children from the criticism of others, wanting them to be seen as beautiful, as we see them? But Tatterhood stands firm: "No, I will go as I am."

As the prince rides next to Tatterhood, he is silent. When he finally speaks, at her insistence, he doesn't make small talk. He speaks honestly and asks a straightforward question: "Why do you ride on that goat instead of a horse?" When her goat transforms into a horse, the prince notices. He becomes more attentive. He proceeds to ask other questions but stops short of asking about her clothes. We feel his acceptance of her in his silence. She has to ask him, "Aren't you going to ask me why I wear these ragged clothes?" He refuses, saying that it is clear that she has chosen to dress as she is and that when she wants to change them she will. It is in that very moment—when the young prince acknowledges her sovereignty, saying, "That, too, shall be as you choose"—that she is transformed, and in the process, teaches him what is most important about love.

Advocacy, Assertiveness, Accountability

At one point, a friend and I (mkz) had similar experiences of being called in to discuss incidents that happened in school with our daughters. The themes were the same: strong-willed girls say how they feel about something and are seen as "disrespectful."

One afternoon, I was called into the elementary school principal's office. The principal said that my daughter and a group of fifth-grade girls were told by an aide that they shouldn't be playing soccer with the boys and that they had to stop. My daughter told the aide she was being sexist, that the girls had just as much of a right to play as the boys. The principal imitated my daughter's angry, defiant body language by crossing her arms and putting her head to the side, in a manner that suggested she assumed I would agree that her behavior was not acceptable. She went on to tell me that my daughter was brought into a meeting with herself and the recess aides and was told that she was not allowed to behave in a manner that was disrespectful, that the aides had to ensure the safety of the children, and that the children had to listen to them. She assured me that she had asked my daughter for her side of the story and told her she needed to write a note of apology to each of the aides.

I agreed with her that my daughter did need to learn to say

how she felt in a more respectful manner. But I said that it sounded to me as if my daughter had felt angry about what she perceived to be an unjust situation and was trying to communicate her feelings to the aides. It also sounded to me as if her concerns and point of view were not taken seriously and the implication was that she was "bad" for expressing them. I also asked the principal if she thought that had a boy crossed his arms and spoken up for himself in a similar way, it would have been seen in such a strongly negative light.

Later on, I told my daughter she needed to learn how to stand up for herself without being disrespectful, that saying someone was being sexist could feel like name-calling if other people didn't understand what she was trying to say. Also that she had to be aware of how she spoke, of her body language and tone of voice and that not just what she said but also the way she said it was important. I wanted her to see that her actions affected other people and had consequences, one of which was to influence their ability to hear what she was saying.

Learning how to say how we feel and how we see things in a respectful manner is not easy. It takes lots of practice. We have to give children room to do this, to learn from trying, from making mistakes, and from trying again.

The courage it took for her to speak out was not acknowledged. The implicit message she was given was that she should be quiet and compliant. If my daughter kept getting this message when she tried to stand up for herself or for others, and if she didn't have parents who accepted her anger and tried to see her point of view, she might have stopped speaking up and lost some of her self-confidence, as happens to many girls. At nine, girls are often vital and confident, but by the age of fourteen, somehow that strength can become hidden, tentative, unseen, even lost.

My friend's daughter is an extremely gifted student, a perfectionist, and very demanding of herself. She also has clear ideas about things. Her fifth-grade teacher had told her to leave project pieces (puppets she had made and books from the town library) in school over the weekend. She had brought them to class as part of a report she was going to give. She didn't feel that they would be safe left at school over the weekend, but instead of telling her teacher that, she just said, "No, I want to take them home." The teacher felt she was being disrespectful and called up her parents. Although this girl never "acted out" or "misbehaved" in school, her teacher chose to see her behavior in a negative light rather than as a sign that she felt secure enough to say what was important for her to do.

It is true that she could have communicated more effectively and perhaps been seen as more respectful, had she explained her concerns to her teacher. But again, the fine art of communicating requires practice and experience. Even so, as the adult, her teacher could have been more respectful of her by asking about her reasons for wanting to take the project home.

As parents, we need to help our children identify their concerns, encourage them to express them in an assertive and respectful manner, and to stand up for what they think is right, even when they are not understood, or when their feelings are not taken into account. To do this, we may need to advocate for our children at times, and help them make sense of the complex situations in which they sometimes find themselves.

If children sense that their feelings count, that there is an attempt made to understand their point of view, that the adults are sympathetic and inquiring rather than close-minded and judging, so many more essential life skills might be learned in school.

Mindfulness in the Classroom—Getting to Know Yourself in School

For six years in the mid-1990s, in South Jordan, Utah, at the Welby Elementary School, a fifth-grade teacher named Cherry Hamrick incorporated mindfulness into her teaching to support her students in not only being themselves but also in knowing themselves better as they engaged in their lessons. She made time each day for the children to focus inwardly. She spoke of it, in her own unique way, as a time to become "intimate with yourself." Now, many classroom teachers incorporate mindfulness practices in different ways into their teaching. Cherry was one of the first, and a true pioneer. What follows may give a glimpse into her creative genius for bringing mindfulness into the classroom.

*

Each day, a different child is in charge of ringing a bell to signal the beginning and the end of this period of quiet time. The rule is, the child decides how long the class is to sit quietly and attend to their breathing, with an upper limit of ten minutes. The children choose how long they practice, and in what ways. In addition to sitting meditation, they sometimes practice a body scan meditation lying on the classroom floor, as well as mindful stretching, walking meditation in the schoolyard, and standing meditation in line before they go into the classroom. Their stress reduction exercises went from seeming "weird" and "strange" to them in the beginning, to being an important part of their day, and something that many of them love and enjoy sharing with their parents and siblings.

In the process of focusing on their breathing and watching their thoughts come and go, they learn that they don't have to react to every thought that comes into their minds, that just because the mind is jumping around and agitated at times doesn't mean they have to jump with it. With practice, they become more comfortable with silence and sitting still. One boy with ADHD (attention deficit/hyperactivity disorder), after years of problems in the lower grades, was able over the course of a year to learn to sit still and be relatively comfortable and focus on the flow of his breathing for up to ten minutes at a time. His ability to concentrate in the classroom changed dramatically, and for the first time he was accepted by his peers and teachers. His mother told me (jkz) this one day when I visited the classroom. This boy led a ten-minute sitting meditation for the class, including some visiting parents, giving the instructions himself as we sat in silence.

Learning at a young age to relax into silence and stillness within oneself can be extremely valuable in balancing out and dealing with the stimulation and outward orientation of the school day. Among other things, children can discover how to tap into their innate ability to settle into focused attention and inhabit a broader awareness— thereby being more present and better able to learn and participate in the life of the class. One of Ms. Hamrick's students, an eleven-year-old girl, wrote to me, saying:

Doing meditation has become more of a habit at home for me, and I will be doing this for the rest of my life. While I was doing meditation at first, and an itch came, I would say "feeling, feeling" to myself, but after one minute, I would find myself scratching it. But now I don't scratch it because now I can be with it long enough that it just goes away. In my meditation, I've also noticed that my breathing has become deeper and I'm more focused on it. In yoga, I've noticed that I get more energy than before, and I think it's because I'm more mindful on what I'm doing. Because of meditation and yoga, I don't rush everything I do like I used to.

Ms. Hamrick didn't just bring mindfulness-based stress reduction into the classroom. She integrated mindfulness in one imaginative way or another into virtually every aspect of the curriculum, including math, English, science, and geography. She encouraged her students to use their whole selves in their learning. They approached whatever subject they were studying so that they developed not only their cognitive and information-processing skills but also their intuition, their feelings, and their body awareness. In this way, they were engaged in learning the basics of what is now called *emotional intelligence*, as well as developing greater enthusiasm for learning.

A teacher in the school wrote, describing his experience of sharing an open classroom with Ms. Hamrick:

The attitude and climate in her classroom was very impressive, especially as I had not heretofore experienced anything like it before. I became aware of certain vocabulary she used to describe things...She referred to what she was trying to attain as a "functional classroom."

I noticed a peaceful atmosphere in her classroom with the students cooperating and discussing their work together. Talking was encouraged; but only work-related talk and "feeling" talk was allowed. There was genuine interest and concern among the students and the teacher. They practiced talking about feelings and processing them on a daily basis. I noticed the students grow in their self-esteem and their regard for human life as well as all life in general.

The students seemed genuinely happier and more content in the classroom setting than I had ever observed or experienced myself. They expressed their love with appropriate touching (hugs), and they knew how to resolve conflict and problem solve in a loving, caring fashion rather than in a hostile or abusive fashion.

Ms. Hamrick also taught the students how to focus and how to get in touch with their own breathing, and how to control their own lives with that technique. They seemed to be able to work better during the day after a few moments of meditative preparation in the morning. We taught in an open classroom situation, and their ability to focus and not be distracted by all of the noise in that type of environment is a tribute to Ms. Hamrick's application of her training and drive.

Ms. Hamrick described in a letter to me (jkz) a trying time when her class had to move temporarily to a new space while renovations were conducted during the school year:

The fifth grade teachers have all been commenting on the disruption of this move and the radical behavior changes in their students. Actually, the comments about poor behavior can be heard throughout the school. The first day was chaotic for most teachers. I found our daily [mindfulness] practice to have paved the way for some simply beautiful days [in the new environment]....

Our first day of the move was peaceful, with attitudes focusing in on working together as a classroom....While the school was going crazy with teachers and students making efforts to tour their surroundings to find out where everything was located, the Rainbow Riders simply wanted to break in their classroom with what they refer to as "their feeling." They wanted to sit together in the "feeling" they experience when they meditate together. They love the saturated serenity they experience together. They are cute about saying it is something that is hard to explain. They insist that it isn't "words," which is frustrating for most adults if they want an explanation. The students say it is something that has to be felt, and "it didn't come to them for a while and it happens best when they are together."

That first day of the move, I just sat back and let them lead the way. I do that a lot because it gives me the sense of where their understanding and process is really at. They were not interested in knowing where everything was located, just the essentials like the restrooms and drinking fountain. They simply wanted to connect with each other and get involved with our own classroom. I waited until 11 a.m. and I asked them to let me know when they wanted a tour of the school. They simply smiled and said they were all okay. They said, "I could show them the cafeteria at lunch, but that we weren't there yet." The students continued to explain to me politely that I was "using my forecasting talent" and that for now it would be better to stay in this minute of time. I said, "Oh, okay," and wondered what they must think of me. One boy [the one characterized as having ADHD] was upset at the explanation and said, "Don't rescue her thinking. She will figure it out."

We are on our second week [in the new space] and they still have only wanted to see the essentials and the rooms they need at the time. I am loving the results of our practice. I have continued to ask them to tell me when they want to go on a tour and they have said that it might be nice to tour the school upon leaving. They have commented on what they see as "the other classes are caught up in a lot of things that they really don't need and are not focusing in on being and working with themselves or each other." P. said, "They do a lot of running around always trying to get something and it never stops."

These children, under the guidance of a highly skilled and deeply motivated, imaginative, and daring teacher, learned to focus inwardly. As a consequence, they got to know themselves better and experienced working together in ways that were meaningful to them and deeply authentic.

✢

Cherry Hamrick was ahead of her time. Now, almost twenty years later, teachers across the country and in other countries are bringing mindfulness practices into many aspects of the school day. Many different programs and curricula have been developed and are currently being implemented and researched. They aim to promote increased self-awareness, attention, concentration, and pro-social behaviors, including increased empathy and understanding of others. In making such practices an intimate and seamless part of the classroom experience, children are given practical opportunities to get to know and explore the terrain of their own being. This constitutes a promising and potentially revolutionary shift in primary and secondary education.

*

As we taste some of the benefits of greater mindfulness in our own lives as parents, we may find ourselves wanting to teach our children various mindfulness practices, including how to meditate. If so, it is important to be aware of how attached we might be to imagined beneficial outcomes of the practice for them. Our children are very good at sensing when we have hidden agendas. Examining our motivations and intentions is key if we hope to introduce mindfulness in age-appropriate ways that might be helpful to them.

There are times when potentially beneficial applications of mindfulness may indeed naturally arise with our children. In those moments, drawing on our own experience and practice, we might, for example, suggest to our young children to be aware of and look very closely at what "color" their pain is and how it changes from moment to moment when they have hurt themselves, or show them how to "float" on the waves of their breath as if in a little boat when they are having a hard time relaxing or going to sleep, or to see if they can think of times when their minds "waved" because of what other people did or said when their feelings have been hurt.

It seems wise to take our cues from our children and their expressions of interest at different ages. Ultimately, the best teaching we can do is by example, through our own commitment to be present, and our sensitivity to them. When we practice formally, either sitting or lying down, we embody silence and stillness. Our children see us deeply focused and become familiar with this way of being. Many of the insights and attitudes that develop from our mindfulness practice will naturally filter into the culture of the family and affect our children in ways that they may in time find useful in their own lives.

PART NINE

Limits and Openings

Expectations

The unexamined expectations we have of our children can color how we see things and influence our parental choices and the actions we take. While some of those expectations can be useful and positive for a child's growth and development and promote self-confidence, agency, and a sense of responsibility, others may be limiting and confining, causing unnecessary suffering for both our children and ourselves.

We all have expectations—of ourselves and of others, and we are especially likely to have them of our children: ideas about how they should behave, how they should look or dress, how well they should do in school, what kinds of relationships they should have, what they should be doing at this age or stage of their development, and so on. As you've probably seen in many aspects of your life, close on the heels of expectations usually come judgments of some kind. When we bring mindful attention to our thoughts and feelings, we see that expectations and their associated but often tacit assumptions and judgments are an ever-present feature of our inner landscape. They are most problematic when we hold on to them rigidly and forget that they are just thoughts, often freighted with intense emotion, and not necessarily true. Mindfulness brought to our expectations can therefore be extremely illuminating and liberating.

If we start off by examining the expectations we have of ourselves, we may find that we harbor quite a range of them, and that we often judge ourselves harshly when we don't "measure up." Some common expectations we may have are that we should always do things well, or "correctly," be successful in our work, be a wonderful parent and a devoted and conscientious son or daughter, and be liked and respected by other people.

Judging ourselves harshly when we feel that we haven't lived up to our own expectations can elicit a range of emotions, depending of course on the specific circumstances and our own life history. These can include shame, disappointment, embarrassment, anger, humiliation, depression, and feelings of inadequacy. Our children can experience similar feelings when they feel judged. For this reason, it is important to be more aware of our expectations and how we express them, the purposes they serve, and the ways that they may affect our children, both positively and negatively.

Our expectations will be different for different children and at different ages. They may also be somewhat different for boys and for girls. Some may have to do with the day-to-day workings of life in the family, such as who is responsible for doing what, and some are more about how we relate to each other. We can also carry more loaded and potentially problematic, often unconscious and unspoken expectations, for example, that a child will always be obedient, or defiant, or shy, or outgoing. We may mean no harm in doing this, but we may unwittingly end up putting our children in conceptual boxes that can be both confining and disregarding. Again, the real problem comes from a lack of awareness of how easily we can be caught up with our own ideas and opinions and not actually see our children in their fullness and complexity.

As part of our ongoing cultivation of mindfulness, we can remind ourselves from time to time to bring awareness to our thoughts and, in doing so, see into the expectations we hold and the emotions associated with them. It also helps to ask ourselves specific questions, such as: What in fact *are* our expectations for our children? Are they realistic and age-appropriate? Do they contribute to a child's growth and agency? Are we expecting too much or too little? Are we setting up our child to experience unnecessary stress and failure? Do our expectations and how we express them enhance a child's sense of self, or do they constrict, limit, or belittle? Do they contribute to a child's well-being, to feeling loved and cared for and accepted? Are they congruent with this particular child? How do they relate to a child's unique temperament, learning style, and interests? There is enormous creativity just in engaging in this kind of inquiry, both through questioning in this way and in bringing awareness to thoughts as thoughts, emotions as emotions, and judgments as judgments.

It can be helpful to examine whether our expectations take into account the many facets of each child's nature and whether they allow them room to try out different behaviors. For instance, can we allow our children to express their angry feelings as long as they don't harm others? Can we see that expecting a child to always be compassionate and loving, and then expressing disappointment when he or she shows anger or self-interest, may be neither compassionate nor loving?

If you want your children to be generous,
you must first allow them to be selfish.
If you want them to be disciplined,
you must first allow them to be spontaneous.
If you want them to be hard-working,
you must first allow them to be lazy.
This is a subtle distinction,
and hard to explain to those who criticize you.

A quality cannot be fully learned
without understanding its opposite.

NO. 36: "OPPOSITES ARE NECESSARY,"
The Parent's Tao Te Ching

We can practice becoming more skillful in expressing what we expect of our children in matter-of-fact and clear ways. Over time we can support them in being aware of and developing their own expectations of themselves and others that are both realistic and healthy.

*

I (mkz) remember very clearly that my expectations for our first child changed when we had another baby. I expected him to be more responsible and independent in ways that I hadn't before the arrival of his younger sister. The child that had been our "baby" was suddenly seen in a different light compared with the new infant, and our expectations for him started multiplying. Perhaps this common phenomenon comes about in part because it makes our life with a new baby easier, or it may be a by-product of some kind of biological species protection, where we fall in love with the new baby and the older sibling loses his magical aura, because he doesn't need us in the same way a baby does to survive.

When I see other parents having similar expectations of their older children, I wish I could remind them that their two-year-old is still a baby in many ways; that their four-year-old is just that—a four-year-old; that their six-year-old still needs to be held at times, to feel their adoration and loving energy; and that though their eight-year-old can take on more responsibility and may benefit from doing so, he still needs hugs and time alone with them, to be free to still be a child.

Our children also have expectations of us. They may expect us to be on time, or they may expect us to always be late; to be reliable or to be unreliable; to be available for them, or not to be available; to immediately get angry, or to be understanding. Their expectations of us are based on their experience of how we have acted in the past. They can reveal to us our own behavior, to which we may be blind. This gives us a chance to change in ways that may be healthier for them, and for us as well.

When we suddenly become grumpy or short-tempered and speak in a sharp manner, it can be confusing or upsetting to a child. If we can acknowledge in that moment that we are tired and having a hard time, we give him a framework for understanding our behavior. When we act in an unexpected way and we are able to name it for what it is, we are making an unpredictable and confusing universe more ordered and understandable. Then children are not as likely to blame themselves or to feel tense and anxious when a parent's mood changes abruptly. It also teaches them something useful about people in general, and they may eventually come to see aspects of their own behavior more clearly as they get older.

If a child accidentally breaks something, she may expect her parents to get angry about it and be surprised when they aren't. It may be that in the past, her parents got angry in similar situations. However, on this occasion, the parents respond with greater understanding and acceptance, because they are making an effort to be more aware of their own behavior and its effects on their child, trying to keep in mind what is most important. In doing so, they are embodying greater kindness and understanding, breaking out of the realm of limited expectations that they had for their daughter, and, in the process, changing the expectations she has of them.

Our expectations of our children will vary to some degree

depending on the pressures we are under and the depth of the resources we feel we have to draw upon in that moment. When we ourselves are stressed and feeling overwhelmed, we might find ourselves wanting affection and sympathy from our children. While it is very human to have those kinds of feelings and needs, we need to remind ourselves that it is not our children's job to take care of us in this way. That doesn't mean that they will not be compassionate or understanding at times. Sometimes children respond with tremendous kindness and sympathy, but often they just want what they want and they aren't interested in our problems, nor should they be. Nor are young children interested in long explanations with lots of words. But it does help them to know that our behavior is connected to how we are feeling, just as their behavior is connected to how they are feeling.

When children are little, there are some basic expectations and rules that we establish, such as "You're not allowed to cross the street without an adult"; "No matter how angry you are, you're not allowed to hit people"; "You need to speak in a respectful way." We also might expect them to have good manners at meals, when greeting people, and so forth. Each of us has to decide what is important to us and what best serves our children and the family as a whole. Being clear about what we feel is unacceptable behavior and what our expectations are is another way of nurturing our children. Small children particularly feel safe and secure, and a sense of relief when our expectations are consistent and clear and supported through our setting limits when they are needed.

As children get older, they start to assume more responsibility for the things they need to do and the ways in which they behave. It helps them when we hold them accountable for their actions and let them experience the natural consequences of what they have done.

At times, we may find our expectations are in direct conflict with those of our children. When one of our children didn't want us to attend an event at her school, we were surprised and disappointed. We wanted so much to go, and our child wanted to experience it by herself. She wanted it to be *her* experience.

When our son was going off to college for the first time, I (mkz) wanted and expected to drive him there. As his mother, I wanted to see his new home and be a part of this important transition. He wanted something different. He wanted his friend, with whom he had traveled across the country that past summer, to drive him. He wanted to arrive at college as an independent person, not as a son being taken to school by his parents. After he told us this, for some moments I was torn between strong feelings of disappointment and my effort to see it from his point of view. Ultimately, understanding why it was so important for him to go in his own way helped me let go of my long-held expectation and be able to say with sincerity and acceptance, "I understand why you want to go with your friend, and I'm fine with it."

In such situations, children are hoping that their parents will see things from their point of view. They want our understanding and acceptance. Sometimes parents are operating only out of the framework of their own needs and desires, not their children's. It is helpful if we can hold both in awareness, see what is best for our children within the context of what is possible for us, and when necessary, let go of our own strong attachments to how we expect things to be.

We give our children a great if unseen gift when we wrestle with our own expectations and are able to consciously let go of those that don't serve our children well or aren't helpful to their growth and well-being. This is an important part of the practice of mindful parenting. When we are able to do this, the atmosphere in the family becomes lighter, there is a greater feeling of spaciousness and balance, and more room for everybody to grow.

Surrender

Just when I've (mkz) been through several particularly high-pressure, jam-packed weeks, my seven-year-old daughter gets sick. Her face is flushed; her head hurts. I'm straining to be free, and suddenly I'm on an even shorter leash.

I'm angry and frustrated, feeling pushed to the limit. I don't want this to be happening. I want to withdraw, crawl into bed myself and shut the door, but I can see she's feeling awful. She wants me. She needs me. My heart goes out to her. She's not doing this to torture me. She can't help it—she's sick. I feel myself take a deep breath. I feel myself beginning to surrender to what is needed and put aside my expectations and lists of things I had planned to do.

The fever intensifies her experience of everything. Her eyes are bothered by the light, so the curtains are pulled, leaving her room dark and peaceful. Occasionally she sleeps. When she's awake, she doesn't want to be alone. I sit with her. I get her a cold cloth for her forehead. I bring her tea and toast. I read to her. And as I do these things, there is a comfort in being able to do what I can to help her feel better. The moments of reading to her, or just sitting with her, holding her hand, have a quiet richness. She'll look at me with pleasure as I read to her, or she'll say, "I'm happy we're together." Her eyes are especially bright, her face almost translucent. I think about how different her day would be if she were in school, and I'm struck by how this "sick" time can be so nourishing. I've often noticed my children emerge from illness with a different look to them, as if they've somehow grown, changed in this crucible of intense heat we call fever, and in their retreat into quiet and being cared for.

Of course, there are moments when she is irritable, angry, and demanding. Those moments are my laboratory. They put me to the test. Will I take it personally and get mad at her, or will I remember how it feels to be sick and be sympathetic and receptive? Can I let her show frustration and misery without judging or criticizing her? Can I let go of my expectations for what I wanted the day to be and surrender to the necessity and the beauty of what has emerged?

Limits and Openings

Studies suggest that when parents are either very permissive and provide few if any boundaries or limits, or are authoritarian, rigid, and domineering, the children invariably suffer and are less likely to develop their own healthy agency. When we treat our children with respect within a clear framework of appropriate limits and boundaries, they tend to grow up more confident and secure in themselves. Within the context of a caring, connected, and engaged relationship, experiencing limits can be the source of significant openings for our children rather than arbitrary barriers we throw in their paths.

It is not always clear what limits and structure might be most beneficial for a particular child in a particular moment. In general, the limit setting in our family was around things that we saw as having a potentially negative impact on our children's well-being, such as TV, junk food, movies, video games, as well as around behaviors that affected the well-being of others, such as disrespect, hitting, and name-calling. When we set limits, we tried to do so in ways that felt right to us and fair to our children.

But of course, parental decisions and limits often don't feel fair to our children. Recognizing this, we can be a grounded and firm yet empathic presence as they grapple with strong feelings of frustration and anger in the course of coming up against a limit that we have established. Certainly, as we noted earlier, life itself often presents obstacles to children getting what they want and many occasions for experiencing disappointment and loss. Child development experts Gordon Neufeld and Gabor Maté refer to such experiences as hitting "the wall of futility." They posit that this process of coming up against an immovable object or situation is essential for a child to learn that there are limits to his or her ability to change particular situations and to experience the consequent feelings of sadness and loss on the way to adapting to the actuality of how things are. Coming to terms with things as they are is the essence of healing. But to get to feelings of sadness and ultimately acceptance, as pointed out by Susan Stiffelman in her book *Parenting Without Power Struggles*, our children first have to go through a natural progression akin to Elisabeth Kübler-Ross's stages of grief, from disbelief that they can't get their way (denial), to anger, to attempting to bargain or negotiate, to finally experiencing their sadness. When we engage in bargaining with them, we derail this important process. If they can express their anger and then also come to feel their sadness, there is then the possibility of their coming to some acceptance. Over time, our child learns to come to terms with and adapt to not always being able to get what he or she wants.

An essential element of encountering the wall of futility is that our child experience us as a reliable and sympathetic presence. Having a healthy and trusting connection with a parent allows a child to feel safe enough to be vulnerable and feel the depth of his or her sorrow. If we understand how important it is for our children to learn to come to terms with unmovable limits and loss, whether imposed by us or as a natural part of life, it helps us to not get stuck in bargaining with them and unwittingly undermine their ability and need to experience their feelings of sadness, and finally come to accept what they cannot change.

Everything we have talked about in terms of mindful parenting is oriented toward developing our children's agency, self-awareness, and resilience in the face of obstacles. Of course, it is important that our children develop confidence in their ability to change what does need changing in the world around them, without being deterred by apparent limits and obstacles. But understanding the importance and value to our children of coming up against the wall of futility, it is easier to stand firm in our resolve when it comes to setting healthy and necessary limits in the family.

Seeing which limits serve our children and which ones don't requires discernment on our part. With some issues, if we are too rigid, we may inadvertently encourage our children's preoccupation with whatever they are not getting. As our children get older, the stakes get higher. If we are too rigid, they may stop trusting us, or lie to us, or withdraw completely. On the other hand, if we are too loose with them, letting them do and have whatever they want before they are capable of self-regulating, we soon start to see the negative effects on them. These can take the form of exhaustion, tension, irritability, fearfulness, anxiety, aggression, poor judgment, out-of-control behaviors, and an overall imbalance.

When our children were little, we tried to give them freedom to explore, to pursue the things they were interested in, to try on different behaviors. When they did things that were harmful or potentially dangerous, we tried to keep our responses limited to those specific behaviors. We tried to let them know, in a matter-of-fact way, that what they were doing was not okay. At the same time, they could feel from us that *they* were okay, that our love and our acceptance of them was a constant.

At times, our limit setting came out of anger, the feeling of "That's the last straw!" But more often, it came out of what we were seeing and sensing and out of simple common sense: concern for how much sleep they were getting, or for what they were eating, or for their safety. Another way to look at establishing limits of one kind or another is to see it in terms of creating a framework or container, whether it's expectations we have around bedtime or mealtime, or basic manners or chores that need to be shared. Over time, gradually they learned how to take care of themselves and, eventually, how to make their own healthy choices.

With older children, we may have to step in and impose some kind of limit on their activities in the face of strong peer and societal pressures. This requires considerable perseverance, skill, and some degree of wisdom. Parenting teenagers can be emotionally exhausting. Our effort, engagement, and patience are as necessary during those years as when we were getting up in the night with them when they were babies.

There may be times with our school-age children when we find ourselves wanting to say something like, "I won't tolerate this!" in certain situations in which our expectations and their behaviors are wildly divergent. Our protestations can come out with a strong self-righteous tone, which only compounds the problems. At the same time, underneath that, we may be feeling completely helpless to influence the situation. For after we pronounce that we won't tolerate the particular behavior, then what? All of the relatively simple strategies that may have worked when our children were little, like distraction and redirection, or physically removing them from the problematic situation, are not appropriate or possible with older children.

Whatever we decide to do or say, it always helps when we are able to be grounded and in touch with our own energetic state and emotions by bringing our awareness to any tension in the body and to our breathing, intentionally slowing it down and allowing it to deepen. In doing this, we can calm our own nervous system, which inevitably has an effect on our child. When we are present and in touch with ourselves, our children can locate us. Our presence not only supports but embodies relationality in such a moment. Effective communication cannot happen without it. We might, for example, bring awareness to our tone of voice. We might try putting aside the stern, often loud, hard-edged voice that seems to come so naturally to us in such moments, saying the same thing more quietly and matter-of-factly. In these difficult moments, it can be a useful practice to reconnect with what is deepest and best in ourselves, and remind ourselves of what is most important.

Ultimately, our children's response to any limits on their behavior depends in part on how connected they feel to us or to the family as a whole, and the degree to which they sense the limits are coming from our concern and caring—even if they are furious about them at the time.

*

Like many parents who have a child in middle school, there was a time when we were suffering the negative effects of one of our daughters spending all her free time on the telephone. What had started harmlessly enough developed into a situation, where from the second she came home from school to the moment she went to bed, she was either on the phone or anticipating a phone call. Anything she did could be interrupted at any moment, including her homework. Eventually, despite her assurances that her homework was not being neglected, she just didn't have the quiet space to really concentrate on the difficult work she had, and her schoolwork suffered. This unlimited use of the phone also had a negative effect on her relationship to her family, so much so that she began to relate to us as if we were strangers and in an angry and distant manner.

We realized that just telling her that her phone time would be limited would have been autocratic and would have created more distance between us. We decided instead to call a family meeting in which everybody got to speak without interruption and say how they were feeling about the phone issue. Hearing each other, we were all better able to understand each other's point of view. We each said what we could or couldn't live with, and we eventually came up with a phone schedule that was a compromise with which we were all satisfied.

After a few days of having uninterrupted time at dinner and an hour afterward to do her homework, she admitted that she "kind of liked" the new phone schedule. We could see she felt a certain sense of relief at having a quiet, uninterrupted time for herself. It was something she wouldn't have initiated. That had to come from us.

After another week or two, she inevitably started to try to bend and change the compromise we had come up with. She told us she wanted to start on the phone a half hour earlier and we said she could if she ended a half hour earlier. Not being willing to do this, she went back to our original agreement. Being aware of the positive effect of the new phone limits on both our daughter and the family as a whole made it much easier to stand our ground.

Whether the issue is phone time, texting, social networking, or something else, there will always be special situations and times when we need to be flexible, and it is important to be aware of them. In some ways, this makes parenting harder, because our children know the possibility exists for negotiation around some issues, and they are likely to look for a window of opportunity to bend the rules. They can be masters at arguing their case, veritable trial lawyers at times, and it is hard not to take this in as an admirable trait, even as it threatens to thwart our authority. But in general, and especially with young children, learning that no means no and that there is no room for negotiation or our changing our mind creates clear expectations and a dependable and secure family environment.

Some children need more limits than others around particular issues. Bedtime for an early riser will be different for the child who is naturally a night owl. A child who is a good reader will have more resources to rely on at night than a child who finds reading difficult. Children who are able to self-regulate more easily and are less impulsive will naturally need less limit setting from their parents.

Even as we notice changes or shifts in our own tolerances and limit setting with different children at different ages or in different circumstances, part of mindful parenting is to continually reexamine whether what we are doing and thinking is in our child's best interest and to ask ourselves if there might be a better way that we are not seeing.

As our children become teenagers, the road we travel as parents twists and turns, the visibility decreases, and things are not always what they seem. They need their privacy, but that privacy means we don't always know what's going on, what they are really doing, what they are really involved in. Their focus can easily shift to "What can I get away with?" rather than "What is in my best interest?" Problematic signs in older children can be much easier to ignore and deny than the cries of a baby. We may find ourselves tempted to say yes to things we want to say no to, both to avoid a fight and because we may fear that saying no will just push them further away.

Teenagers can benefit from our communicating what we are seeing and sensing and what our concerns are—what we perceive as possible dangers to their well-being. On the occasions when we feel we have to say no to things they want from us, if we are not mindful, that *no* may carry many other tacit messages such as "We don't trust you," "You're bad," or "You have no judgment." We need to be aware of these feelings in ourselves if they are present, and of the automatic reactions they trigger, so we don't create unnecessary distance and alienation in moments that are already difficult enough.

If we say to a teenage daughter, "No, you can't be alone with this boy in his house," her response may be, "Don't you trust me?" We might, with some thoughtfulness, respond by saying, "We don't trust the situation. It's too easy to feel pressured into doing things that are potentially dangerous or that you may feel badly about afterward." This response has at least the potential to be seen not as an arbitrary exercise of power but as a respectful and non-naïve assessment of a situation that does not impugn the integrity of our child. She may not see our point of view and may reject it completely and be resentful and angry. Nevertheless, in that moment, the parent is pointing to something real and understands that this one interaction, however it turns out, is bound to be one of many such encounters. Choosing, with some degree of wisdom, what situations we place ourselves in is one of those life lessons that takes time and experience to learn.

*

A friend of ours got a call from her daughter saying, "Mom, I'm in New York City." This was after many discussions with her daughter as to why she did not want her, at sixteen years of age, to go to New York from Boston on her own to visit a school that she was interested in. Her daughter told her that she wasn't able to reach the person she thought she would stay with and called another young woman she had met recently at a local gathering, and was now staying with her. How might this mother react to such a fait accompli? How can she work with what she is given?

She wisely took a moment and assessed the situation. She realized that her daughter was trying to take care of herself and had been thoughtful enough to call her so that she wouldn't worry. Her daughter was already in New York. No amount of anger about it would change that. She told her daughter, "I'm not angry right now, but I reserve the right to get mad later." In this way, she left her options open for dealing with her emotional upset at a better time. She proceeded to ask her daughter questions about her safety and if she had the things she needed to complete her trip and return home. She realized that her daughter was trying to do something that was very important to her. Although she disagreed with what she did, at the same time she was able to appreciate her daughter's courage and resourcefulness. By remaining clear about her own feelings, but also thinking deeply about her daughter's needs, this mother was able to be understanding and not let their conflicting positions come between them.

*

The inevitable challenge of parenting is that the older our children are, the scarier things can become for us as they move out into the world and encounter potentially dangerous situations over which we have little or none of the control we had when they were little. One important but very difficult aspect of our inner work as parents during this period is to be mindful of our own fears and anxieties. This at least gives us a chance not to get so caught up in them that they completely cloud our vision and sensibilities and make it impossible to see what is going on with our children, or to communicate effectively with them.

This is a time when we can build on the work we have done in the past to create trust and, most importantly, a shared feeling of connectedness within the family. With this as a foundation, it becomes possible, if not always easy, to talk with our children about such things as the costs and risks of alcohol, drugs, and unprotected sex (emotionally as well as physically).

Having more and more freedom and faced with all sorts of choices, some of which are destructive and dangerous, and sometimes with strong pressure from peers, it becomes essential that older children develop their own capacity for self-awareness and self-protection. This includes the ability to be in touch with what they are feeling in difficult and potentially harmful situations that may elicit highly conflicted feelings, and to learn to ask themselves what it is they really need. With some self-awareness, they are more likely to make healthier choices and be better able to set their own limits and boundaries. Developing mindfulness in this domain is a process that unfolds over time. Increasingly, schools are offering mindfulness training as part of the curriculum from kindergarten through high school to develop, among other capacities, just this kind of self-awareness and emotional intelligence.

Many activities naturally build self-awareness, along with self-discipline and self-confidence. Among these are martial arts, sports, yoga, dance, theater, painting, rock climbing, wilderness camping, journal writing. They provide concrete occasions for children to experience limits, real and imagined, and the satisfaction of openings and breakthroughs. An inner experience of self-efficacy and mastery in one area will inevitably spill over into other areas of their lives. Ultimately, our children reach an age when they have to rely on their own awareness and good sense and past experience as they go out on their own and encounter the challenge of continuing to grow as their lives unfold.

Minding Our Own Business

Don't draw another's bow,
Don't ride another's horse,
Don't discuss another's faults,
Don't explore another's affairs.

WU-MEN,

THIRTEENTH-CENTURY

CHINESE ZEN MASTER

"Where did you go?"
"Out."
"What did you do?"
"Nothing."

FAMILY DIALOGUE

It is easy for parents to fall into thinking that we need to know everything that is going on with our children, including in their inner lives. It's only natural that we feel this way, since we are so close to them when they are little. We are with them as they discover and learn about themselves and the world, and experience joy and sorrow. But as they get older, it becomes essential that we leave them psychic room for privacy and for sharing with us what they choose to, when they choose to. This itself is an act of lovingkindness. Then, when they do need or want to share something with us, perhaps they will feel that they can trust us and that we might understand their concerns.

This requires presence and availability on our part and a healthy resolve to mind our own business. It is a delicate balance, requiring a high degree of sensitivity and discernment, and patience.

Of course, since every child is different and every parent is different, and no two circumstances are the same, we need to be aware of the current situation in the family and in our own minds. In order to mind our own business, we will have to know what our true business is as a parent—and what it isn't.

It's not just a matter of knowing either. Patience and presence without prying, probing, or being overbearing can contribute to our having a more positive relationship than if the children feel that we are always minding their business, wanting to know more than they care to share, and broadcasting hurt feelings when we feel left out or cut off.

We might find it enlightening to think back to when we were adolescents. At some point, were there not things that we needed to keep to ourselves, things that were just not our parents' business, and never would be or could be, because they were emerging experiences in our own private inner world?

Our child may tell us at some point that he is in love or is going to get married. We may know something of the outer and have a sense of the inner, but we can never fully know the inner and rightfully so, because it is not ours to know. Our job is to take care of our own inner business, the business of our own mind, our own body, our own relationships, and our own life, according the same freedom and respect to our children as they make the transition from total dependency as small children to independent and interdependent adults.

The quality and warmth of our connections with our children will be proportional to how much we continue to do our own inner work and keep a sense of appropriate boundaries and our willingness to have our older children figure things out for themselves and keep their own council. Presence and openness, love and interest, and a willingness to respond rather than react create a more spacious environment of respect and trust between parent and child. This is part of the business that it *is* ours to mind.

It's Always Your Move

After watching a movie with both girls, my older one goes off to sleep, but the younger one needs something else before bedtime. She gets into her pajamas and asks for a story, then changes her mind and asks whether we might play chess on her bed. One game, we agree, and then lights off and to sleep.

We will have to be very careful not to upset the pieces on this rollout board on top of the mattress. But first, she asks me, princess-like, if I will get her a tangerine, "and also, Daddy, a hot water bottle" to warm up her bed on this cold November night. I am happy to get them for her, once I can find the stopper for the hot water bottle. Then I go and get the chess set.

We have been playing chess again for a few weeks now. Sometimes she asks me, sometimes I ask her. For the longest time, I couldn't get her to play, but Myla thought to get a bigger board and a set of bigger pieces than the ones we started with, and also one of those dual chess clocks that you hit each time you make a move. The clock definitely adds an extra something to the game. It's as if you sign off on each move, affirming that it is really what you mean. She loves playing with the clock, and so do I, although we never do look at the time elapsed. It's that definitive banging of it after each move that appeals.

We settle into our nocturnal game. She has black. She always chooses black. I checkmate her early. We are both surprised. I myself didn't realize it was checkmate at first. She had castled and I brought my queen right down to her king, with my bishop backing it up, and somehow, none of her pieces could take me or interfere. It happened so fast, we decide to play "just one more."

I try to set up a similar opening in this game. She soon sees what I am doing. I can tell, because she moves just the right pawn to just the right place to make my attempt futile. With the tiniest bit of help at a few crucial places, she checkmates me just one move away from my checkmating her. It is so much fun, we decide to play just one more.

I am tired by this point, and there is a major current of reluctance in me to play any more—that is, until we start playing. Then that falls away in the energy of the moment.

This time, we wind up with an elaborate endgame in the center of the board involving both queens in adjacent positions with both kings backing them up, with some rooks and bishops right in close and our kings fleeing through openings here and there as we pursue each other, checking and then losing the checking advantage back and forth. It is wonderful, and like nothing either of us has seen before. She is playing lying down by this time, her head on the water bottle at board level.

We sometimes make amused or suspicious eye contact while playing, silently catching what the other is attempting, or experiencing the sheer joy of engaging over this funny world of elegant archetypes in plastic on sixty-four squares. She never wants me to point out anything, but sometimes I like to let her take back a move if it means losing something important, like her queen, or missing a great opportunity that I know she isn't seeing. And she lets me do that... and then won't want to hear another word.

She wants to figure things out herself, and in each game, I see her seeing more and making better moves. She learns so fast from her experience, much faster than I am learning. She catches me in mindless mistakes and is sometimes gracious, sometimes less inclined toward forgiving. She is learning to see my moves and where they might be going, and how she might interfere with them, as well as forming her own strategies for pressuring my position and moving the game along. There is a spatial wisdom growing here. I can see it in her. Perception is challenged to expand. Risks need to be seen and weighed. Plans need to be formulated but also changed over and over again, in response to changing situations on the board. Strategy and tactics develop of necessity.

Every game is an infinite number of possibilities narrowing themselves slowly down to one inevitable end, the one that we get. But we can and do sometimes replay different possible ends. It's like role-playing alternative scenarios in a personal dilemma. We see the elements involved and their combinations and our own power to make choices and direct the flow of things. We visualize and actually explore different approaches, and see the consequences that unfold from each. All sorts of psychotherapies make use of role-playing to sort out emotional dilemmas and the different ways we might navigate through difficulties. Imagine beginning to learn this while playing a game, and developing the inner repertoire of seeing alternative openings and moves that will further the unfolding of our lives in ways that might embody an element of wisdom.

After this game ends, the flow of things is definitely into sleep. She asks if I will stay with her. I shut off the light and sit on her bed. She is asleep in moments. I know it from her breathing, which suddenly deepens and gets quieter.

Most of the time at this age, if I ask, "Can I put you to bed?" she says "NO!" So her invitation is very special for me, and I feel that it is special for her as well, a chance to revisit a move she used to make a lot.

I breathe with her for a few more minutes and then leave quietly, closing her door.

*

Sometimes we won't mind looking for the stopper of the hot water bottle or its counterpart in our lives when it's our turn to make a move. At other times, usually lots of other times, well, we *will* mind looking for the stopper of the hot water bottle, we won't want to get a tangerine, or extend ourselves in any way. It's too late, we're too tired, we just want our child to go to bed, and we *won't* want to play chess, or anything else.

But, in times when we choose, just as an experiment, to give to our children right in that moment in which we are most inclined not to, and instead of clamping down or closing up, make ourselves available and willingly engage with them, we may find that an entire world opens up for them *and* for us—a shared world that in retrospect we would not want to have missed, could not have predicted, and that might be more important to us than anything else we could have done in spite of our fatigue or how busy and pressed for time we thought we were.

In making the choice to attend to a child wholeheartedly in such a moment, we are not acting like her servant (even though it may feel that way sometimes), but more like a true king or queen, a sovereign, rich with time and generous of heart.

But let's face it. Although we are a sovereign in our role as a parent, at some stages more than others, we also *are* a servant, just as a wise king or a queen or any leader is a true servant of the realm. And it is worth being one in that sense.

It is a tricky business. It is not about our giving limitlessly nor about spending endless time with them. Giving ourselves fully to our children—in other words being limitlessly present for them in terms of our being, which in its deepest nature, as we have seen, is limitless—runs so much against the grain of our society that it is virtually taboo to even talk about. And yet, it is important to talk about, examine, and experiment with as part of our own mindfulness practice. It amounts to making new moves on our chessboard, sometimes bold moves we may never have conceived of before, and learning from what comes of them, as the world—as it so often does when we take the initiative—opens to make room for our offerings.

You are the notes, we are the flute
We are the mountains, you are the sounds coming down.
We are the pawns and kings and rooks
you set out on a board: we win or we lose.
We are lions rolling and unrolling on flags.
Your invisible wind carries us through the world.

RUMI (TRANSLATED BY ROBERT BLY)

Branch Points

Did you ever stop and think of how things might have turned out differently in your life had it not been for the remarkable confluence of unfathomable, minuscule, seemingly random events that so influence our lives and proffer momentous potential openings, as well as limitations? Had I (jkz) decided to go to lunch five minutes earlier or later than I did one December day, or had Myla not run into a friend and fallen into conversation in a particular nearby place, in all likelihood we would never have met. We wouldn't have had the children we did or wound up living the lives we are now living. This points to something precious and mysterious about living itself that may be worth pondering.

Had things not unfolded the way they had, other things would no doubt have happened, and we would now be living other, very different lives. It would also have been a very different me, for the me that I am now is in large measure due to the texture of our relationship together over more than forty-five years, the children we have raised, our grandchildren, and our love for each other.

Life may be generic, but love and beauty are specific. The world continually calls us to celebrate those specifics, in the places where we truly belong and feel most deeply at home. It calls us to celebrate the children we have, the life that is ours to live if we can be here for it and awake to its texture and images and sounds, so that these intimate and always-present aspects of our lives are not merely confined to memories stored away with the photograph albums. Our present actualities are true blessings, and their emergence every day in their unique particulars is nothing short of miraculous.

This observation continually reminds me to hold the virtual "pregnancy" of each and every moment with great reverence and respect. It reminds me that its potential is always momentous, even if we cannot know or foresee the next moment until it arrives, and even if for the most part, so many of our moments seem at first blush only humdrum and bland, and each day seemingly more or less like the last. It is easy to miss the ways in which every moment contains the enormity of the entire universe and can be full of surprises and unthought-of possibilities. It is easy to forget that we can watch them unfold and that we are called to participate in their unfolding. Young children are native to this magical world, in which everything is fresh and new and possible.

Seeing each moment as a potential branch point can be an exceedingly useful way of looking at our lives as they unfold. If, in our own lives, we desire the future to be different in any way, as so often we do with great passion, whether it is to have a better relationship with a child, or make something new happen in our lives, the only time we ever get to act to make it so is the present. For isn't the present actually the future? Isn't today yesterday's future? Here it is already. We have it now, right here.

Seeing the present in this way, we might ask ourselves, How is it? Are we at home here, in this actuality? In this, or any moment of our lives, do we actually know, feel, sense where we are and how we got to this place, to this moment?

The only way to know is to keep our eyes open, and that means all our senses. Even then, knowing may not mean knowing, but rather knowing that we don't know, and yet persisting in keeping the question itself alive because it is interesting and we are curious, and however our lives are right now, they are unfolding now, in this moment. This truly is it.

We know that each moment unfolds out of the preceding one, which colors it in some way. The present moment has a momentum all its own. Our actions always have consequences. If we hope to learn anything, or grow, or express our feelings, or improve the quality of life in the future, *this* really is the only time we ever get to affect the course that the incessant stream of actions and consequences we think of as our lives follows. If we take responsibility for attending to the quality and the possibilities of *this* moment, whether with a child or by ourselves, the next moment will be affected by that awareness, and therefore different.

Mindfulness may thus provide openings that may not have been accessible even the moment before, because the mind is now seeing differently. These openings may have always been here as potential, but their actualizing frequently requires our wholehearted participation. So, when it is time to do the dishes, we do them in that way, with full presence of mind. And that opens up the next possibility. It is the same with everything.

The challenge is to see if we really can embody, fully, the life that is ours to live, with the children that are ours to nurture, right here, right now...and now, and now, and now, each moment, each day, and each night a new beginning, as we encounter and move through light and through darkness.

PART TEN

Darkness and Light

Impermanence

Paddling a canoe across the lake in early morning July in northern Maine, looking for moose while my family sleeps in a lakeside cabin, I (jkz) observe the whirlpools coming off the paddle in the otherwise still water, one from the outside edge of the blade, another off the inside. They spin in opposite directions for a time, slipping behind me as the canoe moves forward. They are just water in motion, separate for a time, their distinct form due to the swirling of the water. As I look back to stay in touch with them, I see that they are soon gone. Their energy of motion passes back into the lake. Others appear with each stroke, each different, unique. They are mesmerizing. Form appearing for a brief moment out of emptiness, due to certain conditions that the lake and my paddle obligingly provide.

To me, these whirlpools are as fascinating as the moose I search for but do not find this morning, and in some ways not too different. Living things, too, appear for brief moments in seemingly separate entities we call bodies, dance in the light of day for a time, and are soon gone. We know life appears in its distinct forms because of certain conditions. We know it is soon gone from those distinct forms and will appear anew elsewhere. We know about death. But we see this particular moose or person as more or less permanent, and its passing takes us by surprise and fills us with fear, or sorrow, or sometimes even horror. Yet we know that its passing is as much a part of the way things are as its arrival. We know that all things are impermanent and fleeting, but we tend to ignore this aspect of things until it is right in our faces.

Several weeks later, I am reminded of this as I look at the pale, emaciated body of a friend dying of lymphoma at fifty, surrounded by family and friends, a shocking almost skeleton with his muscles and tendons exposed in ways we don't see except in death, still able to summon up from somewhere, in spite of his pain and diarrhea and fear-racked, medicated body, the energy to come to a party, lie on the couch, and play with breathtaking virtuosity on the guitar, sending currents of beauty off the strings and into our hearts. His wife and daughter, age eleven, full of life, sit nearby.

I am struck by the poignancy of it all. My children are seeing something they have never seen before. It is not pretty, but it is awe-inspiring, and it is transcendent. We, including his longtime doctor friend at whose house this is taking place, can do little for him other than make him comfortable and honor the life that is still in him.

We cannot stop the process. We find we can hardly even name it, so strong is the impulse to deny or turn away. As his thin fingers pick the strings while the other hand defines the notes, his face contorts with effort. He seems to be transported in these brief moments, beyond time, even as it feels to me that he is showing us, sharing with us, perhaps most for his daughter, the power he still has and the beauty he has known in his life.

I met a woman recently whose son, in his last year of college, was killed when the car he was driving at night in the desert went off the road and crashed. Perhaps he had fallen asleep. She will never know. What explanation would suffice? A life extinguished in its prime, a hole rent in the fabric of this woman's life, the life she had given birth to and nourished, with all its connecting threads, suddenly no more. How to hold this? How to come to an acceptance of the unacceptable? And yet, this, too, has been part of parenthood since the beginning of time.

Perhaps the best we can do is feel the fleetingness of life and of our present moments and live inside them as fully as possible, hugging our children and delighting in their life, and feel at the same time the certainty of death, of life arising *and* passing away. The breath can remind us of this as it arises and passes away, as can our moments, our friends, the weather, and our thoughts. Can we find ways to ride these currents mindfully and let life flow through us? Can we honor those mysteries beyond our knowing, which shape our frail humanity and give it surprising strength and wisdom?

*

BOUNDARIES OF LOVE

Beyond and before
the inequities of passion,
the four halves
are secretly braided.
Dispositions of our truth;
possibilities are born and
in time, buried.
Hidden galaxies and
futile losses,
our impatient hearts forbid this.

Places where the unknown
are exquisite and elusive.

RYAN JON ROBINSON,
AGE SIXTEEN, OCTOBER 1995

This poem was written several weeks before Ryan Robinson died of an accidental gunshot wound to his head at an unsupervised teenage party at a friend's house, where alcohol was involved. The boys had found a handgun, which they thought was unloaded, in the parents' bedroom. It happened to have been a Russian gun. Unlike American models, the safety on this gun allowed the trigger to be pulled back and click. The boys had removed the clip and had "dry-fired" the pistol many times into the fireplace. The safety must have accidently been switched off right before it came to Ryan. None of them had any inkling there might be a bullet in the chamber. His father, who had attended a mindfulness retreat I had conducted the summer before, wrote the following to me:

Ryan had just transferred to a new, much larger high school. On his first day, he insisted on wearing a T-shirt his friends at his former school had made for him. On the front it said "Hi, my name is Ryan," and on the back, "I'm new here, be nice to me." I was in the kitchen as he raced out the door, late again. Frantically he came running back in. "Where's my cape? I forgot my cape." I said, "No, you don't really want to wear your cape. Not on the first day. Why don't you just check it out, get the lay of the land." Cautiously, he replied, "Is that what you think I should do, or is that what you would do?" Well, the answer to that was obvious. He had the ability to really see what was going on with people, although perhaps unspoken, and tell the truth about it. Sometimes that ability could feel confronting. But it was always truthful.

Ryan's death, shortly after his sixteenth birthday, forever ruptured the fabric of our cozy little family. The resultant separation divided a life that I had previously taken for granted from the extraordinary pain of each subsequent day. The grief I experienced in those first two months was far greater than any appreciation for being alive that I could relate to. Being alive simply hurt too much.

A huge part of me died with Ryan that cold October night. During the past four months, my life has felt like a prison sentence; something to be endured, no longer enjoyed. For so many weeks after the accident the thoughts and pictures that raced through my mind were uncontrollable. They consumed my sleep and my waking hours. I would attempt to observe them, notice them, breathe with them, but it was hopeless. Everywhere I turned, I was reminded of him. I was like a thousand wild stallions stampeding out of control....

I am thankful for my mindfulness practice. It has become a road map that guides me over very rough, very painful and yet uncharted terrain. It is interesting, I used to believe my thoughts were who I was. Now, my thoughts are what I have, not who I am. My life seems to have become the context within which all my thoughts occur, within which my emotions run. Throughout the day the thoughts and emotions arrive as always. Some, the most wild of the stallions, continue to run unrestrained, out of control, with me at their mercy. Most of them, however, I am able to observe, experience and let go of, while returning to my breath. With the majority, I can now grab the saddle and hoist myself up before being dragged along behind at the end of a rope, bouncing off of my own rocks called "victim" and "self-pity." For this I am very grateful.

During the day I observe a variety of thoughts. "I can't do this anymore...My life isn't worth living; I failed as a parent." During my sitting meditation, I observe these and other considerations...All the while I attempt patiently to return to my breath. I forget, and return. I go away with my thoughts, and return. I notice my impatience, and return. I can see now that underneath the thoughts and the emotions, underneath the sorrow, the emptiness and all of my grief there is something else. It is the absolute unconditional love that I have for a beautiful young man whom I simply miss very much.

Perhaps the greatest lesson I have learned from this tragedy is the arrogance I had maintained in my relationship with time prior to the accident. I have learned how important it is to tell people when you love them, because tomorrow is just a concept of our minds.

The River of Buried Grief

I (jkz) have been in a room with seven hundred men of all ages, every one in tears over his lost relationship with his father. Before they walked into the room and spent time talking and listening together, most were barely aware that they carried such grief, and hardly any would have shared it with other men.

I have been in groups of hundreds of health professionals where, during intensive training in mindfulness, immense personal sadness from childhood poured out of person after person, men and women. At these retreats, we let such emotional expressions of grief and the stories that contain them occur and go on for some time without any reaction or comment other than our full and silent attention. People have a hard time realizing that making space for deep and unpleasant emotions is as much a part of mindfulness as following the breath.

A veritable river of grief seems to flow through us. Its subterranean course is not always in evidence, so we may have no idea it is there. But this river of grief is never as far from us or as foreign to us as we might think when we see it coursing through the heart of someone else. Seen or unseen, it can color an entire life journey, including our character, choice of profession, and how we parent.

I am convinced that this river runs through us all, carrying deep, perhaps archetypal feelings we rarely come in contact with or even know exist. When we are out of touch with our own grief, it can feel more than a little awkward and strange when someone else gets in touch with theirs. It is easy to feel embarrassed for them, or aloof and a little judgmental, like, "Why are they making such a big deal about something like that?" "It happened so long ago." "Haven't they dealt with that already in therapy?" "I'm certainly beyond that."

We are all to some degree defended against the deepest feelings we carry. If we weren't, we would no longer be carrying them in quite the same way. The real work of mindfulness is making room for whatever is happening while it is happening, with openness, equanimity, empathy, and compassion. It means being patient with ourselves and with others and not jumping to move on prematurely to something else because of our discomfort.

In those rare moments when we do connect with our own grief, when it's *our* feelings that surface in this moment, for whatever reason, the situation is all of a sudden very different. Then the whole world is in pain, our whole universe colored by a sorrow that we feel extends far beyond the personal.

Perhaps we wouldn't be carrying quite so much buried grief as adults had we been parented with greater kindness and thoughtfulness when we were children. We cannot say with any certainty. It is different for each one of us. Each of us has our unique constellation of painful past experiences and our reactions to them, some buried, some unearthed.

It takes years of inner and outer work on oneself to heal from losses of one kind or another, and from a lack of recognition and honoring and of being cared for in childhood. Often it takes years to even become aware of our deepest feelings about our experiences and how we were treated. It is not always that one's parents were abusive, or alcoholic, or grossly neglectful. Much of the hurt for many of us came about while our parents were trying to do the best they could with what they had and within the framework of their world and worldview. They were formed by their own experiences, both positive and negative and by what *their* parents passed down to them, just as we are. Each family has its own unique combinations of love, shame, guilt, blame, withholding, and neediness. These emotions are most harmful when coupled with unconsciousness.

A woman told me that when her mother died—at a time when she was still a young girl with a number of younger siblings—her father refused to allow any further mention of her mother in the household. It was as if, once buried, she never existed. All the children were forced into this emotional closet. The father thought it would be better, less traumatic, to just move on and not dwell on the past. On the contrary, it did enormous harm to the family.

So we see that it is ignorance (in the Buddhist sense of ignoring how things actually are) that so often lies at the root of our suffering. This kind of ignorance can lead to parents not knowing their own children. This ignorance can coexist within a family in which there are many positive accomplishments and a surface appearance of harmony and love. The one does not preclude the other.

Unconscious grief casts a shadow that extends out and down in our psyche. It moves in the dark inner recesses of our memory. It has a life of its own underground, even when the surface seems bright. Indeed, sometimes the brighter the surface, the longer and darker the emotional shadows.

Robert Bly, in *The Little Book on the Human Shadow*, describes the dynamics of our buried emotions using the image of an invisible bag we acquire early in life. As we grow, in our attempts to be seen and accepted by those we love, we progressively stuff into this bag all those parts of ourselves that we are made to feel aren't lovable. This can go on for an entire lifetime, living something of a lie to keep up appearances or to fit in.

It may have started out at home with our parents, when we were infants and young children, and were given messages about what pleased them and what didn't, what was "acceptable" in terms of thoughts, feelings, and behaviors, and what wasn't. But it continues in school among one's peers and teachers, and out in the world. Over time our bag gets longer and longer and heavier and heavier as we stuff more and more of ourselves into it: our anger, our impulsiveness, our spontaneity, our softness, our strength, even our intelligence, in our sometimes desperate efforts to be likable or accepted or well thought of, or to fit a certain framework we believe we are called upon to reflect—the stoic, the martyr, the wise one. It is truly dark in the bag, because we are unwilling to let in any light and see what's going on in a large part of our own psyche.

If we pretend we don't have this bag over our shoulder, and we therefore refuse to open it from time to time for thirty or forty years, except to stuff more things in, those shadows we have stuffed inside—which are valid and important, if unaccepted, parts of ourselves—fester and grow toxic from lack of acknowledgment and expression. They can linger there and influence our life trajectory in momentous ways we may not know but only see on occasion in dreams, or when the fabric of our life seems to fray or suddenly disintegrate. What we don't want to look at in the inner world is often visible on our face in the outer world. The inner reflects the outer, and the outer the inner. To come to harmony requires marrying inner and outer, bringing them together again, in the light of awareness and acceptance.

Perhaps it is time to educate ourselves to this burden we carry once and for all and to consciously make ongoing, moment-to-moment efforts to accept all aspects of our being, to listen to and speak with our shadow and our subterranean river of buried grief, and hold them, as best we can, with unconditional acceptance and kindness. This is tantamount to parenting ourselves on the way to what we might call true adulthood.

If we can "parent" ourselves in this way, maybe—just maybe— we will have a clearer view of our children and will be able to see and accept them in ways that will occasion less lopping off of parts of themselves in their heartbreaking attempts to be accepted by us and by the larger world.

✻

> Ring the bells that can still ring.
> Forget your perfect offering.
> There is a crack in everything.
> That's how the light gets in.

LEONARD COHEN, "ANTHEM"

Hanging by a Thread

When our children are suffering, we suffer. When our children aren't hurting, parenting can be difficult enough. Sometimes it feels as if we are hanging by a thread.

*

Kids fighting with each other, temper tantrums, "I'm bored!" teething, fussing, illness, sleepless nights, long winter days, dark rainy days, days when we are feeling low, tired, trying to meet different needs, balancing, juggling work and family and a hundred other things, peacemaking, coming up with yet another creative idea, or uncreative idea, or even dinner…by the end of the day I (mkz) am feeling exhausted, exasperated, tremendously limited, and confined. My world has become too small. I feel an overpowering urge to run outside, to get some air, some distance, some space.

When the weather doesn't allow for outdoor activity and we are cooped up inside for long stretches of time, that's when I become most acutely aware of my own limits as a person and all the skills I never acquired and thus can't teach my children.

I'm also very aware of the limits of our culture. It seems like all there is to do is to consume in some fashion. Whether it's shopping or eating or going to the movies, so often it all feels empty and lifeless. Where are the centers in our towns for dancing and music, storytelling, and conversation for all ages?

They say it takes a whole village to raise a child. But where are the villages in our society? We still see important vestiges of the village of old in extended family, community centers, support groups, cross-generational friendships, and communities of faith. Nevertheless, all too often parents find themselves isolated and alone. This may be especially true for single parents, who may not be able to share their day-to-day struggles, get a different perspective, or just have someone to commiserate with—although from another vantage point, it might be said that sometimes partners can be unsupportive and create more work. Even with friends or supportive partners, the hardest times usually happen when we are on our own. Parenting can be lonely work.

We need community to round out our individual resources and necessarily limited skills, provide a critical mass of ideas, enthusiasm, and life experience in the form of people with a variety of backgrounds and talents to back us up when our own repertoire feels exhausted. As parents, we have to provide the bedrock in the family, but we can't provide everything ourselves.

*

As our children enter the teen years, with all their complexity and problems, having babies and younger children may seem simple by comparison, and we may find ourselves confused, discouraged, even despairing at times. As we have seen, it can feel as if we are losing our teenage children as they pull away from us, influenced more and more by their peers, and are sometimes drawn to potentially self-destructive behaviors. We also understand that in some way, we *are* losing them as they move out into the world. We feel anguished by their vulnerability and our inability to protect them, and sometimes angry at the ways they express themselves—or don't.

The intuitive, elemental, and very physical parenting we did with young children is no longer appropriate. We may find that our physical exhaustion gives way to mental and emotional exhaustion, in part because we are continually adjusting our roles as parents, as our adolescents struggle with their needs for autonomy, connection, love, and meaning.

They grow and undergo metamorphoses in various astonishing, unexpected, and sometimes trying ways, and we are called upon to grow and change as well. As they become independent and need us less, we can find ourselves slipping into a business-as-usual routine where they are concerned, which can feel superficial, unsatisfying, and disconnected to us and to them. They need more time alone, more space from us, and a different kind of sensitivity from us. In some ways we are irrelevant to them, and we are also not irrelevant to them.

It can be hard to see that they still need us when they are angry and critical and closed off from us, and even harder through the veil of our own anger and worry. Refusing to disappear and completely disconnect from them when we feel marginalized, confused, frustrated, and despairing takes tremendous intentionality on our part.

Inevitably there are times when adolescents find life is unsatisfying, when their innermost needs are not being met, when they are unhappy and questioning: "What's life about? Where is the meaning? Isn't there more to life than this? Where do I fit in?" They may become moody and withdrawn, and feel more distant from us than we could ever have imagined when they were little. They may actively push us away with hostile, angry behavior. We see them hurting, but it's hard to reach them.

When they are feeling alienated and alone, they need to feel that we are still with them. We may see them looking at us as if from across a large chasm. Reaching them can be difficult. The gulf can feel scary, to them and to us. We may feel powerless in a way that we never felt when they were little. They inadvertently give us a glimpse of our own fragility, our own doubts and fears, our own feelings of vulnerability that are often buried deep inside of us and shielded from daily examining.

When our teenagers are questioning the authenticity of feelings, of people, and even of themselves, we would do well to locate a place within ourselves that is authentic, grounded, simple, and real. At such times, we might take a few moments to focus inwardly, bringing our attention to our breathing, to the body, and to our feelings. We may not feel very connected or close to our child in such moments, but we can be a sympathetic presence and reach for any threads they may be holding out to us, however thin.

We might also extend some threads of our own, however tentative and delicate, if appropriate. It might involve just listening and acknowledging the reality of the difficulties they are experiencing, or their pain and uncertainty. Or it may call for something more dramatic, such as taking them off by themselves for a day, or a weekend, or a week. This may not be possible or feel possible, but truly hard times call for truly creative solutions. Choosing something they might like to do, and making some time to be together in whatever ways we can, can remind them of the deeper meaning that resides below their busy and sometimes monotonous everyday routines. And stepping outside of our everyday lives, even if precipitated by a crisis, can serve the same function for us as well, and can help us renew our connection with them.

There are times—when our older children are feeling stuck, limited, unhappy with their lives—in which taking some action may be appropriate and necessary. This is particularly true when we sense that they are leaning toward doing things that are dangerous or self-destructive. They need to know that we are concerned about them, and what our concerns are. They may need us to problem-solve with them, or even advocate for them, helping them find ways to make their lives more satisfying, more meaningful.

Teenagers often have their own clear insights into the heart of the matter. But there are also times when they know something is not right but don't know what it is, and at those times they may need us to bring whatever wisdom we have gleaned from our own life experience to the problem at hand. It takes a long time for children, for any of us, to understand how the world works (do we ever fully "understand?") and how to make things work for them.

Helping them in any way may be especially hard to do if we are seen as part of the problem. Although we can be open to making changes in our own behavior, we may or may not be able to help them make changes in their lives. We may or may not even agree on what is needed or even what the problem is. But sometimes, just acknowledging the hard time they are having can make the difference between their feeling isolated and feeling connected, between feeling judged and feeling cared for. When they feel concern and loving acceptance from a parent, it can give them a more meaningful context within which to view their difficulties.

*

There are times when our children, no matter how old they are, seem to "regress" to a younger age. A friend's sixteen-year-old boy had been emotionally withdrawn from his family and got very sick from an infection about the same time. His parents could have chosen to see his sudden illness as purely physical, having nothing to do with his emotional state or the difficulties he and the family had been experiencing. Instead, they were able to view his illness within a larger context, and began to examine the stresses, both physical and emotional, in their son's life and within the family. They then made use of this time in which he was sick and convalescing to promote a broader healing. They accepted his need to regress by being at home—slowing down, turning inward for a time, eating special healing foods, and reconnecting with his family—and recognized the restoring and transformative benefits of this to him and to their relationship with him.

Regression is a word with strong negative connotations. It usually connotes maladjustment, failure to act one's age, going backward to a more infantile stage. But there are times when children, not just young children, need a period of being cared for, read to, sung to, a time in which to go inward in order to be able to move outward again. Responding with kindness and acceptance and without judgment when our children are needing such a time nurtures that part of them that is struggling to grow. It ultimately helps them to move on, to shed an old skin. It can be a true gift to them.

Being able to give this kind of time is not always easy, or even possible. Work and other demands may make it difficult or impossible. But it helps if we can remember that what our child is presenting on the outside is not all that there is. Perhaps, with reflection, we can find a way to trust that some kind of inner transformation may be unfolding and make space for it with kindness, as best we can. Over time, we may come to some understanding of what our child is struggling with.

When a child is unhappy and out of balance and perhaps regressing, he or she can be very hard to live with. But when we take the difficult behavior personally and wall ourselves off, put on our armor, get stuck in our own fears and hurt feelings, the walls between us just get thicker and higher. These are the times when it helps to see with eyes of wholeness. This means viewing what is happening in the largest possible context, with an intention to examine, to be fully present, and view it within the seemingly paradoxical framework of both distance and compassion. When the crisis has passed, if we can let go of any hurt, resentment, or anger we may be feeling, we have the possibility of moving into a truly new moment with our children.

At the end of a day that felt like it was filled with unending criticism and negativity directed at me (mkz), one of my daughters, at the age of ten, snuggled up to me and told me very sincerely that she loved me. This wonderful capacity to be fluid, to let go of anger, changes as children get older. They need us to remind them through our own behavior that it is possible to be aware of ongoing issues at the same time that we meet each moment with a willingness to start afresh.

Ultimately, it is not our ideas that will count the most. Rather, it will be the authenticity of our being and our embodiment of caring that we bring to the gut-wrenching moments all parents find themselves in and that make us question everything.

> You do not have to be good.
> You do not have to walk on your knees
> for a hundred miles through the desert, repenting.
> You only have to let the soft animal of your body love
>   what it loves.
> Tell me about despair, yours, and I will tell you mine.
> Meanwhile the world goes on.
> Meanwhile the sun and the clear pebbles of the rain
> are moving across the landscapes,
> over the prairies and the deep trees,

the mountains and the rivers.
Meanwhile the wild geese, high in the clean blue air,
are heading home again.
Whoever you are, no matter how lonely,
the world offers itself to your imagination,
calls to you like the wild geese, harsh and exciting—
over and over announcing your place
in the family of things.

MARY OLIVER,
"WILD GEESE," *Dream Work*

Losing It

Parents all lose it sometimes. We lose our temper. We lose our minds. We can lose our balance, our way, our dignity, our self-respect. When it happens, it is very painful, no matter what provoked it.

It usually happens when we are exhausted and have been pushed beyond our limits. Intense feelings of frustration arise and we may not recognize them in time, or we just don't know how to shift gears in that moment and may be too tired to care. Sometimes losing it takes the form of screaming and yelling or mean-spirited speech. Sometimes we lash out with a smack or slap. As soon as it happens, we feel terrible—angry with ourselves, sad for our children. All of a sudden, we're in the middle of a nightmare. I'll (mkz) give you an example.

I'm putting one of my daughters to bed. She has always had a hard time going to sleep, and at eight years old, she is still a night owl and can stay up forever. I'm at my worst after 10 p.m. I don't function well. I'm not patient. She often becomes especially sensitive to all sorts of things at bedtime—she'll want something to drink or she won't want to be left alone, she wants the light on, and the night-light is not enough.

When it's time for her to go to bed, I sit with her for a while. When I see, as I do on this particular night, that it's going to be one of those long hauls and I'm too tired to stay up, I say to her, "Sleep in my bed tonight." So off she goes. But I say, "You have to wear a shirt in my bed, that's the rule, because I don't want to spend the night keeping you covered so you won't get cold!" She knows this, objects anyway, but does put on a shirt. Then she immediately starts fussing about it and kicking and punching the bed. I get her another shirt, a softer, more comfortable one. By this time, she is even angrier and swearing at me. She wants the light on. I want the light off. It is turning into a battle of wills. I am afraid she'll wake her sister. I feel trapped. I feel controlled. I feel helpless. Things are moving in a certain direction and I can't seem to change it.

Then I hear her sister yelling at us to be quiet. She's been woken up. I am even angrier now. I yell at her to be quiet. She continues to make noise and pound the bed and fuss, and I finally feel so frustrated and angry and helpless that I slap her on the cheek. She starts crying and then screaming even more loudly. Her sister yells again for her to be quiet. I feel sick that I've smacked her. She's shouting that I'm a child abuser and that she's going to call the police. I'm paralyzed with shame and remorse. I'm in the middle of a gigantic nightmare. After about twenty minutes of screaming and crying that I'm sure the whole neighborhood can hear, she calls for her dad. Her dad's not home. Finally she starts sobbing, "Mommy."

I bring her ice and a washcloth and sit there with her, telling her what I did was very bad, and telling her I'm really sad I hurt her. Finally, an hour later, she's asleep in my bed, snuggled up to me. I lie there wide awake, feeling terrible.

✻

Each child is so different. For some, the transition into sleep is resisted every night and the transition to wakefulness in the morning can be just as hard. With others, it may be as easy as a bedtime story or a quiet song. Sometimes, no matter what we do, it seems like we're headed for disaster. That night, putting my daughter to bed started with reading stories by the fire, followed by sketching pictures sitting on her bed—a lovely beginning, ending in collective misery.

I later ask myself, what could I have done differently? At times, the answer to this question is very clear. In this situation, it wasn't at all clear. Perhaps if I hadn't made an issue of her wearing a shirt we could have avoided this conflict, or maybe she would have objected to something else. Sometimes these night storms feel inevitable, as if they just have to play themselves out. But did this really have to happen the way it did? Is there something that could have made the transition to sleep less difficult for her? How can I work with my anger and frustration so that I don't make things worse? When do I bend? When do I bend too much? Could I have done something to change the direction we were moving in? At times we need to look at what's happening from a larger perspective. In retrospect, I think the whole framework of our bedtime ritual needed to be simpler and much more consistent than it was, and starting at a younger age.

In the midst of the storm, it might have helped if I had stopped for a moment, brought awareness to my breathing, and realized I didn't have to solve anything in that moment. In doing so, I might have avoided reacting with out-of-control anger, which only worsened the situation.

Showing remorse for my actions and concern for her feelings, rather than leaving what happened unacknowledged and unexamined, was important for there to be some healing and some kind of learning. For me, this meant acknowledging the awfulness of what happened and not trying to minimize it nor blame her for it. The next day, when things were calmer and the storm had passed, we were able to talk about what happened and how we felt. Hopefully, each time an incident like this happens, I learn something that makes it less likely to happen again.

Losing our temper and being hurtful as a consequence is horrible. The last thing we want to do is cause harm. When we find ourselves becoming reactive, we always have the option—if we can remember to pause in the heat of the moment—to ground ourselves as best we can in the body and in the breath and bring awareness to whatever we are feeling—whether it be frustration, fear, anger, or something else—with some kindness and acceptance. Our willingness to soften and open in this way in such moments contains the possibility that a wiser way to respond will emerge.

No Guarantees

Parents know all too well that there are many things we cannot control, and that no matter what we do, there are no guarantees. Part of mindful parenting is facing our own expectations and our own limitations and working with each situation as best we can, without trying to force a certain outcome.

From the moment we become pregnant, to the birth of our child, and in the years that follow, there are a myriad of factors affecting each child's life trajectory and development. Some we know about, others we may not. Some are straightforward, others deeply mysterious. We can do all the "right" things, only to find out later that they were not so right, and that there were factors we were not aware of, perhaps that no one was aware of at the time. When it comes down to it, we can only rely on a combination of intuition, common sense, awareness, information, and, most importantly, our love. Even with our best efforts to meet the needs of our children, it is important to recognize that there will be many things that can have an impact on them that we cannot necessarily control, prevent, or even be aware of, in spite of our best efforts and intentions.

The most obvious examples are tragic accidents and traumatic experiences that can leave a child forever changed and the family struggling to adjust their lives to meet their child's needs; or the death of a child, leaving a gigantic hole in the lives of the survivors. Others include being harmed by exposure to various environmental toxins. New information about such hazards is coming out all the time. Many chemicals in the environment are known to cause cancer and birth defects. Some are neurotoxins. Alcohol, smoking, drugs, asbestos, lead, radon, and pesticides, among others, are known to have a detrimental effect on human health and exert their strongest effects on children. But many more have not been studied for their long-term effects on health. As parents, we have to strike some kind of balance between recognizing and accepting the limits of our knowledge and of what we can do to protect our children on the one hand and on the other, being reasonably informed and doing the best we can to protect them. This whole issue can be anxiety producing and intimidating, because we often feel powerless and so much is at stake. It can be easier to just ignore the whole domain of environmental risk.

Sometimes environmental hazards are right in front of our eyes in our own homes, such as asbestos disintegrating on heating pipes or peeling lead paint. Sometimes our noses alert us to hazards such as formaldehyde or other volatile organic compounds, including those venting from newly installed carpeting and furniture. Some are undetectable by our senses, like lead and various chemicals in our water. Environmental hazards such as chemical pollution of wells, pesticides in foods, and poor indoor air quality in schools may require us to organize in groups to lobby and speak out to preserve or restore environmental safety for our children.

While it is of paramount importance for our children to feel emotionally safe, it is also our responsibility as parents to do what we can to make our children's physical environment safe as well.

＊

There are many other factors we don't control as parents, such as the unique physical and emotional characteristics our children are born with. For instance, all parents know that each child is born with unique qualities that unfold and change over time. One of these is their temperament. Rudolf Steiner, the German philosopher and educator, identified four major categories of temperament: the *choleric* (fiery, energetic, often athletic, intense, willful), the *melancholic* (inward, solitary, pessimistic, sensitive, loves rainy days and sad stories), the *sanguine* (easygoing, forgetful, changeable, sociable, dreamy), and the *phlegmatic* (loves to eat and be cozy, inwardly focused, cautious, observant, deliberate).

We all have a mix of different temperaments, and at different times different aspects predominate over others. An infant who is very choleric—demanding, intense—may grow into a child who shows more sanguine qualities at times and also may have a melancholic streak. A sanguine baby may grow into a teenager with a strong will and a fiery temper.

The temperamental features that make a child unique can sometimes be very trying for parents. They can be made even more difficult by our unconscious expectations or by our own temperaments. Different temperaments in families can create situations in which tremendous friction, unmet expectations, and anger come into play. An athletic, high-achieving parent may have trouble relating to a child who is more phlegmatic and prefers to curl up with a snack and a book. An articulate, verbally oriented parent may feel at a loss with a deeply feeling, nonverbal, artistic child. Being aware of such characteristics in our children and in ourselves can help us be more understanding and accepting, and to work with situations with greater insight.

We may have had one baby who nursed easily and was very social, setting up expectations within us, and then have another baby who is a disinterested nurser, harder to reach and connect with, or one who has colic or allergies. An easygoing, flexible child may be followed by a child who finds every transition difficult and is always pushing the limits, whatever they are. A well-organized student and avid reader may be followed by a child who has trouble organizing himself and finds reading difficult.

Some children have a harder time than others in all sorts of ways. They may be born with developmental syndromes such as Asperger's, autism, or ADHD, or with schizophrenia or bipolar disorder. Others may suffer from trauma and its often enduring and painful aftereffects. Some children may be drawn to paths that are worrisome, perhaps even dangerous or self-destructive. In situations like these, parents are dealing with extremely difficult, complex, unpredictable, demanding, and exhausting realities within their family. Being more mindful will not magically make things better or prevent our children or ourselves from suffering. But what it gives us is a practice that fosters greater acceptance and compassion for our children and for ourselves, a source of some comfort and strength.

Parenting mindfully asks a lot of us. There is deep inner work and deep outer work to be done. Our awareness has to encompass the whole. We do this for our children, with the understanding that there are no guarantees.

Lost

In the opening lines of the *Divine Comedy*, Dante speaks to something deep within us as human beings: "In the middle of this road we call our life/I found myself in a dark wood/With no clear path through"—in other words, lost. To really know where one is, his poem tells us, allegorically at least, one has first to descend, go underground, into the darkness of hell. Only then can one make the ascent to heaven.

When we feel that we have lost our way, perhaps during a time of darkness, or despair, or confusion, we might ask ourselves, "How did I get here?" "Where am I?" "What is this place I find myself in now?"

As soon as we start attending, we are no longer lost. We are simply where we are. Where we actually are is always a good place to begin, both physically, when we've lost our bearings, and metaphorically, when it feels as if we no longer know what we are doing as parents, or in our work, or in our lives in general.

Perhaps, in some way, we are always lost, to the degree that we are not fully awake. Perhaps what is most important is our willingness to be where we actually are and dwell here fully, in darkness or in light, without having to go somewhere else. Only then may we know where to place our foot when it is time to move.

The poem "Lost" by David Wagoner, based on the Northwest Native American tradition, captures this spirit. It is what the elder might say in response to a young boy or girl who comes and asks, "What do I do when I am lost in the forest?"

> Stand still. The trees ahead and bushes beside you
> Are not lost. Wherever you are is called Here,
> And you must treat it as a powerful stranger,
> Must ask permission to know it and be known.
> The forest breathes. Listen. It answers,
> I have made this place around you,
> If you leave it you may come back again, saying Here.
>
> No two trees are the same to Raven.
> No two branches are the same to Wren.
> If what a tree or a bush does is lost on you,
> You are surely lost. Stand still. The forest knows
> Where you are. You must let it find you.

The poet reminds us that our lives depend on our sensitivity to the particulars, that if what the forest or a tree does, or the look of a child, is lost on us, then we are surely, in some deep way, lost. The call is to pay attention, to wake up to where we are, to what is before us and all around us, here, now. Can we learn to stand still? Can we hear the forest of life and of the world breathing, calling to us to be still for a moment, to wake up, to feel the interconnectedness of all things, to realize that no two moments are the same? Can we listen in this way to our children?

This is the challenge of bringing mindfulness into our parenting, especially at those moments that seem the darkest, and when we feel the most adrift, without bearings, lost. Can we stand still right there, right then, which in actuality, is always right *here*, right *now*, and be in touch with and guided by what is most basic, through our own attention?

It's Never Too Late

We are all to some degree a product of our times. The choices we make as parents are influenced by the era in which we parent and its values, and by the people around us, our own parents, our friends, and, of course, the "experts." We tend to take authoritative pronouncements at face value and not see past their social contexts, whether it is the way our parents raised us or well-meaning advice from a pediatrician. It's very hard to nurse a baby in a time when everyone is bottle-feeding, in an environment lacking support, guidance, and role models. Or we may have grown up in a family that didn't hug, where feelings were not acknowledged, or where love was always tied to conditions and expectations. We may have carried that way of being into our own parenting, relying on what was familiar and comfortable, without much thought, or unable to muster the will or courage to go against the prevailing tide.

At times, we may not have been comfortable with what we were doing as parents, and our intuition may have voiced discomfort or yearned for something else, but we may not have felt that we had options, that there was any other way. Our feelings, our instincts, and our intuitions may have been buried, and now, later in life, we may be left with regret, sadness, loss, or pain.

We do the best we can and, being human, our view of things is always partial and inevitably changes. We all have regrets and see things later that we didn't see and wish we had done differently.

*

A mother of grown children sent us the following reflections, which she had written several years before we met her:

I am but a baby myself when I give birth to my first child. Twenty-three is wanting to be tripping off in Europe somewhere or going to grad school or dating more than one guy in the same week. Twenty-three is not wanting to change diapers, sterilize glass baby bottles and have cotton lap pads across my thighs. But it is the early 60s, and what's a nice Jewish girl to do at 20 but to marry a nice Jewish boy and produce a grandchild...

It is the early 60s and my husband simply drops me off at the hospital as I go into labor. The doctor says he will call him at home...not to worry and to grab some sleep. "Good-bye, hon," he says. The nurse wheels me off in the wheelchair and looks at my small frame. "What are you here for?" "To have a baby," I say. "Where is it?" she asks, looking at my belly. It is the early 60s and the less gain the better. I am 15 pounds over my normal weight. It is the early 60s and hiding a protrusion is in...showing, as in blossoming, is definitely out.

I am wheeled into the labor room. It is the early 60s and consciousness is out...being unconscious is in, and I am given an injection to create twilight sleep. In the delivery room I feel nothing, I see nothing. My only recall is of someone shaking my arm, and I vaguely hear, "You have a boy." It is the early 60s, and I never get to see my son until many hours after the birth. It is the early 60s, and rooming in (mother and child) is not permitted in hospitals. Fathers can only visit during hours. Breast-feeding is out...formula is in...having a nurse for four weeks is in...bonding with the baby is...well, no one really even talks about the bonding process.

My husband and I may be parents, but we are still kids ourselves. Neither of us has worked out our deeper issues, and when the nurse leaves after four weeks, I begin to cry. The impact hits hard. At twenty-three, I am tied down. I am on a schedule of feeding, changing, bathing, sleeping. I am ripe for the advice that I hear..."Don't spoil him... don't pick him up...let him cry. That's what we did with you. Listen to us...we are your parents and after raising two children, we know what is right. The worst thing is to give in when he cries...Oh, you can see if he needs to be changed or fed, but if he doesn't need that, then let him cry and eventually he'll go to sleep."

I buy their advice...I want to be a good mother and have an unspoiled child, and so I feed, I diaper, I bathe and when I hear the crying, I let him cry.

The word *spoiled* hits hard...It brings back some unpleasant memories of when I was called spoiled by my parents...

"You should be grateful for what you have...for what we do for you...other children don't have it as good as you do...we've spoiled you..."

I look at my infant son...No, I won't give in to his crying.

It's the early 60s and live in house-keepers are in; joining a country club is in; playing indoor tennis as part of a league is in. I don't do any of the forementioned, but I also don't meet my son's primary need for closeness and contact. I don't even learn about bonding until almost twenty-five years later.

At some time during the early 80s, I begin to notice women breast-feeding their babies in public places and in the quiet confines of their homes. On the *Oprah* show I learn that having wants and needs is OK. I am hearing words like *contact* and *warmth* and *the bonding process*. Something in me is painfully sad. Something in me is wanting to cry. I long to return to my infant son and pick him up and kiss his baby tears; I yearn to cuddle him and coo him to sleep, but having that second chance is out.

It is the 90s...my son is a grown man and for me, feeling the pain and the feelings is in.

✷

The grief of lost opportunities, for how we were or weren't in another time, lies deep within the human psyche. It can cause us to yearn for some way to heal our children's pain and our own and bring us closer. We are forced to acknowledge that what is past cannot be undone, only known and known deeply, felt and felt deeply, and thereby, in a glimmer of new possibility and hope, perhaps transformed by our very recognition and our acceptance. It is only in the present that new possibilities exist. Acknowledging our anguish and grief and the pain we may have caused is part of the shaping of those possibilities, of giving birth to something new in ourselves, which may require the shedding of something old, however tenaciously it clings to us and we to it.

In our view, it is never too late to try to heal relationships with grown children who may have been hurt by us through our past ignorance, however innocent or understandable, or through lack of attention, or busyness, or neglect, withholding, judgment, or abusiveness. It is never too late to work toward creating healthy new connections, even if they are distrustful of us, or angry about past attitudes or actions, omissions or commissions on our part that they feel were harmful to them.

One way we can begin to heal these wounds is by sharing our regrets and our awareness of the things we did that were harmful or neglectful, either by letter or in person with our adult children. Doing this in a letter may be a more sensitive way to communicate at first, particularly if a child feels we have been intrusive or thoughtless about boundaries. To be of any real value, reaching out in this way must be a genuine overture, with the well-being of our child foremost in our mind, and, as hard as it might be for us, accepting the possibility that irreparable harm may have been done and that reconciliation may not be possible. We need to stand in a place beyond looking for sympathy, understanding, reassurance, or affection, beyond any desire to be absolved of guilt. We can recognize these feelings when they arise in us, and yet bring our attention back to the question, "What is in the best interest of my child?" even when he or she is an adult.

*

In bringing mindfulness to our relationships with our adult children, it is important to be aware of the ways in which our assumptions, expectations, and judgments may be limiting or disrespectful. It is equally important that we try to be a little more empathic and cognizant of the demands and stresses that they may be dealing with in their lives.

This does not mean that in our interactions with our adult children, we should not voice our feelings or express our needs. When something happens that bothers us, we can be aware of the various feelings we are having and bring them up at what feels like a relatively good time rather than letting things build up. At times, we may decide not to bring up particular issues, whether because they are not that important or because they are too loaded. It can be helpful to keep in mind a larger view of the relationship and to notice how attached we may be to expressing what in the end may just be an opinion. When we need something from them, it is helpful to remember that they are adults and are free to say no and express their feelings in response.

Can we look at our grown children as if we were seeing them for the first time, seeing each not as a newborn, but as a new being? Any moment together, even on the telephone, is a new chance to be present, to build trust, to attune to them, to be sensitive, to be empathic, to accept them as they are, and to honor their sovereignty.

If, on occasion, we lapse into an old familiar pattern, if we find ourselves critical, or unkind, or judging, or demanding, or withholding, or any of the myriad ways negativity can manifest, we can take a moment and look at what has happened. We can acknowledge what we did, hopefully learn from it, and apologize for our behavior. And then...begin again.

*

Western medicine is founded on the cardinal principle, dating to Hippocrates, to first do no harm. Perhaps we need to collectively affirm a Hippocratic Oath for parenting: that we will, above all, first do no harm. This would be a practice in itself. Without mindfulness, how would we even know whether we were doing harm in a particular moment, or upon reflection afterward?

Mindfulness is about living the lives that are ours to live. This can only happen if we make room for our true nature—what is deepest and best in ourselves—to emerge. While we may all be born miraculous beings, without proper nurturing, our innate genius may be smothered, snuffed out for lack of oxygen. The oxygen that feeds our true nature is found in stillness, attention, love, sovereignty, and community. The challenge of mindful parenting is to find ways to nourish our children and ourselves as we make our way along the ordinary and extraordinary journey that is a human life lived in awareness, and so to grow into who we all are and can become for each other, for ourselves, and for the world.

Four Mindfulness Practices, Seven

Intentions, and Twelve Exercises for

Mindful Parenting

Four Mindfulness Practices for Everyday Life

I. DROPPING IN ON THE PRESENT MOMENT

This is the core practice to cultivate mindfulness in daily life. Whenever you care to, no matter what is happening, you can always experiment with dropping in on yourself in the present moment. Can you be still, even for a moment, and simply take in what is unfolding inwardly and outwardly?

You might start by becoming aware of the *feeling* of the breath moving in and out of your body. Sometimes touching base in this way, even for one inbreath and one outbreath, can help you be more present. If you like, you can always extend it to a few breaths or even longer...It is a way to "befriend" the present moment and hold it gently in awareness.

You can then expand your awareness to include a sense of your body as a whole, including that it is breathing...noticing any salient sensations...any tension or tightness...

Experiment with expanding the field of awareness to include any thoughts that might be arising...recognizing and acknowledging them *as thoughts*, as events in the field of awareness, like clouds coming and going in the sky...

Notice as well whatever moods or emotions may be present, and whether they are pleasant or unpleasant or neutral...putting out the welcome mat for them, as best you can, without judging them. If you do find yourself judging them, just notice that, as well...

Where, if at all, do you feel these emotions in your body?...

At this point, simply resting in awareness as best you can, moment by moment by moment...experiencing life unfolding here and now...

When you see that your mind is carried away by thinking or anything else, which of course will happen frequently, just notice what is on your mind, whatever it is, becoming aware of it, and then, gently redirecting your attention back to your experience of the breath and the body in this moment...resting in awareness once again...

2. AWARENESS AND PRESENCE WITH A CHILD OR CHILDREN

Choose a time in the day to experiment with bringing your full presence and attention to whatever is unfolding. It could be waking your children up in the morning or helping them get ready for school, or the transition when they first come home from school, or bedtime, or diapering or nursing, or any other time.

The most important thing is to simply experience what is happening in this moment and to be fully present for it without having to have anything happen next...just this timeless moment as it is...

If you get lost in thought, as happens at times for all of us, you can always return to the sensations of breathing and of the body as a whole to ground yourself in the present moment, and then bring your attention back to your child or children. Each time you notice that your mind has gone off to one thing or another, or has become distracted or preoccupied, notice where it has gone and gently bring it back to the present moment. Work with this practice as frequently as you care to.

3. PRACTICING ACCEPTANCE

You may find it useful to pay particular attention to the inner landscape of the "judging mind" whenever it arises—the mind that is attached to ideas and opinions, black-and-white thinking, the urge to hold on to what you like and push away what you don't like. Whenever you notice the mind engaged in judging, just note the content of the thought and then gently bring your attention back to the breath, to the present moment in all its fullness, and to whatever is happening in that moment, with your child, with your partner, at work, whatever.

Remember that mindfulness can be described simply as the awareness that arises when we pay attention on purpose, in the present moment, and nonjudgmentally. That doesn't mean you won't have judgments. Of course you will—plenty of them! We all have. But for once, we won't judge them, and instead we will simply see them as thoughts, often coupled with strong emotions of one kind or another, again, like clouds moving across the sky, coming and going or sometimes lingering, but nothing we need to oppose or struggle with, or judge in this moment.

You can choose a time in each day when you intentionally work with accepting things just as they are (children, yourself, what is happening in that moment)—and practice letting go of having to have things be different or change in any way. Experiment with bringing an openhearted and discerning presence to this "accepting" time.

4. RESPONDING VERSUS REACTING TO OUR CHILDREN

It can be very helpful to distinguish between the times when you *react* automatically and unconsciously to something a child says or does, and when you *respond* with greater mindfulness and intentionality. Can you bring attention to what is happening in those moments when you find yourself reacting mindlessly? Such reactions can involve a range of thoughts and feelings, from mild irritation and annoyance to being emotionally hijacked by anger, frustration, fear, and the like.

At times like these, you might take a moment to settle yourself by becoming aware of your body and your breathing. This can include bringing a curious, open, "affectionate" attention to whatever thoughts and feelings may be coloring that moment. Can you notice whatever is arising, and experiment with breathing with the thoughts and emotions that are present—neither holding on to them nor pushing them away, nor thinking more about them—but simply, as best you can, embracing them in awareness and with some degree of kindness. While this can be quite challenging in emotionally charged moments, over time such a practice can lead to new insights and openings.

Accepting the intensity of this moment, can you see some way to respond that is less automatic, and more appropriate? It can be particularly helpful and even illuminating not to jump to fix or change the situation, even if you have the strong impulse to do so. You might try to see things in that very moment from your child's point of view. What might he or she need from you in this moment? Can you find a way to stay connected, listening to the feelings behind their words, perhaps acknowledging what you are seeing and sensing from them, and as best you can, residing in your own groundedness, an island of some stability amidst these momentarily rough seas? Perhaps it will become clearer what is actually called for in this moment, if anything.

If you find yourself bewildered or confused about what to do or how to respond to a challenging moment, consider not *doing* anything—at least for now.

If you become reactive and find yourself carried away emotionally and unable to change course, you might try taking a few moments afterward to reflect on what happened. As a parent, you will be given many opportunities to practice breaking out of habitual patterns.

Seven Intentions for Mindful Parenting

INTENTION: An aim that guides action.

The intentions we set for ourselves remind us of what is important. It is like having an internal compass. When we form the intention to be more mindful, that intention focuses and shapes our choices and our actions, including in those moments when we might easily be carried away and fall into unawareness. It increases the likelihood that we will be more present and able to stay in touch with what we most care about. It is never too late to introduce mindfulness into our lives. The very moment that we make the conscious commitment to do so becomes the perfect moment to begin.

Here are some intentions that you may find helpful. Of course, what's most important is to create your own.

I   To see parenting as an intentional practice, a way of being in relationship to experience that provides me with countless opportunities to cultivate self-awareness, wisdom, and openheartedness.

2   To see parenting as an opportunity to embody what is deepest and best in myself and express it with my children and in the world.

3   To bring greater mindfulness and discernment into my daily life, especially with my children, using awareness of my body and my breathing to ground me in the present moment.

4   To remember to see and accept my children as they are, and not simply through the lens of my expectations and fears.

5   To try to see things from each child's point of view and understand what my children's needs are, meeting them as best I can. This includes keeping in mind their need to learn by doing things on their own, and their need to come up against immovable limits at times.

6   To see whatever arises in my own life and in the lives of my children, including the dark, difficult, and stressful times, as "grist for the mill," allowing it to deepen my capacity for empathy and compassion, including for myself.

7   To bring these intentions into my heart and commit myself to putting them into practice as best I can, in ways that honor my children's sovereignty and my own.

Twelve Exercises for Mindful Parenting

1   Try to imagine the world from your child's point of view. Even doing this for a few moments every day can remind you of who this child is and what he or she may be experiencing in the world.

2   Imagine how you appear and sound from your child's point of view. In other words, what does it feel like having *you* as a parent in this moment? How might this awareness inform how you carry yourself in your body and in space, how you speak, what you say? How do you want to be in relationship to your child in *this* moment?

3   Practice seeing your children as perfect just the way they are. See if you can stay mindful of their sovereignty from moment to moment, and work at accepting them with kindness, especially when it is hardest for you to do so. Keep in mind that this has nothing to do with having to like or approve of their behavior.

4   Be mindful of your expectations of your children and consider whether they are age-appropriate and truly in each particular

child's best interest. This is an ongoing process that involves questioning your assumptions and trying to see what you might be missing. You might try listening closely to how you communicate expectations and/or limits, both verbally and nonverbally. Be on the lookout for ending statements you make about how things are (e.g., "It's time to go to bed now") with equivocation, such as following it with, "Okay?"

5   It can be very helpful to purposefully cultivate altruism, defined as unselfish concern for the well-being of others. When children are little, this necessarily means putting their needs above your own. As they get older, altruism may mean according them more responsibility and agency in meeting their own needs. At the same time, knowing what your needs are and communicating them to your children in appropriate ways is also important. You may be surprised at how much overlap is possible between your children's needs and your own, especially if you are imaginative and patient.

6   When you feel lost, or at a loss, remember to stand still, as in David Wagoner's poem: "The forest breathes." Listen to what it is saying: "The forest knows where you are. You must let it find you." Meditate on the whole by bringing your full attention to the situation, to your child, to yourself, to the family. In doing so, you may go beyond thinking, even good thinking, and perceive intuitively, with your entire being (body, mind, and heart) what most needs to be done. If that is not clear in any moment, maybe the best thing is to not do anything until it becomes clearer.

7   Try embodying silent presence. It will grow out of both formal and informal mindfulness practice over time as you develop

greater self-awareness and are more in touch with a sense of comfort and ease within yourself.

8   Experiment with making room for tension without losing your own balance. Do this by practicing moving into any moment, however difficult, without trying to change anything and without having to have a particular outcome occur. Simply bring awareness and presence to this moment. Practice seeing that whatever comes up is workable if you are willing to turn toward whatever is arising, trusting your intuition and instincts as best you can. Your child, especially when young, needs you to be a center of balance and trustworthiness, a reliable landmark by which he or she can take a bearing within his or her own landscape.

9   Consider apologizing when you have acted in some way that is disregarding or hurtful. Apologies can be healing. An apology demonstrates that you have thought about a situation and have come to see it more clearly, and perhaps also more from your child's point of view. That said, we have to be mindful of being "sorry" too often. It loses its meaning if we are always saying it, or make regret into a habit. Then it can become a way for us to not take responsibility for our actions. It's good to be aware of this. Cooking in remorse on occasion is a worthy meditation practice.

10   There are many times when we need to be clear and strong and unequivocal with our children. Let this come as much as possible out of awareness, openheartedness, and discernment, rather than out of fear, self-righteousness, or the desire to control.

11 You might experiment with making regular use of the practice of lovingkindness, holding each child in your heart for a moment and wishing him or her well, voicing inwardly: "May he or she be safe and free from harm;" "may he or she be happy;" "may he or she be healthy;" "may he or she live with ease."

12 The greatest gift you can give your child is your self. This means that part of your work as a parent is to keep growing in self-knowledge and in awareness. Can we be grounded in the present moment and share what is deepest and best in ourselves? This is a lifetime's practice. It can be supported by making a time for resting in awareness in stillness and silence each day in whatever ways feel comfortable to us. We only have right now. Let us use it to its best advantage, for our children's sake, and for our own.

Suggested Reading

Mindful Birthing, Nancy Bardacke (HarperOne, San Francisco, CA, 2012).

Attachment-Focused Parenting, Daniel A. Hughes (W. W. Norton, New York, 2009).

The Mindful Child, Susan Kaiser Greenland (Free Press/Simon and Schuster, New York, 2010).

Wise-Minded Parenting, Laura S. Kastner (ParentMap, Seattle, WA, 2013).

Building Emotional Intelligence, Linda Lantieri (Sounds True, Boulder, Colorado, 2008).

Hold On to Your Kids, Gordon Neufeld and Gabor Maté (Ballantine Books, New York, 2006).

Mindful Discipline: A Loving Approach to Setting Limits and Raising an Emotionally Intelligent Child, Shauna Shapiro and Chris White (New Harbinger, Oakland, CA, 2014).

Brainstorm: The Power and Purpose of the Teenage Brain, Daniel J. Siegel (Jeremy P. Tarcher/Penguin, New York, 2013).

The Whole-Brain Child, Daniel J. Siegel and Tina Payne Bryson (Bantam, New York, 2012).

Parenting from the Inside Out, Daniel J. Siegel and Mary Hartzell (Jeremy P. Tarcher/Penguin, New York, 2004).

Sitting Still Like a Frog, Eline Snel (Shambhala, Boston, 2013). CD with guided meditations voiced by Myla Kabat-Zinn.

Parenting Without Power Struggles, Susan Stiffelman (Atria/Simon and Schuster, New York, 2010).

Guided Mindfulness Meditation Practices with Jon Kabat-Zinn

Guided Mindfulness Meditation Practices of varying
lengths and on various platforms are available
from the following websites:

www.mindfulnesscds.com

www.jonkabat-zinn.com

www.mindfulnessapps.com

(Please note: These are NOT mindful parenting practices. They
are for cultivating mindfulness through periods of formal guided
meditation practice.)

Copyright Acknowledgments